The ELEGANT CANADIANS

LUELLA CREIGHTON

With a New Introduction by **DONALD WRIGHT**

OXFORD
UNIVERSITY PRESS

Oxford University Press is a department of the University of Oxford.
It furthers the University's objective of excellence in research, scholarship,
and education by publishing worldwide. Oxford is a registered trade mark
of Oxford University Press in the UK and in certain other countries.

Published in Canada by
Oxford University Press
8 Sampson Mews, Suite 204,
Don Mills, Ontario M3C 0H5 Canada

www.oupcanada.com

Copyright © Luella Creighton 1967
Material New to this Edition © Oxford University Press Canada 2013

The moral rights of the author have been asserted

Database right Oxford University Press (maker)

First Edition Published in 1967

All rights reserved. No part of this publication may be reproduced, stored in a retrieval system, or transmitted, in any form or by any means, without the prior permission in writing of Oxford University Press, or as expressly permitted by law, by licence, or under terms agreed with the appropriate reprographics rights organization. Enquiries concerning reproduction outside the scope of the above should be sent to the Permissions Department at the address above or through the following url: www.oupcanada.com/permission/permission_request.php

Every effort has been made to determine and contact copyright holders. In the case of any omissions, the publisher will be pleased to make suitable acknowledgement in future editions.

Library and Archives Canada Cataloguing in Publication

Creighton, Luella, 1901–1996
The elegant Canadians / Luella Creighton.

(The Wynford Project)
Originally published: McClelland and Stewart, 1967.
ISBN 978-0-19-900852-0

1. Canada—Social life and customs—19th century.
I. Title. II. Series: Wynford Project

FC88.C73 2013   971.04'9   C2013-902033-0

Cover image: "Ball at the Windsor Hotel, Montréal, in Honour of the Marquis of Lorne, 1879,"
Library and Archives Canada / C-001830

Image page 68, top: with permission of the Royal Ontario Museum © ROM

Printed and bound in the United States of America

1 2 3 4 — 16 15 14 13

To Donald Grant Creighton, C.C.

Publisher's Note

The Elegant Canadians was first published in 1967. This facsimile edition faithfully reproduces the original text of the first edition. In the four decades since, society's attitudes toward Canada's First Nations peoples and indeed the very terms used to denote those societies have changed greatly. So have historical views of first contact between Europeans and the First Nations, relations between French and English Canada, as well as social attitudes in general toward gender and ethnicity. *The Elegant Canadians* is, like any creative work, an artifact of its time, and it is only fair to say that the twenty-first century reader may stumble across the occasional expression no longer in common use.

Contents

FOREWORD
9

1. Rendezvous at Charlottetown
11

2. The Canadians Entertain
16

3. The Travellers and the Towns
36

4. Christmas In A Village, Canada West, 1866
45

1.
Montmorenci Falls,
circa 1867

Ontario Archives

2.
Westminster Palace Hotel,
London, England

Public Archives of
Canada

5. Winter Time and "The Cone"
53

6. Spacious Days
73

7. The Chatelaine
83

8. The Fashionable Years
90

9. The Sixties and the Simple Faith
96

10. Canadians in Paris, 1867
100

11. Concerning the Duty of Women
113

12. Literary Life
119

2.

13. The Sound of Music
132

14. The Glamour of the Garrison
145

15. Summer Time
149

16. Mr. Lawson Comes Home
160

17. Old Grey City
163

18. On the First of July, 1867
169

NOTES
173

The New Houses of Parliament in Ottawa at the Time of Confederation
Public Archives of Canada

Introduction to the Wynford Edition
Donald Wright

I

For as long as she could remember, she had wanted to be a writer, her "obsessive urge to put words on paper" beginning when she was seven years old.[1] Like many children, she filled notebooks and scribblers with stories, poems, and secrets as a way of insulating herself from a confusing and sometimes painful adult world. Books also helped, especially Frances Hodgson Burnett's *The Secret Garden*. Perhaps she saw something of herself in the story's main character, a lonely, difficult little girl who eventually finds happiness in a once beautiful garden that had been locked and allowed to become overgrown. Perhaps too she gathered consolation from the book's themes of a fallen adult world, a garden's regeneration, and a happy, redemptive ending.

Luella Sanders Bruce Creighton was born in Stouffville, Ontario on August 25, 1901. Two days later, her mother died from puerperal fever, a violent and indifferent infection that hits quickly and almost always fatally. Raised by her maternal grandparents, Luella had a happy early childhood: to her grandparents she was a daughter and to her uncles she was a sister. Meanwhile, her father moved to Winnipeg, returning five years later to marry a local woman and collect his daughter. In a new city and in a new family, Luella had to navigate an unfamiliar and unhappy home life. Her father may have been well meaning but he was ineffectual; and her stepmother may have accepted her new assignment but she was ill-equipped, using religion as a weapon to discipline a precocious and willful child. She once forced Luella to feed strychnine to the alley cats she had befriended, telling her that the grotesque contortions of the cats were the same contortions that awaited sinners in Hell. On another occasion, she burned a set of children's ivory-handled cutlery—presumably a gift from Luella's grandparents—because it represented a worldly and unnecessary luxury. These two incidents, however, punctuated a longer and more insidious form of emotional and psychological abuse. The female body, Luella was told, was a site of shame, its normal desires sinful: "You do not know yet that you are wicked, and it is my business to teach you."[2]

In 1915, the family returned to Stouffville where Luella was expected to finish high school, get married, and start a family. But she had other plans. Determined to escape the limited horizons of small-town

---

1. Luella Creighton, Luella Creighton, "Prelude," n.d., ca. 1968–1970, University of Waterloo, Doris Lewis Rare Book Room, Luella Creighton fonds, GA 99, Series 5, Box 9, file 86.
2. Cynthia Flood, "The Meaning of Marriage," in Cynthia Flood, *My Father Took a Cake to France* (Vancouver: Talon, 1992): 10.

Protestant Ontario, she wanted to become a teacher and, eventually, go to university. When her father and stepmother refused, she ran away from home, at one point landing in Toronto where she became part of its "girl problem": working as discounted labour at a shirt factory, she represented a perceived threat to the city's and, ultimately, the nation's moral fabric.[3] Finally, her father and her stepmother relented and, in 1920, Luella received her Certificate of Qualification as a Public School Teacher from the Toronto Normal School which qualified her to teach in a tiny school in Siloam, a village not far from Stouffville, where she counted her pennies and bided her time. Two years later she achieved her goal when she moved into Annesley Hall in September 1922, the women's residence at Victoria College, University of Toronto.

Although a medical examination by the College nurse determined that she had a "weak heart," Luella took the place by storm. Everyone knew the energetic and "permanently unsubduable" girl from Stouffville who represented Vic in the intercollegiate debating series and who once organized a Fancy Dress Skating Carnival featuring some 250 "gaily costumed" historical figures and fictional characters. An English student, she read voraciously and widely as part of her larger plan to become a writer and close the door on her childhood and adolescence. In one of her undergraduate papers, she explored the supernatural in the poetry of Keats and Coleridge. Inspired by Frances Hodgson Burnett, she wrote that every man has his secret garden, a place of "poignant yearning for fulfillment" and "far-off ineffable longings."[4] Was she talking about herself, her notebooks and her journals? Perhaps they were her secret garden. They were the one place her stepmother was refused entry, where she could express her own yearnings and longings, and where she could be herself.

Not surprisingly, Luella attracted the attention of would-be suitors, including the attention of a brilliant history student. Donald Creighton had known Luella in the way that everyone knew Luella, but they were in different years and travelled in different circles. When his sister invited Luella to lunch, Donald was smitten. Playing the role of matchmaker, his grandmother gently encouraged him: "Don't you think Miss Bruce is nice?"[5] On their first date to Toronto's Centre Island, they fell in love on the short ferry ride across the harbour. They both just knew, and what followed was "sudden," "headlong," and "absolutely sure." Luella, Donald said, possesses "an intense, vividly-coloured personality" and an "inexhaustible store" of love. Falling in love was "like a recognition—as

---

3. See Carolyn Strange, *Toronto's Girl Problem: The Perils and Pleasures of the City, 1880–1930* (Toronto: University of Toronto Press, 1995); Ruth Frager and Carmela Patrias, *Discounted Labour: Women Workers in Canada, 1870–1939* (Toronto: University of Toronto Press, 2005).
4. "Luella S. Bruce," *Torontonensis* 1926, University of Toronto Archives, University of Toronto Yearbook Collection; "The Monocle," *Acta Victoriana* 49, no. 6 (March 1925): 30; Luella Bruce, "The Supernatural Element in Poetry," n.d., University of Waterloo, Doris Lewis Rare Book Room, Luella Creighton fonds, GA 99, Series 1, Box 1, file 1.
5. Author's interview with Cynthia Flood, June 3, 2005.

if you must have been two people who knew each other a long time ago." [6] Meanwhile, letters were exchanged, promises were whispered, and plans were made: Donald would go to Oxford in September; Luella would complete her final year at Vic; and they would be married in London in June.

Donald and Luella spent their honeymoon in a small, out-of-the-way fishing village on the Brittany coast. Luella chose Paimpol because of its connection to the French writer, Pierre Loti. She had read his novel, *An Iceland Fisherman*, a romantic if also tragic story about love, death, and nature's indifference, and she now wanted to see Paimpol's granite hills leading down to the ragged edges of the coast, its stone houses with small doorways and clay flowerpots, its little graveyards, and its men in the taverns singing their songs of woe. Perhaps too she saw something of herself in the novel's heroine, a young woman who had been raised by a grandmother and an absent father when her mother died. Luella made a point of visiting Pierre Loti's house.

In September, Donald returned to Oxford and, because women weren't welcome at the all-male Balliol College, Luella moved to Paris where she found an apartment on the Left Bank. Writers, artists, musicians, and ex-pats of all shapes and hues poured into the City of Light, found cheap digs, pursued their passions, and suffered for their art. Scott Fitzgerald, Man Ray, Josephine Baker, James Joyce, and Gertrude Stein turned Paris into what Ernest Hemingway would call "a moveable feast." For her part, Luella took a course or two at the Sorbonne, hired a French tutor, and explored one of the world's great cities. An aspiring writer, she absorbed everything. Paris, she said, "is spinning."[7]

In 1927, Luella and Donald returned to Toronto where he began his 40-odd year career at the university and where she struggled to balance writing with the imperatives of being a wife and, after 1929, a young mother. It wasn't easy and she found herself overwhelmed. Of course, hers was the lot of all women writers, something Virginia Woolf understood: if women are to lead full, creative, and intellectual lives, they must first kill the Angel in the House, that inner voice instructing them in the "difficult art of family life," in the ways and means of self-denial and self-negation. "Killing the Angel in the House," Woolf said, "is part of the occupation of a woman writer."[8] By hiring a maid and refusing to vacuum, Luella killed the angel in her house.

II

Initially, Luella Creighton wrote children's stories for the Boys and Girls Page of the *New Outlook*, the newspaper of the United Church. The first

---

6. Donald Creighton to Harold Wilson, December 11, 1925; Donald Creighton to Harold Wilson, December 16, 1925; Donald Creighton to Harold Wilson, January 16, 1926. Originals in possession of Philip Creighton.
7. Luella Creighton to Harold Wilson, December 4, 1926. Original in the possession of Philip Creighton.
8. Virginia Woolf, "Professions for Women," in Virginia Woolf, *Selected Essays* (Oxford: Oxford University Press, 2008): 140–45.

series featured Gutrik, a 600-year old gargoyle who lives at the top of Paris' Notre Dame Cathedral. From his panoramic perch, he observes the city and, in the process, he teaches children about Paris and its many sites and sounds, its boulevards and its parks, its squares and its fountains, and even its Bird Market where people gathered once a week to buy and sell animals. In one story a little boy and his mother select "a warm and friendly kitten," just the kind of kitten "who might sleep in a hump on your bed."[9] Another series featured Blue Rabbit, a stuffed rabbit belonging to a little boy. Blue Rabbit and a small cast of stuffed animals teach him about the meaning of friendship; they help him overcome his fear of going to the hospital; and they offer him advice on how to plan his first sleepover. A third series centred on a little boy named Peter and his kitten named Spuddie. In her life and in her writing, Creighton was always protecting cats, an atonement, perhaps, for being unable to protect those poor cats from her stepmother's strychnine.

Creighton also wrote short stories and, in these, her themes were darker. In "Miss Kidd," the main character is a respectable church-going school teacher who marries a rough, brutish man. Trapped in a loveless marriage, she endures her husband's drinking, swearing, and forced sex because "it is the duty of a good wife to submit."[10] Only when they are both killed in a car accident is she released.

Creighton next explored a ten-year old girl's dim and inarticulate awareness of her sexuality in "The Cornfield." When Virginia arrives at the Mennonite farm of her step-aunt, she puts flowers in her hair but is told by her scripture-quoting step-aunt that it is "vain and wrong." Women should "adorn themselves in modest apparel, with shamefacedness and sobriety," Paul wrote in his first epistle to Timothy, "not with braided hair, or gold, or pearls, or costly array" (1 Timothy 2:9). At once confused and defiant, Virginia understands that "what the woman said was false." Later, she feels her first romantic interest in a 14-year old boy while playing hide-and-seek in a cornfield. Although nothing happens, there is a connection and, as they walk in silence, she could see "his rough, light hair near the tassels of the corn." Coming out of the field, they are confronted by her step-aunt. Instantly enraged, she slaps Virginia "sharply on the cheek," screaming that she "ought to be ashamed" for walking with a boy. Next she pulls at Virginia's dress, peering into it "with her hateful eyes." Virginia's prepubescent, flat chest elicits demeaning laughter. Virginia stamps her foot "furiously": "Don't you dare touch me," she shouts. For once silent, her step-aunt cannot respond. During all of this, Virginia's uncle does nothing. A pathetic figure, he remains passive and unresponsive.[11]

Published in the *Canadian Forum* in 1937, it won the prize for the best story published that year, the judges acknowledging the difficult subject

---

9. Luella Creighton, "The Observations of Gutrik the Gargoyle," *New Outlook*, November 27, 1929.
10. Luella Creighton, "Miss Kidd," in Bertram Brooker, ed., *Yearbook of the Arts in Canada* (Toronto: Macmillan, 1936): 137–47.
11. Luella Creighton, "The Cornfield," *Canadian Forum* (June 1937): 97–99.

matter and the challenge of depicting "the subtleties of a child's inner life."[12] What Morley Callaghan, Earle Birney, and Bertram Brooker couldn't know is that Creighton's story drew on her own inner life: the step-aunt was her stepmother; the uncle was her father; the sexual humiliation was her humiliation; and Virginia's refusal to be defeated was her refusal.

Encouraged by the award and the validation it brought, Creighton undertook a more ambitious project. But her first novel took longer than she had hoped because, in 1940, she had a second child, meaning, she said, that she had to become all over again "a cook, dressmaker, doctor, mentor, and diplomat" to a young family.[13] But in 1951 she published *High Bright Buggy Wheels*. Set in the fictional town of Kinsail—which was really Stouffville, she later admitted—it follows Tillie Shantz, a beautiful young woman who leaves both her Mennonite family and her Mennonite faith when she falls in love with George Bingham, the owner of the local drugstore. Thinking about his own journey from the family farm to the big city, Harold Innis described it as *the* Ontario novel: "We have all been lured to George's drugstore."[14] Although Tillie's journey may have been part of a larger pattern, it was still the journey of a young woman determined to lead her life on her terms. Three years later, Creighton again mined the themes of family, religion, hypocrisy, and a young woman's awakening in her second novel, *Turn East, Turn West*.

Now in her early fifties, Creighton was enjoying success as a writer but, as a writer, she also needed to push herself. Despite an earlier promise to try something new, to explore the interior life of a middle aged woman, her third novel took her back to Kinsail. But when "Music in the Park" wasn't published, she set it aside and turned instead to other projects and other genres. As a way of avoiding the hard work of writing fiction, she wrote a two-volume history of Canada for children in grades seven and eight.[15] Following a familiar narrative of discovery, exploration, settlement, and nationhood, neither volume was particularly interesting. "I wish I had not wasted my life on triviality," she confessed shortly before the publication of volume two, "but had really worked at writing."[16]

Of course, it would have been easier to give up. But Creighton needed to write for the same reason that all writers need to write: it was her way of making sense of the world and negotiating her place in it. When McClelland and Stewart invited her to write a book marking Canada's one hundredth birthday, she quickly agreed.

---

12. Earle Birney, *Canadian Forum* (June 1937): 97.
13. "New Novel *High Bright Buggy Wheels* Release of Local Authoress," *Stouffville Tribune*, September 6, 1951.
14. Harold Innis, endorsement printed on book jacket of Luella Creighton, *High Bright Buggy Wheels* (Toronto: McClelland and Stewart, 1951).
15. See Luella Creighton, *Canada: The Struggle for Empire* (Toronto: Dent, 1960) and Luella Creighton, *Canada: Trial and Triumph* (Toronto: Dent, 1963).
16. Luella Creighton, Diary entry, January 14, 1963, University of Waterloo, Doris Lewis Rare Book Room, Luella Creighton fonds, GA 99, Series 3, Box 2, File 9.

III

On October 26, 1967, Jack McClelland launched *The Elegant Canadians* at Mister Tony's, an appropriately elegant restaurant on Toronto's Cumberland Street. Over champagne, strawberries, speeches, and toasts, Creighton's many friends celebrated her depiction of the 1860s and her attempt to identify what she called "a kind of cadence of the times" through the genres of history, fiction, and epistolary fiction.[17]

As a writer, Creighton was more interested in people's daily lives, in how they lived and what they did. John A. Macdonald makes a handful of cameo appearances and Confederation waits in the wings, but otherwise the stage is left to, among others, the real Mercy Ann Coles and the fictional Isabella Moore. Coles' diary allowed Creighton to describe in detail the elaborate dinners and fancy balls that accompanied the Charlottetown and Quebec Conferences, while Moore's letters allowed her to imagine the private life of a young woman from Ireland who comes to British North America and falls in love with a handsome gentleman of some means.

Combining three distinct genres gave Creighton the freedom she needed as a writer. It allowed her to depict an era of elegance and opulence, of ladies and gentlemen, of crinoline dresses and brocade waistcoats, of picnics and croquet parties, of religious observance and scientific advancement, of noblesse oblige and deference to authority. It allowed her to attend the Paris Exhibition of 1867, where she imagined a surprised Frenchman opening a box from Canada. Thinking that it might contain the scalp "of some ill-fated whiteman who crossed the path of the savage," he was stunned to discover milled soap so delicate and so fragrant that it could compete with the finest milled soap from France. "Shaken, the Frenchman repaired to his two hour luncheon, eating his thin soup with loud sups and striking his thick slices of bread petulantly into his bowl." And it allowed her to describe the rich literary life of her *dramatis personae*, their personal libraries and their reading habits. Children too, she said, were challenged to improve themselves through fiction and natural history. "Words like 'contumelious' and 'phantasmagoria' were dropped into the children's minds like lumps of enriching fruit. Children in the 1860s were fed words large enough to frighten a modern child, trained in two-syllable words, out of its tidy little mind."[18]

If the 1860s was governed by a spirit of improvement, it was also governed by "the hand of God" and that hand could give or take. In a veiled reference to her own mother, Creighton described how an otherwise "strong and healthy woman" could deliver her baby but die a few days later from "a mysterious fever." But, on balance, the 1860s was marked by "public order, social discipline, and private restraint," by bonnets and crinolines, and by

---

17. Luella Creighton, *The Elegant Canadians* (Toronto: McClelland and Stewart, 1967; reprinted by Oxford University Press, 2013): 10.
18. Ibid, 101–102, 126.

"fashionable years" and "spacious days." The French were "gay"; the Indians were "romantic"; and the one African Canadian—"a tall and ancient negro" named Jefferson—was "devoted" to the family he served.[19]

In other words, Creighton's 1860s was not the 1960s, a decade marked by wars, protests, and revolutions, by liberation movements and angry demonstrations, by civil rights and women's rights, by "years of hope" and "days of rage."[20] On the morning she wrote the foreword, which was, in fact, the day she finished the manuscript, the *Globe and Mail* carried articles on the war in Vietnam, race riots in Nashville, air pollution in Toronto, a labour dispute in Montreal, the availability of birth control in Ontario, and a study linking a woman's ability to enjoy sex to her ability to enjoy food.[21] Confused by the pace and direction of the 1960s, Creighton turned to a highly selected and largely invented past.

As a result, her elegant Canada and her elegant Canadians represent a tiny cross-section of English-speaking British North America. Despite her assertion that British North America had been "released" from the "exigencies of pioneer poverty,"[22] it was every inch a place of poverty, of desperate immigrants, itinerant labourers, impoverished widows, dislocated First Nations people, and marginalized blacks. In Canada West, for example, blacks attended segregated schools, the *London Free Press* reporting in 1861 that some citizens did not want blacks admitted to London's Central School because they were "rude in speech," "uncouth in manners," and "untidy in appearance."[23] On the rare occasion that blacks were admitted to white schools, they were forced to sit on separate benches.

Yet *The Elegant Canadians* struck a resonant chord because it offered a respite from the 1960s. "It calls up an atmosphere that contrasts so agreeably with the supersonic world of today," wrote one reader. Indeed, he added, the 1860s "grows more attractive the further we penetrate into our smog bound future."[24] Meanwhile, the *Montreal Gazette* called it a "finely produced" "blend of historical fact and historical fiction"; the *Saskatoon Star-Phoenix* welcomed its "vivid picture" of the past; and the *Regina Leader-Post* described it as "a charming and imaginative reconstruction" of "manners, morals, fashions, and day-to-day living." To the *Ottawa Citizen* it was "sophisticated"; to the *Victoria Daily Times* it was "delightful"; and to the *Executive* it radiated "feminine grace."[25]

---

19. Ibid, 98, 9, 158, 135, 46, 52.
20. See Todd Gitlin, *The Sixties: Years of Hope, Days of Rage* (New York: Bantam, 1987).
21. See *Globe and Mail*, April 10, 1967.
22. Creighton, *The Elegant Canadians*, 73.
23. Quotation in Kristin McLaren, "We had no desire to be set apart: Forced Segregation of Black Students in Canada West Public Schools and Myths of British Egalitarianism," *Histoire sociale/Social History* 37, 4 (2004): 33.
24. Norman Creighton (no relation) to Luella Creighton, April 5, 1969, University of Waterloo, Doris Lewis Rare Book Room, Luella Creighton fonds, GA 99, Series 4, Box 5, file 50.
25. *Montreal Gazette*, January 6, 1968; *Saskatoon Star-Phoenix*, January 6, 1968; *Regina Leader Post*, March 11, 1968; *Ottawa Citizen*, December 18, 1970; *Victoria Daily Times*, November 25, 1967; *Executive*, April 1968.

However, the famous, flamboyant, crusty, and deliberately controversial journalist and curmudgeon, Gordon Sinclair, criticized it for the same reason that the *Executive* praised it. It is written in "quite a feminine way," he said, and, as a result, "there are no great issues in this book to agitate the mind," only lavish dinner parties and ten-course meals. In a backhanded compliment, he concluded that "Mrs Creighton has not only given us a splendid look at a vanished Canada, but a look that could only be seen through the eyes of a woman."[26]

Creighton dismissed Sinclair's review as "ham-fisted," but, ham-fisted or not, it unwittingly raised an important point: history isn't what happened, it is the record of what happened, and that record will be different when it is written by women.[27] Creighton wasn't ahead of her time in writing social history, women's history, and the history of private life. But when she asked questions about women's lives and women's roles, when she pointed to the unfairness of marriage, property, and inheritance laws in Victorian Canada, when she exposed a sexual double standard which laid women "open to suspicion" for merely walking with a man, and when she asserted women's agency through diaries and letters, she decentred politics and male politicians and, ultimately, expanded the definition of history.[28] It was this decentring, more than the bonnets and crinolines, that annoyed the "ultramasculine" Gordon Sinclair: confined to what he called "great issues," his definition of history didn't include women.[29]

Speaking at the University of Prince Edward Island, Gail Cuthbert Brandt used her 1992 presidential address to the Canadian Historical Association to locate the connections between national history, political history, and women's history, at one point referring to the many social events associated with the Charlottetown Conference of 1864. Few historians, she said, "have bothered to ask who organized these events, who presided at them, or whose labour went into the painstaking production of the seemingly endless courses of food, or the making of the elaborate decorations."[30] At her home in Brooklin, Ontario, was a 90-year-old woman. Although she had stopped writing, she still kept a diary and maintained a magnificent rose garden. Had she heard Cuthbert Brandt's address, Luella Sanders Bruce Creighton might have responded, "My dear, I did that 25 years ago."

---

26. Gordon Sinclair, CBC Radio review of *The Elegant Canadians*, copy in University of Waterloo, Doris Lewis Rare Book Room, Luella Creighton fonds, GA 99, Series 4, Box 5, file 50.
27. Luella Creighton, Diary entry, November 3, 1967, University of Waterloo, Doris Lewis Rare Book Room, Luella Creighton fonds, GA 99, Series 4, Box 5, file 50.
28. Creighton, *The Elegant Canadians*, 115.
29. Marjory Lang, *Women Who Made the News: Female Journalists in Canada, 1880–1945* (Montreal and Kingston: McGill-Queen's University Press, 1999): 145.
30. Gail Cuthbert Brandt, "National Unity and the Politics of Political History," *Journal of the Canadian Historical Association* 3 (1992): 7.

Foreword

British North Americans in Canada and the Maritime Provinces had come out of the woods and into the sunshine by the eighteen sixties; the day of the isolated settler was done. Cities worthy of comparison with the cities of the Old Country had risen on the shores of the New Country. No longer dependent on the waterways for highways, inland cities were rising too.

A sophisticated society grew up with the cities, a leisured, much travelled, well read society, with an awareness of and a sensitivity to the thought and culture of Europe more real than exists with us now. Sophistication reached into the areas of architecture, education, transportation, costume, and the choice of food and drink. A traveller might be offered a choice of a dozen fine champagnes on a hotel wine list, with no mention of the raw whisky which our journalists would have us believe to have been the unique liquor of the time. Johnny Cake with Maple Syrup had yielded to Charlotte Russe and Claret Jelly. Oxcarts no longer rumbled through the city streets; high-stepping hackneys drew glossy carriages of elegant design.

The sixties were years of tremendous creative activity, literary, artistic, scientific throughout the world. Canadians responded to the spirit of the decade with astonishing alacrity, enthusiasm, and success.

Canada had its aristocracy in the sixties, and the members of it lived as one feels patricians should live: lavishly, but without ostentation, elegantly, and with grace. The Canadian aristocracy drew its members from Commerce and the Law, from the Church and the halls of Education. They were known to each other from the nature of their business or their professions, whether they lived in Montreal, Halifax, Toronto, or in one of the smaller cities.

It was a period when the terms "ladies" and "gentlemen" had some significance. A lady writing one of the long letters which the leisure of the time made possible might comment tartly that there were not many ladies and gentlemen at the ball, although there were plenty of people.

The image of the sixties is one of public order, social discipline, and private restraint. There existed in these years a definite code of conduct, social and moral, known to all men. Within the precepts of the code ladies and gentlemen could walk with a serenity of mind and manners as in a gracious garden bounded by a tall hedge. They were conscious of their absolute rightness of behaviour; peaceful content reigned in the garden. But the thorns and thistles of social ostracism awaited the gentleman, and with awful certainty would mortally wound the lady, who ventured beyond the hedge.

I owe much gratitude to a small army of friends and acquaintances who have helped me find the material from which this book was created. They have loaned me letters from Confederation times, family albums, treasured daguerrotypes, many, alas, too dark for reproduction, but full of significant social detail. They have given me hours of their time to recall that "my grandmother said when she was young that her mother . . ." I have been permitted to read and quote from unpublished diaries, and to look over and make use of private family papers. From these hundred-year-old diaries and letters I came to identify a kind of cadence of the times, and this I have attempted to reproduce in the sections of *The Elegant Canadians* which the imaginary people dominate.

The Bradys, the Lawsons, the Moore girls, Elizabeth Gibson, Mr. Townsend, Mr. Andrew, Madame de Trouville, Mrs. Truman and Mrs. Adams, the Burnhams, and the officers exist only between the covers of *The Elegant Canadians*. But their counterparts did live in Canada a hundred years ago, and behaved as they behave.

Among those to whom I am grateful for pictures, recollections, family diaries and private research are Mrs. Ross Baillie, Dr. Robin Harris, Miss Patricia Gilpin-Brown, Miss Cicely Blackstock, Mrs. Arthur Boyes, Mlle. Marguerite MacDonald, Mrs. C. K. Sissons, Miss Muriel Sissons, Mrs. Norman Swanson and Dr. Guthrie Grant. I am indebted to Professor Robert Finch, Professor W. L. Morton, and to Colonel C. P. Stacey, who helped me with information drawn from their particular areas of study.

LUELLA CREIGHTON
Brooklin, Ontario
April 10, 1967

I

Rendezvous at Charlottetown

*It was the first great convivial occasion
in British North America.*[1]

The *Queen Victoria* was just a little ship with a tonnage of two hundred and eleven and the drawing power of three hundred strong dray horses. She was smaller than the ship of her name which ran the Ottawa River and much lighter than the pleasure ships which steamed along the great River of Canada and across the Great Lakes and small, for the pleasure and convenience of travellers.

But the Fates, laughing perhaps, as they plotted the days of the little ship, pleased with the thought of great destinies for small creatures, marked her out for fame, and remembrance. They chose the tiny *Queen Victoria* to take the mighty men of Canada down to the sea with "The Plan" in the dying days of August, 1864.

Where are now the remembrances of the *Heather Belle*, although she carried great men from New Brunswick and Nova Scotia in her day? Who knows of the *Princess of Wales* or the *Lady Elgin*, or remembers anything, any name of the many other pleasure ships famous in their time? Who could name the *Jenny Lind*, chartered for the Prince of Wales on his tradition-shattering visit in 1860?

But the schoolboys know that it was the *Queen Victoria* which carried to the conference table the men who had the immense new dream, a dream of a great country to be made of bits and pieces of scattered colonies. Gaily she carried them down to the men of the seaward provinces to make the dream come true.

The men with the plan were lighthearted travellers. M. Cartier, Mr. Macdonald, Mr. Brown, and Mr. Galt, Mr. Campbell, M. Langevin, Mr. McDougall, and Mr. McGee, most of whom had never been to the Maritime possessions before, set out, with their secretaries, to make an occasion of it, an occasion worthy of their mission. On that late August night, open-minded, open-hearted, they embarked in the *Queen Victoria*, almost incredibly hopeful and confident, self-invited guests ready to be pleased. The little ship left Quebec behind, and the river was open before them.

The magnitude of the enterprise,

> *as decisive an enterprise as ever the white-coated and red-coated soldiers of the past had sailed to undertake*[2]

has stimulated artists to depict the little ship as a monster, a leviathan, a ship seven decks high. Sometimes Mr. Macdonald, with Charlottetown in sight, his tall hat in hand, his ready deputation behind him, is pictured descending a ship's ladder of terrifying steepness and narrowness. He is apparently just ready to step down into a rowboat already equipped with a quota of sailors manning the oars, a barrel of flour and two jars of molasses in it.

It was not quite so. Charlottetown was clearly visible, and there was a small flat-bottomed boat; the barrel of flour was there, and the two jars of molasses. But the boat was rowed by just one fisherman, and the much-embarrassed Provincial Secretary of Prince Edward Island, Mr. Pope, was the other occupant. The elegant Mr. Pope, whose official function it was to greet and play host to the Canadians, stunned by the sight of the *Queen Victoria* at anchor (it had not docked), was forced "to get himself rowed out to the Canadian steamer in one of the disreputable small boats which seemed unfortunately to be the only conveyances available." There was certainly no room for eight stalwart Canadian delegates, with secretaries.

But the *Queen Victoria* was equal to her duty. She hoisted her flag and readied her boats.

When the ministers had brushed their hair and whiskers, perfected the bow on their narrow black satin ties, and given a final pull to their flowered-silk waistcoats, she was ready for them. They gave a final flick of a silk handkerchief to the toes of their already-gleaming shoes, rubbed a broadclothed arm over the nap of their tall hats, and stepped into the little steamer's own two boats. Ministers and secretaries took their seats, and "the boats were lowered, man-of-war fashion." Each boat was manned with four oarsmen and a boatswain. They were dressed in smart blue uniforms, with hats, belts, etc., "in regular style."

So the Canadians came gloriously to Charlottetown, with the Provincial Secretary of Prince Edward Island ignominiously set in the middle distance, toward the shore – flat-bottomed tub, flour barrels, molasses jars, and all.

There was no room in Charlottetown either, for the Canadians. For the first time in more than twenty years of rewarding Island self-contemplation, a violent intrusion had been made. A circus, a proper circus, with clowns and troops of acting dogs and monkeys and marvellous trick riders, had entered into Charlottetown. The populace of the Island surged to the capital. Storekeepers looped their buildings with bunting; banners screamed the wonderful news; and the people from the country, dressed in their best, beamed through the streets, took rooms in the hotels and boarding houses, and filled the place to bursting.

First the circus, and now the Canadians!

The town fathers, the members of the government, looked at each other in consternation and counted the Canadians, the New Brunswickers, and the men from Nova Scotia. Heavens! There might be beds for some of these people, in private mansions, but not for ALL! Tolerable accommodition was found for a few at the Franklin House. Mr. Brown of the *Globe* accepted hospitality from Mr. Pope, now safely at home from his molasses journeying and as willing and able as was Governor Dundas to offer the bountiful hospitality which the Islander reserves for his special guests.

Governor Dundas entertained most of the delegation to an Island dinner, which meant that the riches of the sea were offered in prime condition and great profusion. For at Government House, where the dinner was given, "the sea was washing gently up to the very door." Mr. Pope gave a most sumptuous buffet at four o'clock the next day, built (to top Island taste) on lobsters, oysters, and champagne.

And because there was no room at the inns, however hospitable the people, the *Queen Victoria* herself became hotel for her travellers and host to the Maritimers.

The delegates set out from the ship to the Legislative Council Chamber in the Colonial Building. Smiling, affable, as distinguished in dress and manner as was the spacious sweep of the stairs they climbed, they entered a lofty white-panelled room with slender, fluted columns and wide-swung, graceful arches. There could not have been a more dignified and elegant setting anywhere in British North America for the meeting together of the men from the Canadas and the men from the Maritimes. And here they talked and proposed and discussed and, for many hours of every day, laboured with the astounding idea of creating a whole from the parts.

But when the parleying was over for the day, there were *déjeuners*, dinners, balls. Wives and daughters of Maritimers were caught up in a round of wholly unprecedented gaiety. Middle-aged ministers and ministers much more than middle-aged danced through the night after hours of eating and speeches and were fresh as daisies at three in the morning.

The *Charlottetown Islander* ecstatically reported the quality of the menus offered to the delegates.

> ... *substantials of beef rounds, splendid hams, salmon, lobster, salads, oysters prepared in every shape and style – all the different kinds of fowl which the season and the market could afford – all vegetable delicacies peculiar to the season, pastry in all forms, fruits in almost every variety – wines of the choicest vintage.*[3]

The *Queen Victoria* became banquet hall and celebration centre. The little ship was host for more than one party, and they were lavish ones. The day after Mr. Pope's party the *Queen Victoria* entertained at a luncheon which the newspapers recorded with something approaching awe.

Champagne cooled in tubs of ice; jellies flanked with Charlotte Russe and fragile meringues quivered on the long damask draped serving tables. Lobsters boiled and chilled and piled on great platters, the gleam of freshly polished glasses, flowers, and fruit, welcomed thirty-three hungry and elated men at three in the afternoon.

Hours later they were still there, flushed and exalted, raising their glasses high to the Queen, the Prince of Wales, the Prosperity of the Confederation, The Canadian Provinces, The Maritime Provinces, the Maritime Guests, the Canadian Hosts.

Perhaps they toasted "The Confederate Cruiser," their little ship herself. In the gaiety and optimism inspired by that memorable luncheon, all hearts seemed united, and it was easy to forget that there must almost surely be violent disapproval of the great idea that became more and more acceptable to them as the days passed. United in spirit, they moved off the ship to dinner with Colonel Gray of the Island in his lovely country house, and there was more celebration, more feasting, and more toasts, until the moon was high in the sky. Then the men who had beds in Charlottetown sought them, and Mr. Macdonald and his men returned to the *Queen Victoria* and thankfully sank to sleep in the hard but hospitable beds of their little ship.

And so the banquets and dinners and dancing went on. Island ladies found that their one evening dress, which had done duty for long enough now, was by no means enough, and rushed to have more dresses made. Or at least a waist or two, to combine with an existing skirt and give it a new look.

The ladies of the delegates were entertained in the *Queen Victoria*. A small flotilla of row-boats billowing with crinolines moved over the water, and the ladies who had been hostesses were now guests of the Canadians. There was a gentle teasing of the young ladies who had come with their mothers, and badinage, coy jokes, and the not inconsiderable charm of the Canadians were brought into play that Wednesday afternoon. The Maritime ladies laughed, felt young, and decided that it might be most diverting to go on to Canada with the group. Mrs. Pope, with "eight strong intelligent, good-looking children," who herself had never crossed to the mainland, prepared to be a credit to her husband when the Conference should move on to Halifax, Quebec, Ottawa, Montreal, and even, it was rumoured, right into Canada West— Toronto, certainly, and maybe even Niagara, all as guests of Canada.

George Coles, the Island Opposition Leader entertained at dinner. Mr. Brown of the *Globe* found the Coles establishment a "handsome set-out, several attractive daughters, well educated, well informed, and sharp as needles." Mr. Coles decided to take his wife and his daughter Mercy along, when the cavalcade should move west. Mrs. Coles suddenly found herself considering a wardrobe for herself and her daughter which must be of much greater scope that the Island had ever demanded of her. There was her own dinner on Monday, a ball at Government House on Tuesday; on Wednesday the Canadians received the Governor and his lady, and the delegates and theirs. Thursday there was the grand farewell ball in the Colonial Building. What gown could be splendid enough for that? Never in the Island's history was there such a party.

The Lieutenant-Governor formally received the guests in the beautiful white Council Chamber itself, which had been decked out with flags and flowers and greenery for the night. At the other end of the building, the replica of the Council Chamber was transformed into a ballroom. Long mirrors reflected the glorious lighting effects which the superintendent of the gas works had personally designed. Clusters of globes of light winked back from reflection to reflection, until the dancers thought they saw a million lights glancing from ceiling and walls. Evergreens, transparencies, flags, and the music of two bands beckoned to the dancers. In case both bands should tire at the same time, there were relief violinists and pianists at hand to ensure that there would always be music.

Between reception room and ballroom, in the library, tea, coffee, sherry, claret, and champagne were set out for the refreshment of all.

Until after midnight the crinolines swayed, multi-coloured and seemingly endowed with independent life of their own, only lightly attached to the tiny waists and the bare shoulders where ringlets bobbed in time to the music. Coat-tails flew; old men and young joined with enthusiasm in quadrille after quadrille. And when Sir Roger de Coverley, true to tradition, ended the dancing, there was the supper.

Like so many exotic birds the ladies glided down the stairs – stairs in fact which might have been designed for such a descent. The Supreme Court Chamber by the magic wand of hospitality had been transformed into a festive banquet hall. A vast and formal dinner – silver, damask, crystal complete – was set out. Great cold roasts of beef, hams, the inevitable oysters, lobsters, salmon, salads, fruits, and pastries were there to dazzle the eyes of ladies and gentlemen who had danced for hours now.

The toast list was long. The speeches which followed the toasts were almost, in total, three hours long. It was nearly four when the party broke up, and the delegates in evening dress grasped their belongings and trooped back to the *Queen Victoria* faithfully waiting for them. They went aboard, embarking to go to Pictou on their way to Halifax.

> *and so ended the episode of Charlottetown, the gayest whirlwind courtship in Canadian History.*[4]

There was feasting and fêting in Halifax, with a dinner at the Halifax Hotel of such sumptuousness that after a hundred years it is spoken of with reverence still. What Halifax could do, St. John could do, and did. Fredericton was not to be undone. The Lieutenant-Governor was visited, a journey made up the magnificent St. John River, and when all the banquets were eaten and the speeches made, the Canadians came down by train to Shediac, where the *Queen Victoria* waited for them in the rain, with steam up, to carry them back to Quebec. There had been three weeks' continuous work for the little ship. In three weeks more she was off again, this time to bring the Maritimers as honoured guests to the Canadas.

2

The Canadians Entertain

> *If the delegates will survive the lavish hospitality of this great country, they will have good constitutions – perhaps better than the one they are manufacturing for the Confederation.*[5]

"Gales, thick with snow," swooped roaring down the river valley as the little "Confederate Cruiser" nosed her way up the St. Lawrence with her cargo of Maritimers, their wives, and marriageable daughters. She was hard put to it to gain her way at all, but on the ninth of October she brought her passengers into a snow harbour at Quebec.

Mr. Russell's St. Louis Hotel became a home in Quebec for the delegates. Every night the company sat down to what Mr. Brown called "Company dinner of the first class." Between the banquets, the dinners, the balls, and the *déjeuners* and supper parties, Mr. Russell's waiters flew about at all hours of the day and night, with tea, coffee, and small collations, as well as unlimited supplies of sherry, port, champagne, and brandy.

The weather was appalling. Snow gave place to rain and rain and rain. Outdoor excursions were impossible. There were no drives to the celebrated Montmorenci for Mercy Coles. But dances can be held without benefit of fine weather, and night after night the dripping carriages waited to take the fascinated Maritime ladies to yet one more ball. Or perhaps to take the delegates to the dinner given by the Board of Trade of Quebec, or to the dinners at Spencer Wood, where the Governor General was "easy and affable." And towering above all the entertainment, there was a "Drawing Room" in the Legislative Building.

Mr. Whelan of the *Examiner* found the Quebec women too short, fat and plain. He was perhaps made uneasy by the sight of so many French women behaving in such a French way. There is a defensive note in his report.

> *I have seen more pretty girls at a Government House ball in Charlottetown – more at the late banquet in the Province Building there – than I witnessed at the great Drawing Room*[6]

was the news that he sent home to his Charlottetown newspaper.

But Mercy Ann Coles did not agree with Mr. Whelan. She had made her preparations for entertainment, and was determined to be pleased.

> *I bought an Opera Cloak paid 8½ dollars for it, it is very pretty. I am sewing the trimming on my velvet jacket. Mr. Drinkwater has promised to get me a bouquet for tomorrow night.*
>
> WEDNESDAY MORNING, OCT. 12
> *We all went to the Drawing Room last night, quite a crowd when we all got together, all the ladies looked very well and were quite a credit to the lower provinces. Pa, Ma and I went to-gether. A half dozen gentlemen wanted to take me into the room, but I preferred to go in with Papa. The Governor General stood in the middle of the room with his private secretary on his right hand. We did not require to have any cards. The Aides announced us each time. The Governor shook hands very friendly with each one. After all those who had the privilege of entree were presented they formed a half circle the rest of the people then walked in at one door bowed to the Governor and passed out at the other. There were about 800 people presented and I was very tired before it was all over. Mr. Tilly took charge of me and walked about with me the whole evening. When we came home Ma and I went immediately to bed and were so tired. Ma wore her grenadine over black silk. I wore my blue silk. There were only 2 or 3 trains there.*[7]

The dinners, banquets, and *déjeuners* were entertainments worthy of the name, of the delegates, and of the hosts themselves. Sometimes the Maritimers felt that they were being feasted off their feet, between the strenuous conferences which took most of the hours of their day. The attitude of continuous celebration might blur the issue of confederation, some of the doubtful members felt. Mr. Whelan voiced the dichotomy of the situation.

> *The first and only public occasion on which the delegates from the Lower Provinces had an opportunity of expressing their opinions on the question of confederation was at a dinner given to them by the Quebec Board of Trade on the evening of the 15th of October. It took place at Russell's Hotel on Palace Street, and was pronounced as the most successful publick banquet ever witnessed in Quebec. The attendance was very numerous, including the leading members of the mercantile community, the principal officers of the army in garrison, the heads of the civil service, several members of both Houses of Parliament, and nearly all the Canadian ministers. The banqueting room was superbly decorated, displaying on its walls mottoes in reference to the several provinces. The viands were of the best description, including everything which a rich and populous city like Quebec could afford, to*

> *gratify the taste of an epicure. A. Joseph, Esq., president of the Board of Trade, occupied the chair, and the vice-chair was occupied by S. S. Scott, Esq. The stewards arranged themselves at different tables, and by the most judicious and delicate management, provided for the comfort and convenience of their numerous guests. When the cloth was removed, and the usual patriotic toasts had been duly honoured, the chairman proposed, amid loud cheers, "The Health of His Excellency the Governor-General." It was drunk with all the honours, the band playing "The Fine Old Irish Gentleman."*[8]

Every town of any size longed to entertain the Conference; invitations poured in from Montreal, Ottawa, Belleville, Kingston, Toronto, Hamilton

> *and other places to the remote western boundaries of the province – proffering their hospitalities. To the distant corporations and cities answers of acceptance were returned through the chairman conditional as to the time when the business of the conference should be completed.*[9]

Little Mercy Ann Coles missed much of the festivity in Quebec. Her throat was desperately sore, and Dr. Tupper, all but convinced of diphtheria, kept her in her bedroom. But the other girls went to the parties, and brought her back reports. And the gentlemen were most attentive to her, and many of them sent her their cartes – there was a general distribution of cartes, the feeling being strong that this was a unique occurrence, and there must be something tangible to act as a souvenir that it had really happened.

> *All the gentlemen are having their likenesses taken. Pa's is only tolerable.*
>
> MONDAY AFTERNOON, 24TH.
> *I did not go out yesterday after all. Dr. Tupper said my throat was not well enough. . . . Mr. Bernard was up for a few minutes Saturday just as I was dressing for dinner. Mr. J. A. McDonald dined with us last night after dinner he entertained me with any amount of small talk when I came to bed at 9 o'clock he said he was just going to a party at Mde. Duvals she always gives parties Sunday. . . . This afternoon I have been making visits with Pa and Ma. We did not go in any place but Mrs. Roys at the Manne Hospital. She is a very pretty woman she gave me her own and her husband's carte. Mr. McDougall sent me his to-day.*
>
> TUESDAY AFTERNOON.
> *I was so ill last evening after my drive I was obliged to go to bed. I did not feel so bad since I have been ill. Dr. Tupper came in to see me. I had a black draft and felt better as it was all over. Mr. Bernard came to dinner. I was so disappointed when Ma told me he sent me his carte, this morning Mr. Livesay has*

just given me his, his white hair looks so venerable. I shall have quite a collection for every one of the gentlemen have had theirs taken.... When I get to Montreal I will have mine taken. I had some raw oysters the first thing I have enjoyed since I have been ill.

The Miss Heves seem to be in possession of the parlour down stairs I think they never leave it. There is a Mr. Carver who seems to be the attraction. He is a beau of Miss Fisher's, but they monopolize him. We are positively to start for Montreal on Thursday.

WEDNESDAY
I went for a drive to-day We went through the Lower Town to see where the rock fell and crushed the people to death.

I went to dinner in the evening John A. sat along side of me, what an old Humbug he is, he brought me my dessert into the Drawing Room. The Conundrum.[10]

Montreal was in a frenzy of social preparation for the visitors from the Maritimes, the delegates from the Canadas, their wives, and daughters. There was to be a steeplechase, a military review, a fireworks display. But the rain which sheeted Quebec followed the party to Montreal, and only the great ball was possible. What was to have been the crowning piece of a magnificent structure of entertainment became the only festivity, excepting only the famous six hour *déjeuner*.

Six hours of eating, drinking and speech making.[11]

FRIDAY MORNING, MONTREAL.
Oct. 28 St. Lawrence. We arrived here last night and 8/2 past 10. We left Quebec at 4 o'clock. I felt better as I got away. Ma would not let me talk, but I met such a nice old gentleman Mr. Malcom Cameron who recited poetry for me and then entertained me with riddles. This hotel is an immense place. We had a very nice supper when we arrived in the Hall in which we are to dance to night ... I went to breakfast Mr. Tilley sat alongside of me – Dr. Tupper, Mr. Henry and about 9 other gentlemen came. It is pouring rain so there is no going out for me to-day. Mr. Crowther is here he came to call on me this morning he wants to hold me good for the dance I promised him at Quebec!

SATURDAY MORNING, OCT. 29
I feel quite well this morning. I went down to the Ball last night such a splendid affair. Mr. Crowther danced with me the first Quadrille. Sir Fenwick Williams was here looking as well as ever he called on us all in the afternoon. I did not stay very late at the Ball. I was engaged for every dance but I was afraid of being knocked up....

I have just come in from Notman's my photograph was not good, I don't think, so I would not take it. However, the man said he would send me two down to the Island.... All the Gentlemen are in Conference. Sir Fenwick Williams called [on] me and I saw him in the drawing room.[12]

The party went up the Ottawa, and Mercy Ann recorded for posterity the wonders of that journey.

> MONDAY, (morning), OCT. 31 On board the Prince of Wales. I have just seen the Rapids mentioned in the Canadian Boat Song. Yesterday at breakfast we made the acquaintance of a Mr. Robertson who offered us his seat at the Cathedral such a nice service. We walked around after. We saw the Church plate and the Bible presented by the Prince of Wales. We walked up to see McGill College Such magnificent residences are in the vicinity. We went back to the Hotel in a street car. At three o'clock we went through the Grand Victoria Bridge. Sir R. McDonell and his lady went with us. We stopt in the middle and got out. We saw the rivet the Prince of Wales drove in, they opened the windows and we looked down on a raft just passing under the bridge.

> NOVEMBER 2ND. WEDNESDAY Aboard the Corslet. Prescott.
> We have been travelling ever since 8 o'clock. Yesterday we had such a gala day. We went to see the Parliament Buildings in the morning, they are magnificent such a splendid – of everything that is grand. The Picture Gallery is the only room that is finished fit to – and it was there we had the luncheon. We saw the model of the library which will be a most splendid building it is made of plaster Paris and is kept in a room to show what the library will be. We went quite to the top and saw such a nice view of Ottawa, the Chaudiere Falls are very pretty and can be seen very well from there in the halls are some marble pillars the marble is got near Ottawa and is the prettiest I have seen, when we came out we walked round the grounds and saw the Rideau Canal which has 8 locks. We saw the place where the new barracks are to be built. We went there at 2 then to luncheon. It was a grand affair.... We went to the ball in the evening it was a very grand affair. I had to refuse six gentlemen the first Quadrille.... I had been engaged the day before. I have kept my card which has all the names of my partners written by themselves. I had to come away with half a dozen gentlemen not danced with.[13]

Kingston, Belleville, Cobourg – all the big towns on the line became part of the triumphal procession to Toronto. Mercy records it *en route*.

> ½ PAST TWO.
> We have just dined at Kingston such a delicious dinner given by Mr. Bridges.

> 8/45 Just arrived at Belleville all the voluntary turned out. The Mayor presented an address. They drank the health of the

mayor and started the moment after. Mr. Crowther has just given me a likeness of himself and Mr. Drinkwater. I will have to lie down again. Won a pair of gloves from Mr. –

TORONTO QUEEN'S HOTEL
THURSDAY NOVEMBER 3 – We arrived at Mr. Cockburn's place last night at eight o'clock – such a beautiful place, he gave us a magnificent supper the only pity was we had such a short time to stay. They had illuminations and all sorts of grandeur. We arrived here at 10 o'clock such a grand affair torch light procession 5000 people were in front of the hotel. Dr. Tupper, Mr. Tilley and Mr. Brown made speeches from a gallery just beneath my bedroom window.[14]

And so with music and feasting the Maritimes came to Canada.

Toronto turned out to greet them with a deafening welcome. Some people from the western towns where the visitors would go later, joined with the people of Toronto to roar their greetings too.

Young Mr. Lawson from Hamilton was there, the weight of his newly acquired mercantile empire heavy on his shoulders. He pondered the significance of the marriage of the provinces, should it take place, to his expanding business. Perhaps his father had handed the Lawson Emporium over to him a little too soon. He thought of the grist mill at Ancaster which was now his responsibility, as well as the retail clothing, furnishings, small wares, and implements business. All the men in the mill and in the store depended upon him now for wages. What would this confederation mean to him – and to them? He thought they would take their lead from him, as they had from his father. Unless, of course, there was politics in it, and then they would vote as they had always voted.

Jack Brady from Bradsbrook came in from the country fifty miles northeast of Toronto, to rest his mind about the galloping idea of a Confederation. He saw young Mr. Lawson, and made his way towards him. Although he was ten years older than the merchant, they had married sisters; they met seldom, but with pleasure.

Jack Brady motioned to where a young man stood with his childlike wife. She was so small, so almost lost in her mantle, she seemed about to be drowned in her crinoline.

"Andrews the brewer from London, isn't it?"

"I shouldn't have noticed him, unless you had brought him to my attention. Surely he's changed? He must have lost two stone?"

"I'm sure he has. Very worried about his wife, I think perhaps. Has no reason to be worried with his business, I hear."

Mrs. Andrews clung to her husband's arm and bowed with a kind of fragile grace to her husband's acquaintances. Mr. Andrews bent to speak to her, and they went slowly off towards the Queen's Hotel.

"Doesn't look as if she'll live the winter out, does she?"

"I never thought to see her live to marry at all. She is quite a friend of Amelia's, and told her that her doctors thought it might be a healthy thing for her to marry."

Young Mr. Lawson thought of his Amelia, not to come with him because she was too near her time, and he could not allow her to travel. She loved a spectacle, and would have seen things here which he might not. She was full of ideas for expanding the business. She thought a drapery department – not just flannel and turkey red, but silks and fine things, would be profitable. People had to travel to Toronto, or even Montreal, for really good patterns, she said.

Thousands of people jammed the streets in front of the Queen's Hotel, swamped the station and the approaches to the station, and flowed over the Esplanade and into York Street. The band of the Queen's Own marched along Front Street, playing as if music were about to go out of style and they must make the most of it now. Ladies in vast crinolines were handed down from high-wheeled carriages; the doors flashed shut, and the glossy hackneys, reflecting the torchlight, stepped high and were gone into the shadows again. The roars of the crowd rose in thunder, as the delegates in carriage after beleaguered carriage, finally pressed their way to the hotel door. Someone shouted, "They're coming out on the balcony now," and the crowd roared again.

Three hundred men of the Fire Brigade, torches high in their hands, flamed down the street in torchlight processions, terrifying the horses. They reared and snorted; hostlers leapt for their heads.

Then the band of the 10th Rifles as loud and stirring as the Queen's Own marched by, mingling their music with the fiery golden jets and silver fountains and rockets which sprang now into the dark sky, and came down in red and blue and green bubbles of fire.

Then a sudden silence fell over the crowd waiting to hear the men speak. The crowd stood still almost as if expecting a sign from the sky. There was something in the torchlit air of that early November night in Toronto which could not be seen nor touched, but which was making its real presence known. Among the people there came a stirring, an expectation, a quickening of the heart and spirit. A magic was at work, so that it seemed to the men gathered in the torchlight with the music all about them, that all things could be done now, and royally done, when before, perhaps, they had been afraid.

People told themselves wordlessly, that there were great things in the air, and they promised themselves to do great things.

Young Mr. Lawson lifted his shoulders. He would be worthy of the great responsibility laid upon him. He would make of the Lawson Emporium and the Lawson Mills, in this great new country, an enterprise which would be a source of pride to it. Mr. Andrews looked down at the face of his young wife, glowing with excitement. There were places in Germany, in England, where miraculous baths sometimes worked miraculous cures for ailments such as hers. He pulled her arm closer within his and promised that he should take her there to the best one. Jack Brady thought, strangely, of his godchild in Ireland, a young woman now, whom he had never seen. Her father, his cousin, had died at sea – seven years ago, it must be. Every year he had said that he would go and see how she was. Now he would go next year, perhaps, and bring her out to stay with them. He would write to her at once, or to her mother, to see if it could not be done.

The men on the balcony finished speaking, waved their hands again in response to the thunder of applause, and were gone.

And so, to the sound of much music, to the bubbling of much champagne, with the feasting on many oysters, with the clasping of many hands, with the drinking of many toasts while the band played, the bargain concluded. There were still to be a thousand more hours at the conference tables, violent opposition, the breaking of hearts, the scratching of many pens, the signing of many papers, and the crossing of Atlantic water. But the vows had been made and the contract approved in the minds and hearts of the men with the limitless imagination. And in torchlight and parade and cheering, the Canadas greeted their brothers from the Maritimes to whom all Canada was new.

●

Letter One.

JACK BRADY, BRADSBROOK, CANADA WEST,

TO ISABELLA MOORE, DUBLIN, IRELAND.

· · · ●●●● · ·

Bradsbrook, C.W.
24 June, 1865

Dear Cousin Isabella,

It is possible that my name may not be favourably known to you, yet your father and I were cousins, and I have been alas, a very negligent godfather to you. Once, about fourteen years ago now, I visited your home in Fitzwilliam Square. You and your sister were on holiday then with your mother, and you must have been just a very small girl. But although Desmond, your father, was some twenty years older than myself, we had a very cheerful time together, and I have promised myself many times that I would go again to Dublin, and hope to see the rest of Desmond's family. But now he has been gone these seven years, and I have not returned. I had hoped (and indeed I know that Desmond had intended to make the journey across the Atlantic) to see your father here. But these plans retire behind immediate concerns, as well I know.

However, to come now to my point. You bear my mother's name, and have, according to your father's opinion, much of the look of the Bradys about you – the auburn hair and blue eyes which distinguished my father's people. The last time I wrote to Desmond I asked him if he would send you to us for a year, when he considered that you were old enough to come. Now by my calculations you must be nearly twenty years of age. Before you marry (and had you already done so I feel sure you would have sent us news), we hope very much to have you here. We think that we can make you comfortable.

My wife Maude who has not been abroad now for some years because of her duty to her children, still young, thinks that she can not yet leave them. Otherwise she would hope to visit you at home and accompany you here. You see that you are expected to accept our invitation. In a twelvemonth, or at most eighteen months from now, I shall be in Europe, and will come to Fitzwilliam Square, and arrange for you to come to Canada in the same ship as I. It will be a privilege for us to welcome you here, and I need not say that Desmond Moore's daughter will be our guest from the moment she steps out of her own home.

    Your affectionate cousin,
    JACK BRADY.

●

Letter Two.

ISABELLA MOORE TO HER SISTER CONSTANCE,

IN DUBLIN, IRELAND.

· · ∘ ● ● ● ∘ · ·

On Board the *Scotia*
29 November, 1866

Dear Constance,
    You will have had assurance from our friends that they saw Cousin Jack and me safely aboard the *Scotia*. I had intended to keep a sort of Journal, which at the end of the voyage I should send to you. Alas I have found myself so occupied that I have had little recourse to my writing desk. It had never occurred to me that life on board an Atlantic steamer could be such a busy one. Conversations with many new acquaintances fill in the hours most pleasantly. And there are daily contests and guessing games about how many knots we go and how far in a day and when we shall land.

We have been perhaps more than usually fortunate in our company among the hundred and eighty passengers. There is a large cargo of freight on board, and of course, we carry much mail. There are Germans, Dutch, French, Spaniards, and Bavarians on board, Canadians, Americans, and about thirty English, I believe. The ladies are in a minority, there being not over a score of our sex, including a number of American ladies, and three lively French women. A number of Jesuit brethren are among us, and most of the others seem to be rather quiet gentlemen, for whom an Atlantic crossing is obviously no novelty.

There is a Mr. Andrew, for example, who is in the habit of crossing twice a year – on business, I presume. Cousin Jack is an acquaintance, and has introduced Mr. Andrew to me. He is in the distilling business, and has recently lost his wife. He wears only black suits, his tie is black, and he does not affect at any time the flowered brocade waistcoats that

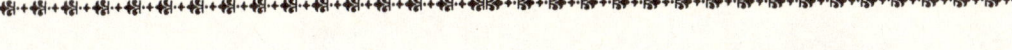

Les dames jouant aux quilles à Cacouna   Public Archives of Canada

Croquet at Belmere, Lake Memphremagog, P.Q., 1870   Public Archives of Canada

La course pour le Prix de la Reine, June 27, 1872

Sous la grande tribune

La grande tribune

La vente de poules

PHOTOS ON THIS AND FACING PAGE FROM PUBLIC ARCHIVES OF CANADA

Running of the Queen's Plate, Whitby, C. W., May 24, 1862   Thos. Bouckley Collection

Saut des barrières

La course à double harnais

1.
The four-oared boat race
between Tyne and St. John Crews
on the Kennebeccassis, 1871

Public Archives of Canada

2.
Cycling, circa 1868

Manitoba Archives

3.
The Ice Velocipede, 1870

Public Archives of Canada

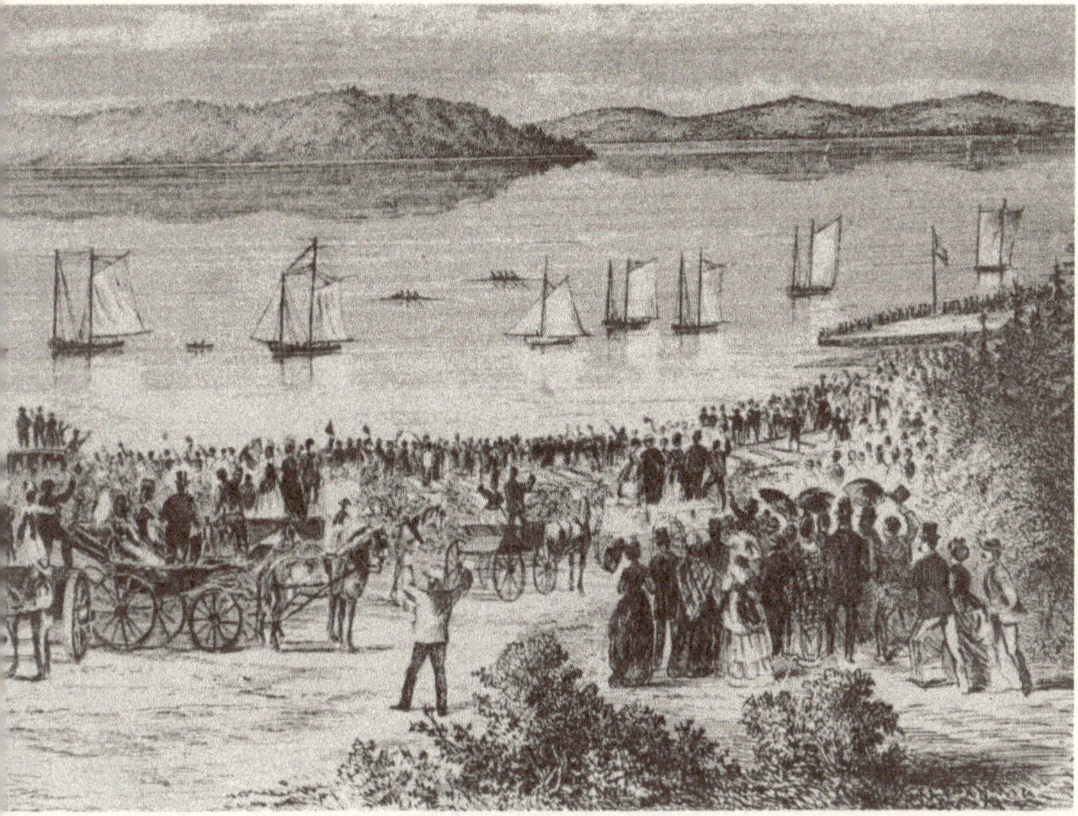

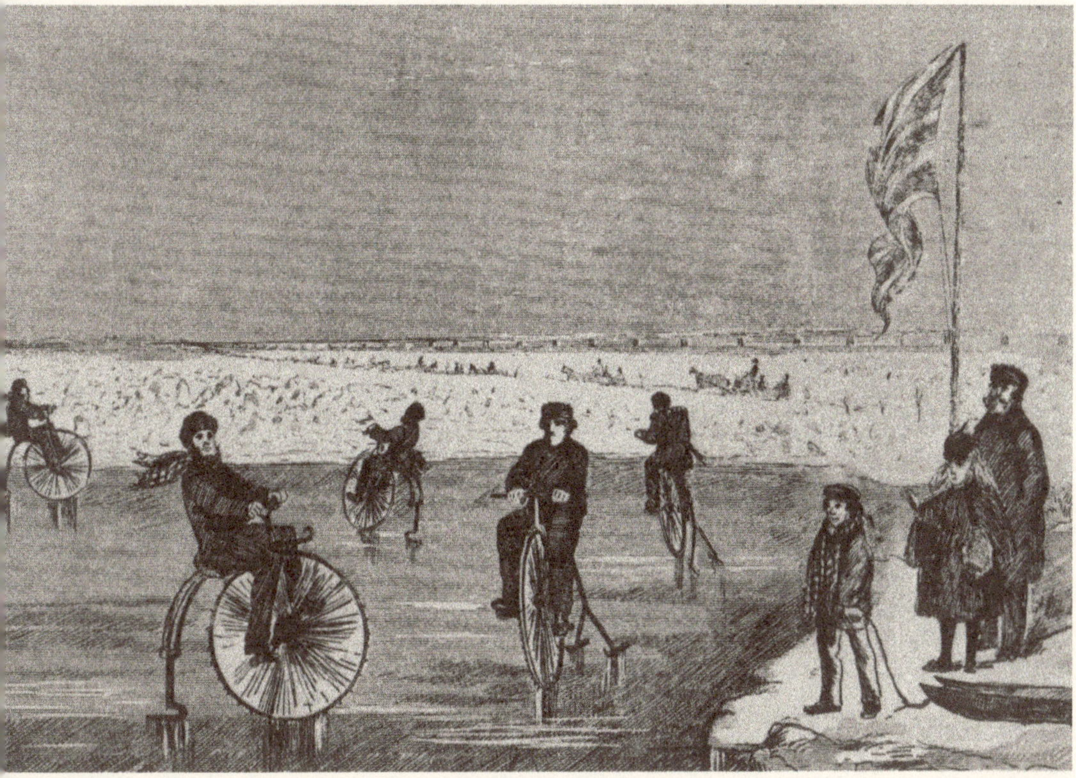

1. *Skating rink interior, St. John, New Brunswick, 1870,*

The Canadian Illustrated News

2. *Dominion snow-shoe hurdle races, Montreal, circa 1870*

The Canadian Illustrated News

3.
Trotting races
on the ice
near Montreal, 1871

Public Archives
of Canada

Picnic at Montmorency, "Captain Buzbie drives Miss Muffin"
Toronto Public Libraries

Picnic at Montmorency, "Coming down is easier but more dangerous"
Toronto Public Libraries

many of the gentlemen wear. He is the most agreeable of conversationalists when engaged in animated converse. But when his face is in repose it wears a most melancholy expression. He is, I think, the youngest gentleman in the ship and rather more distinguished than handsome, with dark chestnut curling hair and whiskers.

When it was discovered by my new acquaintances that I had not crossed to North America before, I might have been smothered by the torrents of advice which flowed over me. I learned what I must positively see, what I must on no account, miss, and what I should guard against wasting time in gazing upon. There was by no means a unanimity among my teachers.

Several of the American ladies assured me that I should be most disappointed in Canada and should alter my plans and travel in the United States instead. I was urgently invited to visit one of the American ladies in California; another pressed the beauties of Chicago upon me.

A gentleman from Nova Scotia who sits opposite us at table by no means agrees with Cousin Jack that it would be a splendid thing for all the British American colonies to unite. He growled into his claret again and again and said confederation would bring no joy to Nova Scotia. Nova Scotia would be swamped. And as for the whole idea, it was a monstrous one and its nature would be a "thing of shreds and patches," neither monarchy or republic, an unnatural thing altogether. He pounds on the table and gets purple in the face and leaves us very abruptly whenever the subject comes into the conversation, which it, of course, very frequently does.

The American ladies were most elaborately dressed, with, to my taste, too much obvious extravagance. The two Canadian ladies whom I have come to know were more quietly costumed, and less pressing in their insistence that I should not fail to visit them in some far distant city. A Mrs. Kirkwood from some small village in Canada West, St. Thomas, I think, has the most elegant travelling costumes I have ever seen. Simple, but perfect in fit and far from ostentatious in colour. When one has looked for a few moments at Mrs. Kirkwood, one does see that the small feathers in her bonnet are of the exact shade of the Van Dyking on her skirt, which in its turn echoes the colour of her fine kid gloves.

Mrs. Kirkwood is returning from a visit to England where her daughter who returns with her, has made her home with her husband, Major Ormiston. Major Ormiston was stationed in London, Canada West, until a year or two ago and made Miss Kirkwood's acquaintance there. Apparently such marriages between officers and Canadian girls of good family are by no means rare. Major Ormiston's regiment has been sent away again to the east, I believe, and Mrs. Ormiston is to spend the winter with her mother in St. Thomas. Mrs. Kirkwood says she does not wish to spend the cold weather in England, because of the severity of the climate there. I was extremely surprised to hear such a sentiment, since I have always understood Canada to be a much colder country than England. I still think myself wise to have brought out mother's old fur coat. I have worn it already to my comfort, if not to my pride in walking the decks.

Madame de Trouville from St. Anne de something, a place on the St. Lawrence, I believe, is in heavy mourning, and although always polite, had little to say with any vigour. Her blacks are the softest richest weaves. I did not know that there could be such heavy bombazine. She wears no jet or feathers, but is wrapped in seal. Had I suspected the quality of the clothes which the Canadian lady travellers wear, I should certainly not have chosen my last year's grey poplin to bring, and the brown alpaca should have stayed at home with our mother's old beaver. Mrs. Kirkwood and her daughter, Mrs. Ormiston, Madame de Trouville, and I exchanged cards. Gossip in the ship runs that this French lady is the widow of a sugar magnate, and lives in a large way in French Canada. She has spent some months abroad now, and has spoken of being anxious to be at home. She travels alone, with only her maid.

All the American ladies on board are most extraordinarily thin. I was so struck with this aspect of their appearance that I spoke to Mr. Andrew about it, as I walked with him and Cousin Jack, on the deck. Mr. Andrew says that the young American women are, in figure, elegant, and almost sylph-like. In the most gentlemanlike words Mr. Andrew indicated that this effect was in fact produced without any harmful artificial restraint. As I buttoned the thirty buttons of my brown alpaca basque before dinner, I pulled the strings a little tighter. I found that there was a certain undue pressure required. I do not think that I could be called sylph-like, although I am but one and twenty. I find it oddly disturbing that I could not so be considered. At dinner I looked at Mrs. Ormiston, wearing the most elegant purple moire. I was forced to confess that "sylph-like" could be certainly applied to her, although she is a married woman and not above two or three years older than I. Mr. Andrew said that American women kept their thinness which often amounted to an angularity as they matured. They age sooner, he thought, than English girls, and do not acquire the attractive embonpoint of the middle aged British lady.

What the reason for this can be I cannot say, but certainly it is difficult to believe that one can cross the Atlantic remaining in good health, and do anything like justice to the food supplied, and still remain thin.

A very large part of the day on board ship is spent in dining, breakfasting, supping.

At eight o'clock in the morning one finds long tables in the dining salon profusely adorned with an immense variety of food. The food is provided until half past nine, and even if only a few passengers appear, the quantity and variety remains unchanged. You will find ham, Irish stew, mutton chops, broiled salmon, cold tongue, crimped cod, eggs, tea, coffee, chocolate, toast, and hot rolls. Lunch is at twelve, when there is cold beef, potatoes, pickles, hotch potch, and a very large consumption of pale ale.

Dinner – four in the afternoon. Long bills of fare are set out on the tables, and there is plenty of good and well-iced water with each meal. The service is exact. When the captain is seated twelve stewards in neat blue uniforms spring to action. Each table steward lifts the lid of the great tureen of soup which stands at the head of each table. There is an amazing variety of soup and fish, game, venison, meat, and poultry of all kinds offered, with French side dishes, a profusion of jellies, puddings, and pastry, and a plentiful dessert of fresh and preserved fruits. Ale, spirits, wine, and liqueurs flow freely at dinner, and there is much consumed.

You will understand that when tea is served at seven, there is little interest displayed. From half past nine to half past ten any passenger may order what he fancies, anything from pickles to punch.

After tea and until eleven o'clock one would easily suppose himself to be in a reception room in a fashionable hotel. Two regularly organized whist parties play rubber after rubber, seemingly without end. Three or four chess boards are employed at one time, and there is no lack of backgammon players.

Cousin Jack comes now to advise me to go to bed, to be ready for tomorrow, when we are due to land. I am both glad and sorry. One makes interesting acquaintances in a ship, and the likelihood of ever seeing them again is so slight that a melancholy must result.

If you hear of a very trustworthy messenger coming out to Canada, will you think of entrusting my small jewel casket to his care? I begin to feel that I have been greatly mistaken in leaving my garnet parure behind, and the tall comb with the garnet and carbuncles. I had not thought, when coming to what we are told is really a country in a bush, that I should have need of such things, but Mrs. Kirkwood says they are very fashionable here.

> Your affectionate sister,
> ISABELLA.

3

The Travellers and the Towns

The cities of the Canadas and the Maritimes had declared their distinct and separate personalities by the sixties. The little river-bound town, the village on the lakeside, and the early settlement back from the water (but never very far) had formed its unique characteristics, moulded by several generations of people who settled there long enough to lay the mysterious pattern of their ways upon it. Each had its unmistakable flavour; its aura and allure were distinct, unique to itself. So strong was this emanation of culture that an astonishing agreement was voiced among the travellers who saw and hastened to pronounce upon the character and aspect of the cities.

The travellers came in scores to the British possessions in North America, in the sixties. There were ladies and gentlemen, military and naval men, active and retired. There came journalists and actors, university men and businessmen, singers and lecturers. More than one officer who had been early stationed in Montreal or Quebec or Niagara came back when he was retired to see the places which he had known when he was young, and where he had been happy. Many were perhaps drawn back because they suffered a nostalgia for the country of the great snows. They went to see their men who had stayed and now belonged to Canada. But they, returning, also felt something of a sense of proprietorship.

The colonies which had defected from the Empire almost a hundred years ago were in the sixties in anguished danger of splitting in two. The travellers went to the United States – to the cities of the North, and, when they could, to the cities of the South. They circled round from Nova Scotia and New Brunswick, some of them taking a few days in the lotus land of Prince Edward Island on their way. They went down through the passionate States to Boston, Chicago, and New York, then by Niagara to Canada.

Comparisons were invariably made with the manners and customs of the republican Americans and the monarchist behaviour on the northern half of the continent.

And since the decade was a very literary one, when not only a professional writing man took his pen in hand, a great many of these travellers wrote down impressions of what they saw and felt and experienced.

During the Civil War, English travellers to the States, particularly vocal ones (and there don't seem to have been many of the other kind), were by no means welcomed. There was rough treatment of English journalists; they were inclined to come back to the British dependency thoroughly prepared to like what they were shown.

Most distinguished among the commentators on Canadian life in the sixties was the celebrated pioneer war correspondent, W. H. Russell. Mr. Russell had so vividly portrayed the Crimean War for *The Times* of London that he was thought to be responsible for the fall of the government and a new policy in the Crimea. He came to Canada fresh from able, effective, and highly unpopular reporting of the American Civil War. Stepping gratefully once more on British soil after a turbulent visit to the warring States, he came in by Niagara.

> *The toll-takers and revenue officers on the bridge showed the usual apathy of their genus. Had the King of Oude appeared with all his court on elephants, they would have only been puzzled how to assess the animals.*[15]

Mr. Russell included Hamilton in his tour of observation, and like all the travellers of the time, fell victim to its magic.

> *After a few hours' ride the train reached Hamilton, one of the most thriving, if not the largest cities of Upper Canada. Somewhat less than half a century ago this flourishing town, or "ambitious little city" as it is familiarly termed, was but a wilderness. Now it possesses a happy population of over twenty thousand souls; is ornamented by several elegant churches – always a pleasing sight – imposing lofty stores, a fine public market, and commodious dwellings, in addition to a "monster hotel" that would be considered worthy of laudation in New York, Washington, or Philadelphia. The town itself is picturesquely situated in Burlington Bay, at the western extremity of Lake Ontario, and is handsomely laid out. The fine wide streets and the extreme cleanliness of the city at once make a favourable impression upon the traveller. To the rear stretches the Mountain, dotted all over with pretty villas; to the upper plateaux of which the prosperous citizens betake themselves during the sultry summer season, in order to derive benefit from the bracing breezes that always play around and fan that elevated locality.*[16]

There was something about Hamilton in the sixties which roused extravagant enthusiasm in the breasts and pens of the travellers. The Governor General's sister-in-law, Frances Monck, a lady not notably easy to please, walked for hours about the city, and applauded it as being airy, clean, and possessing a fine looking Roman Catholic Cathedral. And, in oddly related approval, wrote:

> *The soil is good, and the meat excellent. I was so ravenous I eat first roast beef, then hot boiled mutton, because there was no more beef.*[17]

The gay and exuberant gentleman amateur actor, Captain Rhys, who travelled the country on a £500 wager that he could clear the same sum as a professional in a strange country, in eighteen months, and under an assumed name, is responsible for some of the most spirited comments on the Canadian cities. The nature and inhabitants of Hamilton intrigued the Captain.

> *Some of my pleasantest hours in Canada I spent in Hamilton. Firstly, the hotel in which we were located, the "Royal," was one of the best in which we had yet enclosed ourselves ... Hamilton is curiously inhabited. There are more Englishmen there without any apparent occupation, and living upon apparently nothing, than in any other town in Canada. There are lots of billiard tables, and they (the inhabitants) play; there is a cricket ground – but I never saw any of them there, except in the capacity of lookers on. They seem to be an exiled lot, always looking out for, and expecting something that never turns up. They are constantly in the various stores – i.e. shops – which were and are good, without display, but never seem to purchase anything; and, in short, I never could make head or tail of them.*[18]

Captain Rhys made a special trip to Hamilton for a famous cricket match.

> *Ho! Back to Hamilton.*
> *Why did we go back to Hamilton for?*
> *Why, because everybody was going to Hamilton, of course, to see the great Cricket Match between the All England Eleven and the Canadian Twenty-Two. And which I was not going to miss, if I knew; I couldn't get away to see the game either at Montreal or New York, which I still always regret, that at the latter place especially, as I should not only have considerable benefited my banker's account, but should have had the consummate gratification of seeing the self-imposed invincible New York Twenty-two and their backers, tacken down an infinity of pegs – a result which I publicly prophesied when and wherever I had an opportunity of so doing, during my late sojourn in New York. As it was, however, I did manage to relieve one Republican enthusiast of his odds of four to one, to the tune of eight hundred dollars.*[19]

The playwright and actor, writer, wit, and sportsman extraordinary, gave Toronto full marks for looks.

> *Toronto is the handsomest town we have yet seen. Wide streets, good shops, lovely gardens, handsome public buildings, churches rich in spires and traceried windows, spacious hotels,*

and elegant equipages. We put up at the Revere House, and during our stay there was a grand Scottish gathering. Such piping and dancing, and throwing the caber! Glorious weather, bands playing, handsome women, wonderful calves (the men, I mean – that is, the men's legs)....[20]

Mr. Russell, who filled the columns of the London *Times* with descriptions of American cities (in one of which he had almost met his death from malevolence), and who knew the great Scandinavian cities, as well as those of his own native islands, agreed with Mr. Rhys. He came from Niagara by train, and then

... a sharp smart sleigh-drive, and we were at the comfortable hotel called Rossin House – The people in the streets were well dressed, comfortable looking, well-to-do. The servants here are Irish men and women, with a sprinkling of free negroes. Churches, cathedrals, markets, post-offices, college, schools, mechanics' institutes, rise to imperial dignity over the city.... The shops are large and well furnished with goods.... The city is so very surprising in the extent and excellence of its public edifices, that I was fain to write to an American friend at New York to come up and admire what had been done in architecture under a monarchy if he wished to appreciate the horrible state of that branch of the fine arts under his democracy.[21]

No traveller to Toronto failed to remark on the superb architecture of Osgoode Hall. Men, women, and children all had something to say of the great structure.

Little Mercy Ann Coles, wide eyed with the wonders she had seen on her wonderful jaunt, did a breathless piece in her diary in praise of Toronto and starring Osgoode Hall.

We started for the Lawyer's Hall, a splendid building the centre hall is right up to the roof stained glass in the dome the floor is mosaic. They showed us the Library and all the Judges' rooms. We drove from there to the University. It is a splendid Building nearly as handsome as the Ottawa Departmental Building. There all the students wore caps and gowns, the doctor made a very nice speech to us to which Dr. Tupper replied, we then visited the Museum in which is a very fine collection of birds and small animals. The Butterflies were beautiful we had to hasten away for our time was short, the students formed a line and cheered us as we drove down the avenue, from there we went to the Normal School which is certainly the most varied institution I ever saw, it combines a Picture Gallery, a statutory Gallery all kinds of miniature implements and nearly everything one can think of that is curious. The little boys and girls both sang when we went to their school rooms.... We had to hurry back to the Hotel for the gentlemen had to go to the Music Hall to luncheon....[22]

English visitors much more experienced and travelled than Mercy wrote letters home about the buildings in Toronto. There was no courthouse in England, they reported, to match Osgoode Hall.

> *A massive stone erection with a Hall up to the roof pillared and vaulted; tesselated pavements, carved work and pictures on all sides.*[23]

Anthony Trollope, travelling knowledgeably in British North America in the early sixties, gave Toronto his praise.

> *The two sights of Toronto are the Osgoode Hall and the University. The Osgoode Hall is to Upper Canada what the Four Courts are to Ireland. The law courts are all held there. Exteriorly little can be said for Osgoode Hall, whereas the exterior of the Four Courts in Dublin is very fine; but as an interior the temple of Themis at Toronto beats hollow that which the goddess owns in Dublin. In Dublin the Courts themselves are shabby, and the space under the dome is not so fine as the exterior seems to promise that it should be. In Toronto the Courts themselves are the most commodious that I ever saw, and the passages, vestibules, and hall are very handsome.*
>
> *But the University is the glory of Toronto. This is a Gothic building and will take rank after, but next to, the buildings at Ottawa. It will be the second piece of noble architecture in Canada, and as far as I know on the American continent. It is, I believe, intended to be purely Norman, though I doubt whether the received types of Norman architecture have not been departed from in many of the windows. Be that as it may the College is a manly, noble structure, free from false decoration, and infinitely creditable to those who projected it.*[24]

In Toronto, when the visits to the fine public buildings were done, it was fashionable to join the promenade of the fashionable along King Street. There was the bowing to friends, and perhaps an introduction, when the hosts would present their visitors to appropriate acquaintances. The acquaintances would call tomorrow, leave a card, or perhaps pursue a course to friendships. There was the cutting of the ladies and gentlemen who by some social misdemeanour could no longer be considered worthy of the gracious bow.

The tall, swift wheels spun past, plumes of dust flying behind them. The ladies raised their skirts ever so little to pass over the crossings which would be muddy had there been rain, although, in Toronto, the planks had been replaced by flags in places. And even where there were still planks, the travellers found the streets in better repair than in either Montreal or Quebec.

Before it was quite dark, and the torches were lit, there would be an oyster supper at any one of several well-recommended houses on King Street. Then home again to the hospitable house, after a pleasant afternoon, soon to be recorded in letters to the home parish in England. Toronto, they said, is really (reassuringly) English. There are more stone houses here than in Hamilton. And it is very curious that, although the people look as the people at home do, yet the visitors are always known for English, in whatever place they find themselves.

The Canadians had found their own unique distinction in manners and accent by the sixties, as well as their own distinctive difference in a thousand criteria of taste. It was revealing, not to say disturbing, to the English visitors that no apologies were made for the Canadian manners and customs when they differed, sometimes sharply, from the unquestioned standards of social behaviour at home. It is the women travellers, writing their daily journals of immediate impressions and criticisms who are lofty and superior when there is diversion from English habits. The gentlemen were able, and often obviously rejoiced, to encounter a more spacious social element in which they could find relaxed and spontaneous fun. The lady writers tended to hold up horrified hands at evidence of pejorative democracy. The gentlemen almost never did. They went along enthusiastically with the new ways and enjoyed themselves thoroughly. Which is not quite to say that there was not a pinch of disapproval.

In the late 1850's Isabella Lucy Bird travelled to North America and recorded of her visit to Toronto:

> *At Toronto my kind friend Mr. Forrest met me. He and his wife had invited me some months before to visit them in their distant home in the Canadian bush; therefore I was not a little surprised at the equipage which awaited me at the hotel, as I had expected to jolt for twenty-two miles, over corduroy roads, in a lumber waggon. It was the most dashing vehicle which I saw in Canada. It was a most unbushlike, sporting-looking, high, mail phaeton, mounted by four steps; it had three seats, a hood in front and a rack for luggage behind. The body and wheels were painted bright scarlet and black; and it was drawn by a pair of very showy-looking horses, about sixteen "hands" high with elegant and well-blacked harness. Mr. Forrest looked more like a sporting English squire than an emigrant.*
>
> *After some miles of very bad road, which had once been corduroy, we got upon a plank-road, upon which the draught is nearly as light as upon a railroad. We drove for many miles through woods of the American oak, little more than brushwood, but gorgeous in all shades of colouring, from the scarlet of the geranium to deep crimson and Tyrian purple. Oh! our poor faded tints of autumn about which we write sentimental poetry! Turning sharply round a bank of moss, and descending a long hill, we entered the bush. There all my dreams of Canadian scenery were more than realized. Trees grew in every variety of the picturesque. The forest was dark and oppressively still, and such a deadly chill came on, that I drew my cloak closer about me. A fragrant but heavy smell arose, and Mr. Forrest said that we were going down into a cedar swamp,*

where there was a chill even in the hottest weather. It was very beautiful. Emerging from this, we came upon a little whitewashed English church, standing upon a steep knoll, with its little spire rising through the trees; and leaving this behind, we turned off upon a road through very wild country. The ground had once been cleared, but no use had been made of it, and it was covered with charred stumps about two feet high. Beyond this appeared an interminable bush.

Mr. Forrest told me that his house was near, and from the appearance of the country, I expected to come upon a log cabin; but we turned into a field, and drove under some very fine apple trees to a house the very perfection of elegance and comfort. It looked as if a pretty villa from Norwood or Hampstead had been transported to this Canadian clearing. The dwelling was a substantially built brick one-storey house, with a deep green verandah surrounding it as a protection from the snow in winter and the heat in summer. Apple trees, laden with richly coloured fruit, were planted round, and sumach-trees, in all the glorious colour of the fall, were opposite the front door. The very house seemed to smile a welcome, and seldom have I met a more cordial one than I received from Mrs. Forrest, the kindly and graceful hostess who met me at the door. . . .

"Will you go into the drawing-room?" asked Mrs. Forrest. I was surprised, for I had not associated a drawing-room with emigrant life in Canada; but I followed her along a pretty entrance-lobby, floored with polished oak, into a lofty room, furnished with all the elegancies and luxuries of the mansions of an affluent Englishman at home, a beautiful piano not being lacking.

In a habit which took long to die, if indeed it is yet dead, visitors from abroad felt called upon to assess and evaluate what they saw. Very often one suspects a didactic purpose in the writing – improvement for the mortals who had made the awful change from being a citizen of a sovereign state to a dweller in "our dependencey." One gains the impression that more of a sea change might have been expected, a sinister sign laid on the face. There was surprise (not always delight) to find cities in this new world worthy of admiration. And again it was the ladies who found the little niggling faults. From the height of her absolute incompetence in domestic matters, the sight of a lady supervising her own kitchen was a despicable sight. Or it ought to have been. The indubitable fact that the lady in question was elegantly dressed and composed in mind while she directed the miracles of the kitchen could not but disturb. The gentlemen could assess the grandeur of the achievement in a comparatively short time from the state of a rough, undeveloped pioneer country where subsistence was the aim, to the prosperous civilization which met their eyes in the sixties.

> *I am now here once more after roving for twenty years, and find the country prosperous, loyal and free. Labour and good pay for the million, bread for everyone, and land cheap enough for those that can buy. People whom I left here twenty years past, poor and dependent on their able hands are now residing in elegant houses, elegantly furnished, are wealthy and independent.*[25]

With its own special *élan*, Montreal caught the imagination of the travellers. They could be delighted with the grey and ancient aspect of Quebec, but there was a lively romance, a kind of success story, about Montreal.

Returning travellers, once stationed in Montreal, claimed the city as their own. Quick to praise and compare.

> *I think I may say that in truth Montreal is celebrated for pretty women and fine horses. Our horses go like the wind in harness or under the saddle, and are thoroughly educated.*
>
> *The people won't put up with pipeclay water for new milk, as they do in London. I see a cow attached to almost every good house in the west-end. All under the charge of one herdsman. He drives them into town every morning and evening, to be milked at their respective homes. As he passes each door he blows his horn, the gate opens and the milker knows her crib. In like manner he collects them by the sound of his horn for the field, not over a mile from the city. The priests let their pasture for cattle, $8 or $10 each, for six months.*[26]

The *Times* of London, offering columns from Mr. Russell, brought the beauties of Montreal architecture before its readers. The old French river port on the mighty St. Lawrence supported a population of more than 90,000 people, in the early sixties, the *Times* said, and might well offer competition in any number of ways to cities of comparable size in the British Islands.

> *The quays of Montreal are of imperial beauty, and would reflect credit on any city in Europe. They present a continuous line of cut stone from the Lachine Canal along the river-front before the city, leaving a fine broad mall or esplanade between the water's edge, and the houses. The publick buildings, built of solid stone, in which a handsome limestone predominates, are of very great merit. Churches, courthouses, banks, markets, hospitals, colleges are worthy of a capital. . . .*[27]

The *London Herald* with news from the pen of the jaunty Mr. S. P. Day, conferred more honour on Montreal than a mere architectural bouquet.

> *To speak truly, I was scarcely prepared to find the "Island City" so noble, prosperous, and thoroughly British. The tangible evidences of commercial greatness and social advancement*

> *were unmistakeable. Everywhere my eye lighted upon public buildings, not only substantial, but ornamental and unique. Now, when it is considered that splendid churches, a courthouse, banks, a fine market hall, groups of warehouses, stores and handsome private residences, besides the Victoria Tubular Bridge, have mostly sprung up during the last few years, there can be no hesitation in awarding due merit to the Montrealers, whose social progress has been so unparalleled. It will not be considered an elimination of truth to affirm, that few people on the whole continent of America have manifested so much spirit or enterprise.*[28]

Since Champlain first sighted the great rock of Quebec, no writing traveller has been able to curb a passion to describe it, each feeling that he can give it the glory it deserves. Many travellers have confessed themselves defeated by Niagara, but all had a whack at Quebec. The unexpectedly foreign and antique charm of Quebec enchanted them. The travellers of the sixties were no exception to this rule. The ladies turned out some lofty and sentimental pieces, and almost always found space to say that the streets were rough and dangerous and dirty; that the horses were wild, and the drivers something less than considerate. But the gentlemen were completely carried away by the majesty of Cape Diamond and the river and the grey stone citadel on the crest of the great rock.

> *The majestic appearance of Cape Diamond and the frowning fortifications – the cupolas and minarets blazing in the sun – the noble basin, like a sheet of silver, wherein a hundred sail of the line may safely ride – the river St. Charles, gracefully meandering – the numberous village spires on either side of the St. Lawrence – the fertile fields dotted with clusters of cottages – the imposing scenery of Point Levi and New Liverpool – the charming island of Orleans, and in the distance the bold Cape Tourment and the lofty range of purple mountains, form a coup d'oeil almost impossible to be surpassed.*[29]

Thus were the readers of the *Herald* informed by Mr. Day.

The neatness and symmetry of the pleasure grounds in Saint John were noted with approval by all who passed that way. Halifax was much commended for the dignity of her stone houses and the beautiful Bedford Basin. And yet . . . and yet . . . while there was Toronto and Montreal and Quebec, there was also Hamilton. One could not forget Hamilton. Mr. S. P. Day, who had seen all, had seen Hamilton, and Mr. Day remained enchanted.

> *Few towns or people in Canada have impressed me more favourably than did Hamilton and its citizens. In point of construction and beauty the former is faultless . . . I am inclined to regard Hamilton as the modern "Arcadia" of British North America, where the citizens dwell in happiness and brotherhood, where actual poverty is unknown.*[30]

4

Christmas In A Village, Canada West, 1866

The Brady house in Bradsbrook was a tall, red brick structure. Its seven broad gables were feathered in intricately cut verges, alternating motifs of paired tiny angel wings and the leaves of the shamrock. It stretched back and back, to include a long summer kitchen turned at a pleasant obtuse angle from the main body of the house. Beyond the kitchen a vast room with no ceiling but its tall roof, and brick within as without, provided apple storage for the fruit of the orchards which produced part of the Brady wealth. The mills which answered for most of it hummed away across the stream. Stemming out from the apple storage section, forming a kind of courtyard, the driving shed stood, one storey high, amply large for cutter and fringe topped democrat, double buggy and light sleigh.

Three hundred acres lay with the house. From its hilltop it looked down through virgin pines and a gentle southern slope to a fertile countryside, and a village very pleasing to the eye.

The village lay in a valley. Three grist mills ground away on the stream that gave it its name. A young fellow from Ireland named Jack Brady, two generations ago, leaving starvation behind him, stretched out his thin and eager hands to the bounty of this smiling corner of Canada West, and named the village and the brook after himself. Perhaps he did not intend the contraction. Being of a poetic turn of mind, and finding "creek" to throw up an image of rough untutored and cluttered streams, he conjured "brook" from the memory of the gentle waters of his native country which he knew he would never see again. His "location," the lands which he was given, and the lands which he later bought, became "Brady's Brook." Corrupted by time and usage, when the first Jack was long dead, the village which grew up about his mills became "Bradsbrook." It became a mark of distinction and a confirmation of knowledge of the district to pronounce it correctly.

It was the third Jack Brady who by 1866 had built his great house on the hill at the edge of the village.

The village itself, as a hundred villages like it in Canada West, burst into much building, in the fifties and sixties.

Le Bas Canada led the way to the building of beautiful and enduring churches. But by the sixties the Upper Province had abandoned nearly all the small rough-cast places of worship, and was creating small but beautifully designed and constructed buildings for the worship of God.

There were four such, built within a decade, in Bradsbrook. The worshippers there were more Chapel than Church, and the smallest one of all was a tiny, white, board and batten, gothic design. But so perfect were its proportions that it could have been set with pride anywhere in the islands from which most of its supporters had come. The love of stone which glows forever in the hearts of the Scots who had left their granite hills to come to Canada was reflected in the pink and grey stone which they used to build a kirk for themselves. Square-topped windows, twenty-four clear panes in each, lifted the little stone structure a touch beyond too great severity. John Wesley's name was carved in stone above the door of the biggest church. John Wesley's windows were garnet and blue, and his spire shone tall and slender and silvery into the sky. Beyond the stream to the east, a starkly simple, grey frame Mennonite church upheld by uncompromising lines and lack of ostentation, its doctrines of purity and self-effacement in the sight of the Lord. A mile or two beyond the village, at a crossroad, where there might some time be a village, a small red brick structure raised the cross, and was prepared to serve many Roman Catholic believers, when they should come. So far the Romans had not clanned together as the Presbyterians had, but the flock, although small and scattered, was served. And tonight there were lights at the cross roads.

The snow came early to the Canadas in 1866. In the days before Christmas there was perfect sleighing in Canada West, and in Canada East the towns and villages were smothered in white. Starch-like, crackling snow mortared the patches of corduroy still to be found in low lying spots on the road.

The Bradsbrook Christmas Fair did good business in the Market Building. By evening when the lanterns were lit outside the door and the last of the shoppers came steaming in, there was little left of the ducks and geese, the turkeys, the few chunks of spiced beef, the many wheels of cheese, the crocks of mincemeat, and the mountains of eggs. The tables in the stalls under the green boughs were almost empty, except for a few cakes claimed earlier in the day and waiting to be called for. The biggest turkey of them all, alone now, carried a "First Prize" red ribbon round his neck. He waited to be picked up.

A tall and ancient negro stepped in, carrying his lantern carefully. For most people the brilliance of the snow lit the road enough for easy walking. But this man was old, and perhaps more nearly blind than he would admit.

"Think you can carry the colonel's bird?"

The old man smiled and nodded. "The sleigh's outside there."

"I'll carry him out for you." But the old man shook his head. "Give it into my hands."

"I hear you've got a visitor, up on the hill, Jefferson."

"Yes, we have, too. Young lady from Ireland, she is."

"A relation to the Colonel, somehow, isn't she?"

The negro nodded, staggered under the weight of the turkey,

righted himself, and went out, the lantern dangling from his wrist.

Cutters and sleighs climbed the hill from the Port, seven miles away to the south. They passed at the four corners to pay toll. A slim red cutter with a snorting horse shot past the toll gate before the keeper could close it after the stage went through. The keeper roared and shook his fist, but the driver of the cutter laughed, waved, and drove on. Dashing down from the north with a great tingling of bells a stage coach paused to let his passengers out. A couple of men, two officers glorious in furs, and a sweet-faced woman with a little girl in a scarlet hood came down out of the coach, carpet bags and parcels in their hands. The driver made change, wished his cargo a Merry Christmas, and whipped up his horses towards the toll.

There was light enough on the main street. Beams from hanging lamps in the tailor shop, the doctor's offices, and the general store shone through the frosty windows as from tiny suns. Lights shone warm and yellow from the harness-maker's shop, and through the windows of the general store. The many-paned window of the jeweller's store gleamed with the gold of watches and chains, of lockets and bangles, amethyst brooches and sets of carbuncle buttons.

The blacksmiths were working late tonight. The mighty clang of their heavy hammers striking sparks from the iron added its strong staccato to the sound of the sleigh bells. Bellows blew the fires into roaring light and sparks flew like miniature fireworks into the dark. As the door opened, a strong smell of burning hoof mingled with the frosty pine-scented air, and a gleaming chestnut freshly shod pranced out into the road, to be backed into his shafts and turned, frantic, homeward towards his oats. Horses tethered to hitching posts along both sides of the street sent plumes of steam into the air. Once in a while a sad-faced livery horse quickened his pace as he neared home and slithered his cutter into the narrow lane to the livery barn.

There were two photographers in Bradsbrook, and they were busy tonight. Dripping glass plates were lifted out of dark tanks, and negatives inspected by hands yellow from the chemicals. Christmas orders were being demanded – the baby in his barrowcoat, indecently nude, but with a background of Niagara Falls; Grandmother and Grandfather, rigidly severe, with six inch brass frames; gay lads twirling their canes against an improbable backdrop of mountain and mountain goat.

The three great mills set on the two branches of the brook like giant watchmen over the village were dark tonight, only vast shadows bulking up into the winter sky. Brady's big mill of soft pink brick, built in 1848 in sheer defiance of the act which took the preference off Canadian wheat, defied not only imperial ordinance, but storm and hail and fire. The new mill was fresh from the sawmill, sending out still the unique fresh pine smell. Further down the stream an old, grey, weathered mill still worked its maple wheel. And in all three, the great stones daily ground the grain.

Here are there in sunny half acres protected by bush, a hundred hives of bees were gathered, like a tiny village. Mr. Thomas was the great Bradsbrook honey man. The blossoms of the fruit trees, the wild flowers, the rose gardens, and the patches of clover were the harvest fields for Mr. Thomas's bees. As was Colonel Brady for apples and mills, so was Mr. Thomas for bees. In a neighbouring town a proud newspaper would say of him, when the marriage of the provinces was consummated, "The apiary of Mr. Thomas is very large, and it is probable that his bees, as regards quality and number are first in the province, if not in the Dominion." Mr. Bickle was Bradsbrook's greatest wheat producer, as Mr. Ormiston specialized in the growing of immense strawberries which the Queen's Hotel in Toronto sent for.

In Bradsbrook as in its hundred counterparts, resources for mental exercise and enjoyment were being prepared. Literary societies had been formed, and Bradsbrook had built a little building where books and periodicals were provided. The reading room was free to all. During the winter there would be debates, and public readings, and free lectures.

And as it was in the village of Bradsbrook, so it was throughout the towns and villages of Canada West. The days of severe hardship, the hunger, the bitter cold no longer had to be endured. The wilderness had been conquered. There was time now to reach out and grasp the abundant life, the life of the mind and the spirit.

* * *

All was quiet in the Brady house. The sweet pungent smell of burning tamarack from the woodstoves filled the great house. In the kitchen all was tidied away, chairs and tables pushed to one side, the big centre table carried out to the summer kitchen. Christmas puddings robed in white linen hung from hooks in the ceiling. The oysters were snug in their barrel; the turkey waited in the pantry. Cordials matured in crock and keg; cakes and cookies rich in butter and cream filled the crocks in the swinging cellar shelves and tall pantry cupboards. Mrs. Brady stood at the window looking out towards the bush.

"Watch with me here," she said to Isabella, and slipped her arm about her waist. "We are so happy to have you with us."

Darker shadows moved along the orchard road now, and there was a sharp jingling of big harness bells as the horses started away from their stable.

"There's something almost majestic, isn't there, about the way that team moves?"

Isabella stared after them. "I never thought about it, before," she said, "or really looked at a work horse. You are teaching me to open my eyes, Cousin Maude."

"Your eyes have seen much more of the world than mine have. But my time will come, perhaps. And I am very content here. And so I should be – what else could I need?" She stretched out her arms, as if to include Jack Brady and her children and the beautiful plentiful world which was hers.

"Watch now."

Suddenly a great roar shook the woods, and swift mounting crackle of flame topped the tallest tree. Isabella gasped.

"What is it?"

"They're burning the brush from the Yule log."

"Do you always do this on Christmas Eve?"

"Always, we do, and Jack's father did. Sometimes the snow is too heavy before Christmas, but we try to bring it in on this night. Jack says it's bad luck to wait. There's luck, he says, in a Yule log that lasts the twelve days. Listen now!"

The great fire roared and crackled.

The women at the window could see black shadows mingle and move about the fire. Jack Brady and his children and his men joined hands and danced about the fire. Then the log was canthooked into its chains and onto a stoneboat. Four men steadied it, and the percherons strained to start it on its way. The children heaped snow on the embers of the fire until there was no glow. The horses jingled heavily along the road between the apple trees. Half a dozen men and the Brady children cheered and sang as the log was brought home. With much shouting and heaving the log was canted into place, up against the back of the ballroom fireplace. Dry pine logs flanked it, and dry cedar strips lay before it. For a moment then everyone was silent. Jack Brady, a flaming pitch pine root in his hand, with ceremony and grace set the Christmas fire blazing.

"That beech will last the time out," said Jack Brady, "and give luck to us all, for the year."

Fiddle and accordion in the kitchen tuned together for "Turkey in the Straw." Black John McKenzie thumped out the rhythm with his thick grey-socked heels, while he made the fiddle sing. Young Billy Ormiston, a genius with the accordion since he was a little boy, added strangely gay music to the haunting of the violin. Old Jefferson, seated in a corner beyond the reach of the sets, softly clapped his hands in time with the beat, and John McKenzie called out for the dancers. Mistress and maid, master and man danced together in the kitchen.

So there was music and laughter in the house, this Christmas Eve. And the village and the roads were filled with the music of the bells.

●

Letter Three.

ISABELLA MOORE TO HER SISTER CONSTANCE,
IN DUBLIN.

· · · · ● · · ·

26 December, 1866

Dearest Constance,

I am quite exhausted. The whole story of the Christmas festivity must wait until I see you. But I must just say that after the "Burning of the Brush," which means in this case the small branches and twigs of an enormous beech tree, there was dancing in the kitchen for family and servants alike. A violin (called a fiddle, here), and an accordion made up the band, and a "caller-off" half sang and half shouted the movements of the dances. All of which, of course, were quite new to me. All very very noisy, gay, and perfectly bewildering. And hot. But I was not allowed to feel awkward. And I must confess that it is an exhilarating experience to be lifted into the air by the strong hands of a backwoodsman about one's waist, and to observe that one's feet are flying in circles in the air! I have never felt myself so small and light! These dances are called "square dancing," from the beginning of them, I suppose, when couples do form in a kind of square. Three movements are "called off" at what seems tremendous speed, and then there is the "Breakdown" which is faster than ever, noisier than ever. You should have seen your sister! Stamp! Whirl! Leap! Swung off the ground like a kitten. Then sinking to a hard kitchen chair, exhausted. I never thought I could endure such games. But Cousin Maude danced too, until her ringlets showered over her face, and ended the dance laughing and gay. And she is at least ten years older than I am. I could not let my "old country" stiffness, for so I begin to feel it is, keep me from the fun.

We sat down thirty to Christmas dinner, yesterday – eighteen including children, in the dining room and the others in the kitchen. I had thought to feel sad on my first Christmas out of Fitzwilliam Square, but I was not permitted to mope. Our company was very cheerful, not to say gay. Cousin Maude's sister, Mrs. Lawson, who is very young and very pretty, and I think perhaps too petted a wife, came with Mr. Lawson and their two children, with their nurse. They mean to stay a fortnight, I believe. Not Mr. Lawson, of course. He is a miller and a merchant too, I believe, in rather a big way. I don't think Mrs. Lawson can be much older than I. Three officers of the 25th on Christmas leave from Toronto, joined us. Two of them rather distinguished gentlemen. One reminded me a little of the Mr. Andrew whom I met on the *Scotia*. The Rector and his wife and their visitors from Surrey made up our party.

Our dinner was early, about three, so that the officers could catch the stage which passes through Bradsbrook about seven and meets the cars at the Port. But there was time for a few charades and some music before they had to leave, which they did right after supper. The Rector's family stayed on to tea, and our day ended about eleven.

There was a service in the church, in the morning, but very few people came. Apparently it is not the custom here to think of Christmas as a Holy Day. The church, which is very small, made of white wood, and simplicity itself within, was filled with greenery, and the Rector's visitors had gone to great pains to hang banners with gold lettering, on the bare walls of the church. But there were few to see them. Without our household there would not have been a dozen people there.

You would have been amazed, I think, as I was, to see the table set for our Christmas dinner. We sat down to a splendid table, as well furnished with glass and china and silver as I have ever seen at home. The ewers and cruets were of excellent workmanship. I could not help exclaiming about them since they were of patterns unknown to me.

It seems that there has been beautiful silver created in the Canadas for a century or more. The damask table cloth and napkins were also most unusual, and rich. Looking carefully at the central design, which encircled the centre piece of mounded oranges and grapes and apples, I saw the design itself was of apple blossom, leaf and stem and fruit most artfully woven. Cousin Jack said he had it done in Ireland, many years ago, and that it was saved for special occasions.

Cousin Maude was pleased with the Irish embroidery I had brought for her, and thought the undersleeves and collars very pretty. Cousin Jack gave me a ruby brooch which had, he said, belonged to his mother. He had had it re-set in the modern Etruscan style. I felt that he was wrong in giving it to me instead of to his wife, but both he and she would have it so. It looks most inappropriately rich on my old grey poplin. I long for my royal blue taffeta.

You know that I brought only my second best clothing, not wishing to embarrass Cousin Maude and her family with my best. I should have done much better to have brought the best I had. My brown alpaca and the purple faille begin to look very shabby, here. And that old beaver of our mother's! I came prepared for the absolutely frightful cold which we are taught exists in our North American colonies. It may be that I shall experience this bitter cold later. We are smothered in furs, riding always under a buffalo robe when we go in the cutter. When I compare the beaver with Cousin Maude's sealskin, the softest and most brilliant skins I have ever seen, I am ashamed to put it alongside.

Our cousins' house is much warmer, much more evenly heated, indeed, than our stone house in Fitzwilliam Square. It is a new house, you must know, built only seven or eight years ago, and Cousin Jack has spared nothing in the way of comfort in its construction. It is a large house, such as in England would be the manor house. And even since the building was completed there are improvements. Each of the main bedrooms has a small fireplace, but rather more for the appearance of comfort, than for comfort itself, since the rooms are warmed from stoves – not the stoves themselves, of which there is but one on the front bedroom floor, but a system of "stove pipes." There are, it seems, 91 lengths of these black tubes writhing their way through the house. The halls in the part of the second storey which the family occupies are unduly large, I think, in comparison with the smallness of the bedrooms. Cousin Jack says that he thinks the reason for this, which is common in large houses here, may be a hangover from the time when it was hard to heat bedrooms, or even a kind of tribal memory of how cold the bedrooms often were in the "Old Country." I admit to a certain asperity when people say, almost, if you will believe it, with a hint of pity in their tones, "So you're from the Old Country." It gives the impression that the next word might be "Are you getting enough to eat, over there yet?"

My bedroom is furnished with what is called a "Bird's Eye" maple wood. The bedstead is fairly elaborate, the posts being constructed of what appear to be reels in graduated sizes, the larger at the bottom.

The same design, inverted, makes up the lower part of the headboard. These more delicate carvings are called "tear drops," while the bed itself is called a "spool" bed. It is a treacle-coloured wood, with darker markings through it, and while novel to my eyes, is attractive enough. The chest and wardrobe are made of the same maple, trimmed with a black walnut moulding, and the drawer pulls are white china. All of the furniture was made in Toronto.

Much of the furniture throughout the house is lighter in colour than that to which I am accustomed, and it gives an airiness to the rooms which we do not achieve at home. Canadian furniture makers tend to use a number of different kinds of wood in the same piece. None of them woods that we are familiar with at home, I think – maple (of course) and butternut and black walnut, to mention just a few. Very little oak.

My curtains are of swiss lace, with dull green rep overcurtains. There is a turkey-red carpet on the floor, and the effect is cheerful. In the hall just outside is a charming little reed organ, recently placed there to make room for the new piano in the ballroom downstairs.

My room connects with little Emily's room. There is a square hole in the wall between us, and both rooms are heated by a metal drum, into which apparently the miraculous stove pipes throw their heat. In any case, my bedroom is extremely hot.

The servants (called hired girls and hired men here) have their bedrooms above the kitchen, gained by a back stair. It is not possible to pass from their quarters to ours, except by going downstairs. Among the four servants who live in the house, is an old negro, a runaway slave, now freed, of course. He escaped to Canada by the "Underground Railroad," as the system is called, and has been with our cousins for some years. When asked how he got here, he simply said "I follow the north star." Romantic, isn't it? His face is always very sad, but he is devoted to the Bradys, and seems helpful in the house and with the animals. Cousin Jack has three "teams" of Percherons, very large dappled grey horses. He goes to Europe every few years, he says, to buy more horses.

I started to tell you about the furnishings of the house, but I have written enough. I must only say that most of the beautiful furniture in this house was made in this country. Fine furniture has been made in both Canadas for many many years. The thing that struck me as most unexpected was a very handsome grandfather clock, such as our Irish clockmakers made as long as several hundred years ago, and regarded as treasures. Such a clock stands beside me, as I write. It is mahogany, and exquisitely carved. Made in Quebec.

There is no word of any of our shipboard friends. Does it not seem odd, to be so closely confined together for those eleven days, and then to spring apart forever? There IS something a little sad about it.

Believe me, I remain,

>Your affectionate sister,
>ISABELLA.

5

Winter Time and "The Cone"

> *The winter, which commences generally about Christmas and ends in April, is the chief season of idleness and enjoyment . . . begins a course of protracted outdoor pleasures. These consist of fashionable routs, picnic parties, skating in rinks, and sleighing. Some of the skating rinks are well constructed (such as that at Montreal) and cost considerable sums of money. They are exquisitely fitted up, and at the appointed season become highly imposing from the combined effect of brilliancy and beauty presented to the gaze of the spectator.*[31]

Winters in the Canadas entranced the visitors from Europe and the British Isles in the sixties. Many of them were extremely literate people, and wrote down with feverish haste, of the wonderful things they saw. Whirling snow, a field of ice, the loveliness of a snow clad landscape, snow which blinded all vision from a carriage window, might have been recently invented to astonish them.

It was a time of great sensitivity to natural marvels, and the visitors were seldom disappointed in their search for the wondrous clamour of nature, the vast waterfalls, the majesty of the rivers, and the incredible, unimaginable stretch of the forests. They travelled the rivers and lakes in paddle wheelers, and bore into the country in the "cars" on the very new network of rail.

The worst of winter seemed to call loudest to visitors. ". . . in the midst of bitter winter and the dazzling snow," they came.

The gaiety of the winter scene never failed to exhilarate. Revelry in snow and ice, and the ice and snow in such limitless quantities astonished the visitors. They could not leave it alone. From the lowliest private to the occupants of the viceregal residence, they revelled in the snow. A plaything had been made of an enemy, a menace transformed into a source of pleasure. To the garrisons in the Canadas, heavily reinforced for there was civil war in the nation to the south, winter presented itself as a stupendous holiday. Officers and men in scarlet uniforms, in dark green uniforms flashed with scarlet, the 17th, the 25th, the 60th Rifles, bringing colour and romance and excitement with them, flung themselves with enthusiasm into these strange new plays. What should it be today? Skating, sleighing, shooting the cone? Already they had drilled on snow-shoes, and marched up the mountain in Montreal, shamming battle.

Everybody, it seems, skated. They skated in Ottawa, in Montreal, in Quebec. The glorious "Victoria" rink in Montreal was built in 1862 at what seemed an enormous cost. The Montrealers were not slow to advertise their rink, in 1867.

> *Those unacquainted with the glorious Northern Sport of skating can form no idea of the fascination it exercises over those who indulge in it. After the frost sets in sufficiently severe to set, the ice is seldom empty. At the "Victoria" military bands perform frequently, and fancy dress entertainments take place 2 or 3 times during the season, which are thronged with enthusiastic skaters and spectators. The effect of this stirring crowd, with the inspiring music, brilliant light, render it more like a palace of fairyland than of earth.*[32]

Says an enthusiastic writer in the *British American Magazine* of 1865:

> *I don't like to mention names or I could tell you who are the best lady skaters in Quebec, Montreal, Kingston, Toronto, etc. Montreal has two magnificent rinks, one erected at an expense of over $4000, and the other double that sum!*[33]

Montreal lit up its rinks with gas lamps, decorated their walls with swags of evergreens and flags, and enchanted its visitors, both spectators and practitioners. Some were content to look on and see "hundreds of charming Canadian girls gliding through the mazes of the dance with officers and civilian swells."

In Montreal, Mr. Russell of the *Times* was driven to the rink, and made his penetrating comments.

> *Our destination in this drive, was the Rink, or covered skating-ground, which is the fashionable sporting resort of Montrealers in the winter time. The crowd of sleighs and sleigh drivers around the doors of a building which looked like a Methodist Chapel, announced that the skaters were already assembled.*
>
> *Anything but a Methodist-looking place inside. The room, which was like a large public bath-room, was crowded with women, young and old, skating or preparing to skate, for husbands, and spread in maiden rays over the glistening area of ice, gliding, swooping, revolving on legs of every description, which were generally revealed to mortal gaze in proportion to their goodness, and therefore were displayed on a principle so far unobjectionable.*
>
> *It was a mighty pretty sight. The spectators sat or stood on the raised ledge round the ice parallelogram like swallows on a*

> *cliff, and now and then dashed off and swept away as if on the wing, over the surface, in couples or alone executing quadrilles, mazurkas, waltzes and tours de force, that made one conceive that the laws of gravitation must be suspended in the Rink, and that the outside edge is the most stable place for the human foot and figure.*
>
> *And if a fellow should fall – and be saved by a lady? Well! It may end in an introduction, and by a condition of muffinage.*
>
> *The little children skate, so do most portentous mammas. A line of recently arrived officers, in fur caps and coats looked on, all sucking their canes, and resolving to take private lessons in the morning.*[34]

Puzzling references to "muffins" which obviously do not refer to a flour and egg and milk mixture, appear again and again in the lively contemporary accounts of winter fun in the Canadas.

The Governor General's sister-in-law, Frances Monck finds "muffins" at the first outdoor King's Own Band concert of the year. "They are wearing blue veils with their fur caps, to keep their skin from tanning."

She finds them on the rink, doing "most exquisite skating, wearing red petticoats and stockings, brown dresses and pretty fur caps, flying through the rink like swallows."

Mr. Russell finds that skating "muffins" wear "dandy jackets and neat little breeches, a good many of them."

The "muffins" gladdened Mrs. Monck's eyes on many occasions, adding an unexpected gaiety to her rather sombre outlook. She found them "looking very nice and bright, flying along in sleighs, with their men friends."

Mrs. Monck did not take to the ice herself. Perhaps she was too distressed at the very poor showing made by some gallant and highly-placed officers of the 17th when they put their elegant feet to the ice for the first time. Her husband ventured, but she evidently did not consider the sport for herself. She was not long in Canada, but the time was sufficient, and the stimulation of the intense cold, the extraordinary snow, and the invigorating winter playtime had begun to work on her, before she left. One can see in her journal the gradual breaking down of her initial social rigidity. She took her shocks well on the whole, and maintained a dignified composure when she found that Conway, her maid, had actually received an "invite" to the same party as had her mistress. The girl refused, of course, out of respect to her employers.

Almost every day brought new and surprising experiences. She went, an astonishing concept, to a dance, on ice.

> *After dinner I dressed for the rink ball, by putting on over-stockings and boots, many warm things under my sealskin coat, and my fur cap instead of a wreath – When we arrived I was struck with the very pretty and novel sight; the rink was lit with gas and decorated with flags and ornaments; there*

> *were tables with refreshments on the ice, and the 25th band was playing.*[35]

And before she left Canada Frances herself succumbed to the fascination of just playing on the ice. "I went out sliding this morning, and flew all across the cricket field. I took off my crinolines and tied myself up in a sheet to keep the snow from my petticoats. I begin to think it very exciting."

The winter towns lived under a kind of ecstacy of bells. Frances found it wearying, "Really the bells on the horses bewilder one so much in town, one hears no sounds but 'bells, bells, bells, bells.'" But Mr. Russell, in Toronto, enjoyed the music of the bells.

> *In this winter time the streets are filled with sleighs, he says, and the air is gay with the carolling of their bells. Some of the vehicles are exceedingly elegant in form and finish, and are provided with very expensive furs, not only for the use of the occupants, but for mere display.*[36]

And Mr. Russell himself produced a definitive finding on the subject of the muffins.

> *The fair Canadians may have been too kind in accepting the name and position of "muffins" from the young Britishry; but the latter cannot say that they have suffered much in consequence. A muffin is simply a lady who sits beside the male occupant of the sleigh* Sola cum solo, *and all the rest is leather and prunella.*[37]
>
> *I observed that the young people have a curious custom of going about with small sleighs, which are, to the best of my belief, called "tarboggins."*[38]

Not even Niagara roaring its mighty welcome to its literary visitors in the sixties, ever received the ecstatic acclaim that the falls of Montmorenci did. Spring, Summer, and, more than all these together, Winter at the Falls produced paeons of praise, astonishment and comment. Wide-eyed and voluble, the sightseers saw Niagara and were overcome, saw the local lunatic asylum and were moved to moral paragraphs; then they went to Montmorenci in the winter time, and words all but failed them.

Mr. Russell, the renowned world traveller, was for once, put at a loss. The cone came to him first as a revelation, as if he alone of all the world knew not the Cone:

> *"What is the Cone?" The effect of our ignorance on the waiter was too touching – he was so astonished by the profound barbarism of our condition that we felt it necessary for our own character to proceed at once to a spot which forms the delight of Quebec in the winter season, and to which the bourgeoisie were repairing in hot haste for the afternoon's pleasure. A sleigh was brought round, and in it, ensconced in*

furs, we started off for the Falls, which are about eight miles distant.[39]

It was not just the "bourgeoisie" who rushed to the Cone. Parties from Spencer Wood, with the Governor General's entranced sister-in-law, pen practically in fur-gloved hand, patronised the Cone.

> *The scene is too wonderful, and you cannot imagine you are looking at reality when you see this wonderful sight. As we turned into the sort of amphitheatre of rocks and fir trees, in the middle of which are the Grand Falls, we saw all the 25th in their red coats, and all the R.A. in dark-blue overcoats, grouped about on the ice, and on the cone. There was a large collection of sleighs and harness in one spot, and a little further on were all the ladies of the party, sitting at lunch on the frozen river at a table with forms all round it. The officers were in undress uniform with fur caps, and were attending on the ladies. They were all very civil to us, and gave us lunch. The Cone, as I told you before, is formed by the frozen spray from the Falls falling on a large rock out in the river. The big cone is about eighty feet high. There is also a "Ladies' Cone," a much smaller one. You go down these cones . . . on "Sleds," or little flat forms of wood on runners. [Mr. Russell with his keen eye and ear would have known that she must have been talking of "tarboggins."]*[40]
>
> *We found a large party of people – The R.A. had a large picnic also after lunch the two parties amalgamated, and we had great fun. A fire was lighted on the ice, and we had hot soup. The sun was so hot we did not feel the least chilled eating our food on the river! After lunch we walked off to look at the sliding down the cone. How we laughed! About twelve soldiers all held on one behind the other, and came bumping down the cone, not sitting on sleds, but just bumping or slipping down on nothing. The terrific tumbles they had astonished us, but they did not seem to mind; happily there were doctors present. I saw one head bound up and bleeding.*
>
> *Soon the band of the 25th struck up, and a quadrille was proposed. Col. M. flew to ask me to dance. The novelty of dancing [on ice] was not to be resisted, otherwise I would have preferred to look on at the men sliding. A ring of soldiers was made round the dancers; it looked altogether curious and novel. . . .*[41]

Mrs. Monck's partner had thrust his walking stick down his back, to keep it out of his way. She was "much amused."

> *He implored me to down the cone with him! Of course I refused! The bugles soon sounded; and we set off sleighwards – some water from a fissure in the ice was rising every minute as the tide was coming in, and we must cross it quickly.*[42]

The marvels of the Cone were not all made by nature. Man introduced his skill and imagination within the great ice mass. Mr. Russell, strangely enough, found what Mrs. Monck did not. In search of the strange and beautiful, Mrs. Monck

> went to see the beautiful ice-house out in the Cone, and the curiosities there. There is an ice-sofa and table, an ice-horse, a bird, a dog, and two mummies, they are marvellously cut out of blocks of ice. A drunken soldier there asked Mrs. Rose to come and sit on the ice-sofa "along with a British soldier."[43]

Mr. Russell may have followed the soldier,

> for, obeying many invitations, we walked along a snow path which led to a portal cut in the solid oxide of hydrogen, and entering found ourselves in a hot and stuffy apartment excavated from the body of The Cone, in which there was an Americanised bar with drinks suited to the locality, and as much want of air as one would find in a house in the fifth Avenue of New York. It was full of people, who drank whisky and other strong waters.[44]

Frances Monck and Mr. Russell had at least one opinion in common. The firm conviction that the Cone, either the Gentleman's Cone or the less intimidating Ladies' "solid oxide of hydrogen," presented no challenge to them which they had any idea of accepting. But one of Mr. Russell's companions

> was led to sacrifice himself on a tarboggin, and yielded to a demon guide . . . He was but an item among many, but I knew he was among "the braves des braves" and had received a baptism of fire in the trenches of Sebastopol . . .[45]

The intrepid soldier had fought in India, and in China.

> I watched him assuming the penal attitude to which the young tarbogginner is condemned, and after a balance for a moment on the giddy height, his guide gave a kick to the snow, and down like a plunging blomb flew the de-winged Icarus, he passed me close; I could see and mark him well. Never, to judge from facial expression, could man have been in deadlier fear . . . and yet he had the astounding audacity to say "it was delicious. Never had a more delightful moment," when he came back pale and panting from his flight.[46]

There is no record that Frances Monck tried tobogganing, but she was sorely tempted. And special slides were prepared, at Spencer Wood.

> The slide is up now for tobogganing but no one has begun yet. The slide is a raised wooden platform with an inclined plane placed on the top of a hill upon which the snow falls, and when rolled and frozen over, you slide down on a toboggan, which is flat piece of thin ash wood curled up at the end to

> *receive ones feet; two or three people can go down on one toboggan, one behind the other, as close as one can pack, and one guides the toboggan with a bit of wood; terrible sport, I think, but I must try it once!. You shoot down a hundred yards further than the slide, all across the cricket-ground.*[47]

It would be pleasant to have a picture of the lady, fitting herself into a toboggan. For she provided herself, during her winter in Canada, with clothing which must have assured her warmth, at any rate. Certainly she was equipped for driving.

> *You must have two robes to cover you, in a sleigh. I mean to get a white cloud . . . a "cloud" is a long knitted scarf which goes all over your cap and round and round your throat, and ties in long ends. The cloud was two and a half yards long. "My cap is to be very high, the fashion this year, for we have our cap fashions here." I paid some visits, and I did not really feel cold, as I wore my velvet bonnet for the first time, and two veils, a warm knitted cape, a velvet coat, and my Astrakan-trimmed cloak; besides, we had our bear skin robe and an apron in the phaeton.*[48]

Colonel Monck fitted himself up with astrakhan furs, for winter too, and a handsome pair they must have made, when, with winter deepening, the Governor General drove her to Henderson, the furriers, and she chose

> *a beautiful velvet and sealskin cap which costs ten dollars, (about two sovereigns, English). And Dick ordered a handsome buffalo sleigh robe, which is to be trimmed with a rim of brigade colours.*[49]

One is forced to wonder if the Hunt Ball at home in the "Old Country" may be a little dull, after the social exercises of a winter in Canada, with her sleigh and her own little scarlet cariole, and watching as "the Lancers danced on skates, beautifully." Will there be something to compare with the thrill of seeing the garrison performing in the snow? "This morning the 25th (all in their scarlet) marched up here on snow shoes, a very fine sight."

In the sixties fashionable women wore crinolines, an arrangement of flat, one-inch-wide whalebone, covered with (in some cases) fine linen to prevent damage to the fine materials they were appointed to hold out from the wearer's body. In graduated diameters, hung together by strong linen straps, these "hoops" could swell a small woman whose hips measured perhaps thirty-six inches to a ninety-six-inch circumference (or larger) at ankle level. The ankle did not show, normally (although a compromise was reached for a skating costume). When such a contraption was tied by its strings to the little woman's waist and a number of petticoats superimposed, plus the skirt of a dress which took fifteen yards of poplin or alpaca to make, the resulting structure was a formidable one.

A woman who walked well, whose "carriage," that favourite word in the period, was erect and stately, whose gait swung her crinoline with grace, was an impressive figure, with her beautifully gored skirt hung over her crinoline.

But it was a poor costume for winter sport. The *British American* advises that, in the case of mixed company tobogganing, "First of all seat the leadies – lady tobogannists should not wear hoops."

When the beautiful simplicity of Spencer Wood was abandoned for Rideau Hall, the great tradition of winter fun travelled with the Governor General.

> *The Governor-General gave two evening skating and tobogganning parties at Rideau Hall every winter . . . the parties were wonderfully picturesque. In those days . . . all members of snow-shoe and tobogganing clubs, men and women alike, wore coloured blanket-suits consisting of knickerbockers and long coats, with brightly coloured stockings, sash, and knitted "tuque", invariably pronounced "tuke." The club colours of course varied. Rideau Hall was white with purple stockings and "tuke", and red sash. Others were sky-blue, with scarlet stockings and "tuke", or crimson and black or brown and green. A collection of three hundred people in blanket suits gave the effect of a peripatetic rainbow against the white snow. . . . the rinks were all fringed with coloured fairy-lamps; the curling rink and the tea room above it were also outlined with innumerable coloured electric bulbs, and festoons of Japanese lanterns were stretched between the fir trees in all directions. At the top of the toboggan slides powerful arc-lamps blazed, and a stupendous bonfire roared on a little eminence. The effect was indescribably pretty, and it was pleasant to reflect how man had triumphed over Nature in being able to give an outdoor evening party in mid-winter with the thermometer below zero. The gleaming crystals of snow reflecting the coloured lamps; the Bengal lights staining the white expanse crimson and green, and silhouetting the outline of the fir trees in dead black against the burnished steel of the sky; the crowd of guests in their many-coloured blanket suits, made a singularly attractive picture, with a note of absolute novelty in it; and the crash of the military band, the merry whirr of the skates, and the roar of the descending toboggans had a something extraordinarily exhilarating about them in the keen, pure air. . . . Supper was served in the long, covered curling rink, where the temperature was the same as that outside, so there was a long table elaborately set out with silver branched candlesticks, and all the G-g's fine collection of plate, but the servants waited in heavy fur coats and caps. Of course no flowers could be used in that temperature, so the silver vases held branches of spruce, hemlock, and other Canadian firs.*[49A]

Letter Four.

MR. ALFRED TOWNSEND, TRAVELLING LUMBER MERCHANT,
TO HIS WIFE IN BIDEFORD, ENGLAND.

• • • ● ● ● • • •

Sillery, Canada East
20 January 1865

Dear Carrie:

If I were a younger man, I think I should never come back to Bideford to live my life out. These Canadian folk know how to enjoy themselves. My word. Never a dull moment, as they say. Not here, there isn't. I've just about made my deal with the shipper, and I'm leaving for New York in a fortnight or so, and I don't mind saying I'm a bit loathe to go. We've had a gay time here, and no mistake. And only a little bit of a place, this is, when you come to compare. Eight miles out of Quebec, we are, and only tracks, you might say, more or less tunnels, in the snow – sometimes eight feet deep, they are, between the house and the road, and then the eight miles. But do people sit at home warming theirselves? They do not. Up and at it, night and day. I know what you're say, "It's those Frenchies, there. We always knew they were a gay lot." Well, my girl, you're wrong this time. Not that they aren't gay, of course, but it's the English soldiers that mostly are to blame, in my opinion. And then there's the Governor General, living right here. Fine big house like Buckingham Palace, pretty well, it is. Called Spencer Wood, or some such name. Twice as long as a church, and with a verandah all along the whole front of the house. Posts all along, and arches in between. The house is white, and has a lot of cedar trees growing in front. Might be all right come summer time, but just now, it being all white, and the snow behind it being all white too, it's not so much, only for the size. And there's lots going on there, all the time. Soldiers tracking up there on snowshoes, to show themselves off, in their fur coats and hats, to the Governor, and strings of sleighs, all jingling with bells, and the ladies in them so covered up with furs and veils and cloaks till there might as well be a nest of ferrets in the cariole (that's what they call these little low sleighs) for all a man can see of a face.

The officers of the regiments play pretty high, with the customs of this country, if you ask me. They swank around with sleighs built to order just for themselves, and trimmed here and there with the colours of their regiment. And then, not content with that, they buy great big buffalo robes, or bearskins they might be, and have them trimmed around the edge with their colours. What are they going to do with the likes of that kind of thing when they go home? Ten to one his regiment won't be here more than maybe a few months, the way it seems to be.

Col. Monck, he's the Gov. Gen's brother, he got one of these fancy sleighs, and he's off down to the rink, or off to the Cone, or calling on some nob every day, with a tandem pair. Don't they just lick through the roads, though!

There's no waiting here, for summertime, like Ascot, or the Derby, to start the racing. Canadians race their horses all the time, winter and summer, just as long as the roads are dry enough to set a pair of wheels on. In wintertime, it's sleighs. They tell me it's already eight years since the Queen gave a prize for the fastest horse in her remaining part of North America. The part that doesn't belong to us any more hasn't got any race started that long ago. You might be wondering how they race in the winter, when, as I've told you, they've got six to eight feet of snow in front of every house in Sillery, and in Quebec too, the city, I mean, and nobody does anything about it but shovel a little tunnel through. The city seems sunk down into the snow, I don't know what they COULD do about it, come to think of it. Well, the race is on the river – on the ice, that is. Put up rows of fir trees (mostly what they call spruce, here), to make the race track, and away they go.

There's the English officer, with his blood horse, and there's the French Canadian with his shaggy black horse, hardly bigger than a pony, really. And the officer yells "Hi!," and the Frenchy yells "Avant!" And away they go, running like the very devil. And it isn't always the blood horse that wins either. The little black chap, you see, is maybe more used to racing on the ice. The Canadians do it all the time. The rivers are like roads to them, in the winter. "Ice bridge," they call it, when the river freezes over. I heard about this ice-bridge, and like a fool, thought it would be a bridge built up in the air. I didn't admit that, to anybody though. And even with the "ice-bridge," things can be pretty exciting sometimes. I cut this piece out of the paper, a magazine, that I saw. I didn't suppose you would believe me, if I told you myself. And the man says it a lot better than I could.

> *Occasionally serious accidents occur while driving upon the snow over frozen rivers or lakes in sleighs or carioles. Pleasure parties suddenly become engulphed without the slightest premonitory warning of their danger, when every strenuous exertions become necessary in order to save their lives. Their first object is to make sure their footing upon strong ice, when they immediately seize hold of a noose attached to the sinking horse's neck, when they pull-pull-pull remorselessly with all their might until the poor animal is almost strangled. When his breathing becomes thus checked, he rises at once gently to the surface and is hauled on to the ice. So soon as the noose is relaxed respiration becomes restored; and in a few minutes the horse canters on the snow as nimbly as before. These processes of emersion and semi-strangulation not infrequently take place several times during one day.*[50]

I haven't seen that, myself, yet, but there's no doubt but with all the cavorting that goes on on the little river here (St. Charles) – and not so little either, but only to compare with the St. Lawrence, which is like a sea all by itself – a power of occurrences do take place.

'Tisn't only the racing or the driving just for the fun on the river. There's many a sleigh down there this minute cutting out huge blocks of ice, quarrying it, you might say. This is for keeping the food from spoiling. Every nob has an "ice house," not a house made of ice, though the young folk do that, too, but to keep ice in. What do you think of that, old lady? Mostly they drive their "berlots," down for that job. You say that word "bare low." They dig an excavation in the ground and build half the house more or less under ground. Then there's sawdust put in, and when the ice is some feet thick in the St. Lawrence, out they come with their "berlots." And pretty uncomfortable contraptions they are, to my eye. The driver sits on just a strip of leather, strung up between two uprights.

They make a great hole with a cross cut saw about six feet long, with teeth like a crocodile. Two or three men to a berlot. They quarry the blocks out, and heave it up onto the sleigh. When they've got the load as high as the horse can pull, they track home again. It takes the best part of a week, going on like this, to fill some ice houses. They tell me that properly built, with sawdust underneath and on top, this ice will last until next September. Maybe longer. Taking into account the summer, which is uncommonly warm, in these parts, that seems a remarkable thing, to me. The whole enterprise looks pretty uncomfortable, but the men don't seem to mind. The old sleigh bells are ringing, and the harness creaking away and jingling in the cold, and the men wrapped up with furs pretty well incognito.

Funny thing I saw the other day. Up at Spencer Wood, maybe I told you, the Governor General's sister-in-law is staying just now. Her husband being the G.G.'s brother, Colonel Monck. Well, Mrs. Monck, of course, has a little cariole made up just to suit her. Red as a hunting jacket. Slung low to the ground these things are. A real big dog could just about step over a cariole, would hardly need to leap. I was driving along behind her, the other day. Couldn't see her, of course, her being so smothered up in furs, as I said, but I recognized the fit out. And driving along ahead of her was a very smart turn-out, Colonel somebody or other, to judge from his looks, and a lady with him. (This was a real lady, not one of your muffins.) He was driving "tandem," one horse ahead of the other and very smart they looked. Well, here we were, jingling along like a bell ringers concert, and suddenly the front sleigh, with the colonel in it, tipped over sideways and tossed the col. and his lady into eight feet of soft snow. The horses and the shafts broke from the sleigh, and ran demented along the road. Well, this happens, nobody hurt, and Mrs. Monck right behind sat up straight and sudden in her cariole like a hare out of hole. She laughed and laughed. Surprised me. She doesn't laugh very easily, I hear. Built something in the fashion of the Queen, a bit on the dumpy side. Mind of her own, too. Caught a glimpse of her at the Sergeant's Ball, the other night. No, I wasn't dancing, just looking on to see what I could see. She didn't dance much, fearful of tearing her lace flounces, somebody said. And where every other woman there had about seven pound of hair, false, that is, mounted up on their heads, the higher the better, the Honourable Mrs. Monck had hers parted straight down the middle and brushed back like two blackbirds wings, with only a little knot of her own hair, about the size of a biggish snail, coiled about at the back of her neck. Independent.

Hard to say what these folk do in the summer. A man would almost think they had to have snow and ice and frozen ears before they were enjoying themselves. There's these outside "rinks" for skating, with carpets spread out for the ladies who don't want to skate, and tea and coffee and cakes on little tables, and a band playing away like mad.

I'm too old to learn to skate, now, and I'm telling you what you'd know anyway, I wouldn't fancy myself on one of these flat little sleds that are all about. Tarboggins. But I've broomed a few iron stones along the ice. Too cold here for the granite. Cracks them. And I'd like to take a turn at what they call "ice-boating." What would you think of racing in a boat on a river in the winter time, ice right down to the bottom, I should think. Not done with a proper boat, of course, but what else would you call a vessel with mast and sails, that can go like hell for leather, all down the river? The boat is a kind of floor, shaped in a triangle, set up on great iron skates. One of these skates at the stern is worked with a tiller; this makes a helm. "Wear" and "Tack" is precisely the same, they tell me, as with an ordinary sailing yacht. Maybe it's just tales, having me on, but they say that some have done five miles in five minutes, on one of these boats. Maybe I'll have a try, before I come home.

  Yrs aye
  ALF.

Five or six people lie down flat on the floor, on these boats.

A Gravenhurst Laddie, 1867

Sous les Bois, Chemin St. Louis, 1865

A Soldier of the Queen    The Writing Desk    Thus saith the Lord

Sabbath Black   The Beaverton Belle    The Daily Portion

The Skaters    Their R.H. The Prince and Princess of Wales    The Grandmother

The Aunt from England   The Sisters    "L'Élégante"

1.

2.

3.

1.
St. John's Newfoundland,
Watercolour, circa 1850

The Canadian Gallery, R.O.M.

2.
Nova Scotia Archives

3.
Montreal family carte de visite,
circa 1859

Ontario Archives

Ball at Windsor Hotel,
Montreal, 1878

Public Archives of Canada

*In the seventies
the crinolines
gave place to
the bustle and train*

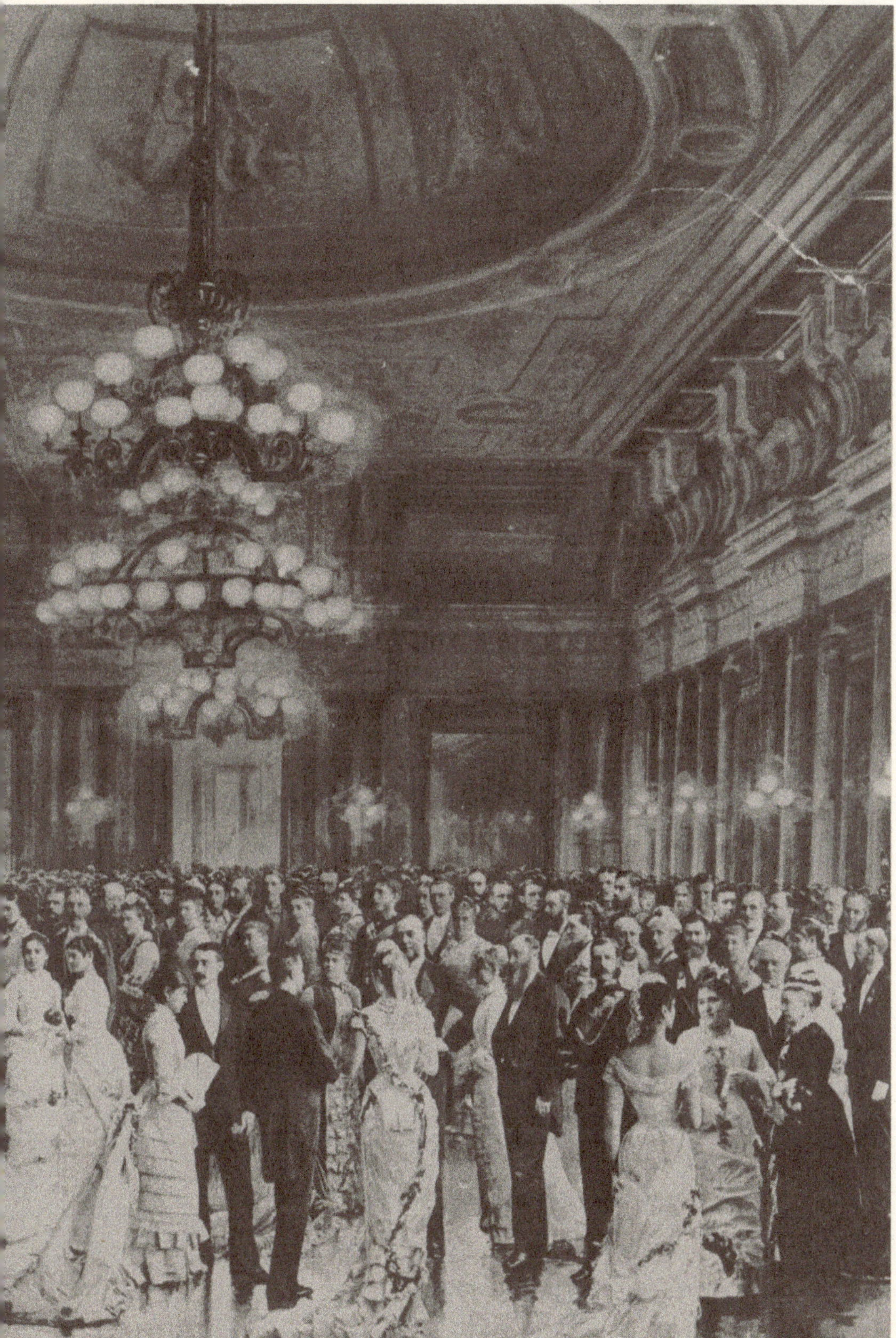

A Moonlight Excursion on the St. Lawrence
Public Archives of Canada

6

Spacious Days

> *The castellated mansion of the sheriff,*
> *with its elegant towers, imposingly situated*
> *on rising ground, is considered*
> *the largest and handsomest detached dwelling*
> *on the whole American continent.*[51]

Thus Mr. Day, on Sheriff Reynolds' house in Whitby, 1862.

They were spacious days, in the Canadas, a hundred years ago.

Released from the stringent exigencies of pioneer poverty, proven able to create a prosperous rewarding life in North America, the builders of the fifties and sixties breathed deep and set joyously about furnishing their land.

These were decades of imaginative, creative building. In public works the architects still called upon Greece and Rome. There was the fluted pillar and the pediment or there was the heavy Roman arch. Often there were both, with a touch of Gothic mixed in for variety. Sometimes a great building would seem to be, in intent, the copy of Gothic building in England. And yet it never came out a true copy. There was an exhilaration in the air in these years that fed the imagination of the builders. Suddenly the British North American felt himself a whole and free man. He must make for himself, he could not be satisfied to copy. And with the lifting of the economic load, he needed no longer stifle the urge to create for the sheer beauty of creation. Decoration was not necessary, and in the time of poverty building for fun was beyond the bounds of consideration. But now the constricting band had been stretched and broken. The builders were free.

There were astonishing structures designed and built in these ebullient years. And most of them had something essentially original about them. The dead hand of tradition had been gently lifted off. They were massive, enormously solid structures, built of great stones to last forever. But almost always, even in the most solemn, monolithic, stately building, there would be found some little foolishness. There was a frivolous stone feather or a swag or a strange bearded face gazing down from the keystone of a massive Roman arch.

The Parliament buildings which housed the first Dominion Parliament is a prime example of imagination set free. A lofty, pinnacled, elaborately complex building, it was appropriately designed and constructed to house the law makers of the new nation. The roof rose in a complexity of towers, pinnacles in variety, elaborate ironwork enclosures, and stripes of green and purple tiles. Gaiety came into the House with coloured tiles. The soft grey stone work surrounding the ranges of ogival windows, large and small, was accented here and there with yellow, black, red, and white. It might have been a stone lace castle, rising there above the river, with three great fountains playing before it, and ladies and gentlemen walking the broad paths in the vast and formal gardens.

All the entrances, the tall windows, the short windows, the pinnacles, and the towers seemed to point straight to heaven. And atop it all, in a touch of inspired fantasy, the Crown itself, a pointed crown.

The warehouses, the counting houses, the shops, wore an aura of prosperity like a wreath about their roof tops. The old proportion of stone to glass was dramatically altered. Shop fronts became great areas of glass two stories high supported by slender iron bars, set in slender mulleins. The sun was shining in Canada West, and the vast windows were built to let the radiance in. The buildings were going up now; clothing shops and carpet warehouses were often four stories high, and some business houses climbed to five. This was far enough to expect customers to walk. But the elevators were coming.

The men who built for the merchants were encouraged to add fanciful details, symbols which would not be forgotten, once seen. So it was possible to walk down King Street in Toronto and find that above your head as you entered a shop, there would be a great lion crouching, all shining gold. And on the parapetted top of this same store, a life-size, perhaps a little beyond life-size beast, a lion *rampant*, ready to spring. "The Golden Lion" marked his owner's dry goods emporium well. And down the street on the other side, a vast fabulous griffin, half bird, half lion, and twice as big as a horse menaced both earth and heaven. He was all beak and tail and devil's wings, and held aloft a laurel wreath to thus proclaim that here were silks.

City and large town houses surrendered usually, during the sixties, to the influence of the "Italianate" or the "Mixed Gothic" styles. Either design usually produced a "tower springing from the middle." It was a wonderful time for towers. Parliament buildings, court-houses, post-offices, and Italianate dwellings all must have their towers. Occasionally the tower was subdued, indeed conquered, and a charming little belvedere sat upon a classically satisfying house. But then you had something else again, and a purity of mass and proportion which the Italianate and the Mixed Gothic, with all their pretensions, and they were many, could not produce.

A wealthy city dweller, his fortune made in sugar, iron, whisky, wheat, or merchandising, built himself a house in which to entertain his friends, and to afford himself an exceedingly comfortable and well-served life. Men who rose high in judicial circles, publishers, and civil servants built city mansions of impressive size and sometimes of great beauty. Here in their castles they entertained each other and friends from across the Atlantic with a lavish elegance.

Privacy was a prime consideration. There were houses taking up a whole city block which were quite invisible to a man on foot outside its garden walls, although a man in a carriage might catch a glimpse of the tower. A small, man-sized gate was cut in the dark red brick walls, and there a tradesman might enter, draped basket in hand, to deliver his goods. The carriage entrance is on another street, and the gates will be opened for a guest who is expected. Stables and driving sheds, the gardener's cottage, the cow shed, and the chicken house are built of the same materials as the house and are discreetly approached from the third bounding street. And life within the great house is, perhaps, as orderly and dignified and discreet as is its environment.

Italianate or Mixed Gothic, the great houses in the cities were built on a scale which makes the twentieth century gasp. A drawing-room seventy-five feet long and twenty-five feet wide was provided in a house which still stands. But before the caller was admitted to the drawing-room, he was received (and his admission considered) in a reception room, equally richly furnished – the heavy silks in the curtains and the chairs fully as crimson, the curtains as deeply swagged, as in the vast room beyond.

Sometimes the visitor needed to climb only a shallow flight of steps before he found himself admitted to a broad hall, with a great swirl of staircase leading up to the drawing room on the floor above. In a house so planned the ladies had to climb the stairs, and then make a stately descent, for the dining room would be below the swing of staircase.

The huge dining table would be in the centre of the room, a white marble fireplace at each end. A glistening damask cloth almost swept the floor, perhaps with a pattern of a "hunt" woven into it, if the master of the house were a horseman. The table might be set for twenty, or forty or more. There was a cluster of wine glasses at each place. The silver glimmered in the candle light which the mistress of the house might find more flattering to her guests and to herself than the gas light which sang in the halls and in the kitchen.

The kitchen, of course, was in the basement, and at the end of the room opposite to the head of the table would be a tall, free-standing screen. Waiters and waitresses served from a long table there, out of sight. A diner strategically placed sometimes could see the anxious face of the cook, peering beyond the screen from her kitchen stairs. "Is it time yet, to let the soufflé out?"

Sons and brothers, grown wealthy in wheat or whisky, vied with each other to produce splendid houses.

> Sarah says the most splendid affair she ever saw. So convenient, hot and cold soft water to be had at any time, day or night, by just turning a tap. The old gentleman's is no house at all in comparison to it – a fireplace in every room in the house. The marble slabs of each cost $200 – at the opening of it they had a party of fifty couples.[52]

Two parties, each of two hundred guests, were held in one week without apparent exhausting of capacity or expense, to open the new house and gardens of a gentleman in Oshawa.

The great houses were built to accommodate many people: the man and his wife who owned the house, their usually very large immediate family, their servants and the servants of their visitors. A daughter, Ruth, married and living in England, might be expected to visit her family with her husband, Mr. Ormiston, perhaps for some months. She would bring her own maid with her, and the hope would be that her Sarah, or Lucy, or Jane would not be "impertinent" to the three or four women already engaged in keeping the house clean and its occupants well served.

So, the married pair came, with their servants, the children, and their nurse. The nursery, vacant perhaps for many years, was made ready for them.

A few days or weeks after Ruth and Mr. Ormiston arrived, if the visit was to be of long duration, Mr. Ormiston's groom, his horse, and his dogs might be expected. Room in the house could be found for the groom — perhaps an attic room freshly plastered for him, room in the stables for the horse, in the kennels for the dogs. It was not unusual for such a pair to bring along their plate and linen, together with enormous numbers of boxes of clothing.

Houses built on this scale were not frequently found in small villages, but almost every established little town and village has its "big" houses. Sometimes there were two or three of them.

The men who built and owned these houses were not the capitalists, the great lumbermen, the financial wizards. These houses belonged to small-town men, to village men, sometimes to farmers. Small-town merchants, foundrymen, country doctors, furniture builders, livery men, built impressive, sometimes beautiful, and nearly always, by twentieth-century standards, very large houses. In the upper province they were usually brick, demonstrating the superlative quality of their workmanship until this day. In the lower province many of the dwellings were stone. In the Maritime provinces there were clusters of great white frame houses suggestive of an infinity of comfort for their owners, an almost faultless symbol of peace.

The men who were able now to build substantial dwellings for themselves in the country chose their situations with an eye for prominence. They sited them often on the top of a gentle hill, sometimes with a lake or river glimmering at the bottom of the slope. Since many of the farms were now at the edge of a village which had grown up to them, the big house enjoyed its eminence and looked down to the bustle of the village below. There are many evidences in what is now Ontario that the owners of the big houses had gained some of their inspiration from seeing building in Europe. Perhaps they had gone back to the "Old Country," and taken advantage of the journey to make a little tour into Italy, to spend a few days in Paris, or make a journey on the Rhine. Some suffered a rush of architecture to the head and produced vast incongruities in brick and stone. They could afford now to leave behind them the memory of the primitive farms and appurtenances of the pioneer dwellings of their fathers and grandfathers. They most emphatically did.

So it is that in the rich agricultural lands of Canada West, a simple red brick broad-gabled house, trimmed traditionally with her strips of white wooden lace, may find herself inexplicably in the grip of a towered creature from some Rhineland castle. Here and there, in such a structure there may be great and intricate coronets of iron, patterned after Irish lace, thrown out from the gentle gables.

There was nothing small, constricted, cheese-paring, about these houses. The entrance hall may be protected by a broad vestibule, with stained glass windows on three sides shedding cobalt blue and crimson light on door and inner wall. A vast verandah may swing half way around the house. The hall will be a spacious one, with a broad and pleasant staircase winding up to the second story. The upper hall is broad too, and may terminate in another glass walled room, conservatory or sewing room. The downstairs rooms are tall, well proportioned, lit with bow windows and generously designed single lights. The fashionable term for the largest room in one of these houses was "ball room," and sometimes this ran the whole depth of the house.

Such a house was often built on a simple plan of two rectangles. The main rectangle provided living quarters for the family, with perhaps four or five bedrooms, a bathroom, "ball room," library, and dining room. The lesser block contained a huge kitchen, pantry, servants' bedrooms and sitting room. A stairway led from the kitchen to the upper quarters in the rear block. A huge two-storey combination woodshed and buggy shed adjoined the kitchen end of the house. In the upper storey the fruits of tremendous drying, shelling, and husking autumn operations were stored.

Here and there throughout the grounds a number of outbuildings were scattered, each with its own particular function. A latticed summer house, near the croquet lawn, a small stable for the carriage horses and the pony, with a loose stall for a visiting horse and a driving shed to shelter his rig. Perhaps the cow would have her own shed for winter occupancy. There would be a chicken house, a root cellar, a housing for the pump and spring.

Smaller again in size, the houses lining the village streets often exhibited a better balance and proportion than their more ostentatious neighbour on the hill. Lacking the size of the big house, gifted builder-architects compensated by achieving outstandingly satisfying effects by imaginatively designed doorways, windows, and roof lines. The little pointed gable which is such a feature of so many houses of the period and earlier usually crowns a house of perfect symmetry. The house may be of white frame, or field stone, or red brick, laid in Flemish bond. Sometimes the red brick has its corners built of a contrasting colour of brick; slim Doric columns may appear in either type, and many-paned bow windows adorn the facade and light the rooms within. Doors were often made beautiful by fan lights above and long lights beside them. Shutters on windows and doors added to the gracious aspect of the little house. The very small white house with its prim gable and meticulous balance suggested order, restraint, a denial of exuberance, a refutation of exaggeration. One is tempted to think that the character of the occupant can be assessed by the outward appearance of his house. The very woodpile of the small white house, split sticks two feet long neatly arranged the full length of its hundred yards of fence, seemed more circumspect, more contained in spirit than did the four foot logs ranging eight feet high like an invincible bulwark behind the driving shed of the big house.

The idea that an interior should surrender itself, in decor, to shades and hues of one colour, or of one colour and its complement is a constipated theory which the men and women who furnished their elegant houses a hundred years ago would have scorned, in utter disbelief. Their criterion was excellence of material, excellence of workmanship, wealth of pattern and richness of colour. The gentleman for whom the house was built took great interest in the furnishing of it. Not infrequently he chose the carpets, the chair coverings, the curtains, the dishes, the wallpaper ("a bright, rich lively pattern"), the table silver, the chandeliers. Very frequently these objects might be all chosen without consultation with the lady of the establishment, who might then be pleased, or at least would accept them. Perhaps this is why the Canadian furniture of these years was for the most part very solid, heavy, highly polished, long lasting; it may explain the lack of flimsiness in curtains and coverings, and also, perhaps, the great abundance of red in carpets and hangings. Although there was gold, too, with the red, and a handsome mixture of mustard yellow and bright blue in stripes, and rose and buff in the blurred bouquets of roses on floors and walls.

The children fared well in their share of the house. Very often a great bright room in the attic, broad low windows looking down over orchard and stables, belonged to the children. A turkey-red carpet on the floor, a doll house with exquisitely made furniture and dishes, a wooden rocking horse as big as the collie dog, and small chairs as carefully constructed as the ones downstairs furnished a play haven for the little ones. To bring the smallest to the level of his relatives about the dining table a special chair was provided. It was walnut too, or mahogany, and could be fitted on a regular dining chair. And in all his possessions the same meticulous care was taken for the pleasure they might give to his eyes and the comfort to his person.

And good new schools were ready now to receive him.

Scores of new schools were built in Canada West in the late fifties and sixties in brick and stone. In almost all of them there was a care for proportion, and a grace and originality in the fenestration. Fan-topped windows and stone lintelled windows with the many panes of good Georgian lights were used in schools throughout the countryside. The belfry was built to top the structure, and again with a design to please the eye. Sometimes the school bell was brought from a great distance, chosen for its exceptional tone, and with little thought of expense. (Although the bill is saved and thought worthy of recording.)

The education of the young was not to be halted at the finish of the little school, no matter how beautiful its architecture. The children of the Canadian aristocracy educated their children according to their own ideas of what was fitting and right, with very little regard to what such education might cost. Occasionally one of the bright boys of a miller, distiller, or merchant prince was sent to one of the great English public schools. The results of these experiments were not always happy. A son was sent to the University if it was considered that the University was an institution to which he should go, but by no means because he would not be fitted for his life without a university training. Some of the wealthy disdained the University for their sons and shot them into the family business at an early age. They put a boy in the mills at seventeen, gave him a salary of $400 a year, and let him prove himself in the clouds of flour dust, and the rough hemp bags, and the broad dusty ledgers. He learned the business from the judging of the fall wheat sprouting brilliant green in the well-tilled fields of Canada West; the sound of the grinding of the great stones was never out of his ears.

At twenty-one, being found worthy, he was turned into a man. No, he was transformed into a gentleman, with a vast party and the gift of gold watch worth three-quarters of his year's salary.

The daughters of the house were not neglected. The older girls from such families in Canada West were sent sometimes to long established schools in Quebec or London or Whitby. The education of the younger children was confided to the care of governess, till it was believed that a boarding college would benefit them. The education of the daughters would sometimes be topped off by a year in Paris, "to learn French to perfection – other branches of course." The thousand pounds which such a year of "running about and schooling" cost seemed no extravagance to the parents, although certainly subject to criticism perhaps, from the branches of the family which put little value on the higher education of young ladies.

The orchards, the great gardens, and the groves of nut trees planted years ago by the settlers provided lavish fare for the table by the sixties, summer and winter. Hickory, walnuts, and butternuts came from the plantings. Beechnuts from the beechwood could be gathered by the bushel. Apples in half a dozen varieties, two or three kinds of pears, the small sweet sugar plums and the big blue prunes, red, white, and black currants, the strawberry bed and the raspberry patch offered abundant fruit for all the year round.

Game was to be had in prodigal abundance, and was commonly found on the table. On a good day's shooting a man might bring down twenty brace of ducks between ten in the morning and four in the afternoon. A "beautiful large deer" could be bought for seven dollars in the sixties. "Six brace of ducks, fresh and in good order" was a gift which a lady might expect from a friend who had "gone to the prairies to shoot." The wildfowl were so easy to bring down that they must have provided something of an embarrassment, at times. "Mr. Ormiston sent me three bushels of ducks."

Wine travelled to the families of the well-to-do in bulk, and no accusing finger pointed at the users of it in these expansive years. The hysterical cult of the temperance worker had not yet been born. Quantities of wine, port, and sherry would arrive from Buffalo, on order to a house where a number of the young men in a family still lived at home. Forwarders in Montreal would send word to Mr. Ormiston that his barrel of wine was on its way to him. Mr. Punshon, the great Wesleyan preacher whose fame still rings round the back roads, "drinks no port wine, but takes a little claret and ale." Sometimes, in a very abstemious mood, perhaps before delivering one of his spellbinders, Mr. Punshon would take nothing but a couple glasses of sherry. Egerton Ryerson was a happy recipient of a dozen bottles of Port Wine, and found it "the best and most invigorating Port" that he had tasted in a long time. There was not the slightest doubt in the country that Mr. Ryerson was, and ought to be, an excellent judge of port wine, and that Mr. Punshon was behaving naturally and well. And when it seemed that the South was winning, in the American Civil War, and that celebration was called for, many dinner tables were furnished with "a few extra bottles of champagne."

Herbs in great variety grew in the sunny hot spots in the gardens, to titillate the palate. They were hung in the winter from the beams of the woodsheds — herbs to eat, pungent herbs to smell, and to lay among the blankets to keep the moth away and make the beds smell sweet. Their very names make a song to sing — pomfrey and borage, hyssop and dill, sweet basil and costmary, sage and apple mint.

No house, merchant prince's or small town harness maker's, lacked its flower garden, within and without, to offer a background to its beauty. The ladies of the household were careful to see to that. "The lilac in the dooryard" bloomed for great and small. In the conservatories of the great houses oleanders blossomed, and lemon trees, and a century plant which bloomed but once, it was said, in a hundred years. Rubber trees and potted palms grew there, shadowy, exotic, mysterious. The harness maker's wife grew her scented geraniums, her boston fern, her fuchsia, her Christmas cactus. The cactus grew ever more enormous every year, from its hot summering in the garden, and poured out its pink cascades from the height of its high bamboo stand, when the snowbanks were billowing outside.

Summer gardens were fragrant with lilies, marching in stately clumps before high cedar hedges. Blue flags, scarlet verbena and sweet faced pansies grew in well-tended patches about the glory of all the gardens, the cabbage rose, and the moss.

Letter Five.

ISABELLA MOORE TO HER SISTER CONSTANCE IN DUBLIN.

· · · ● ● ● · ·

Bradsbrook, C.W.
15 March, 1867

Dear Constance:

    I am sorry to hear that you have had such trouble with your chilblains. Perhaps a more active life would increase your circulation, and you might avoid this trouble. No date has been set for my return.

    We went last evening "tandem style", to a great dinner party in Oshawa, a town fifteen miles from Bradsbrook. The last few weeks have been cold and windy, but without snow, and the roads are hard as iron. Wheels, instead of sleighs. There is, it seems more snow to come, and a period of great mud, but just now the tandem fairly flies along. This is my first drive with this new team, and I've been longing to ride behind them. Cousin Jack has recently bought these horses – a pair of perfectly matched chestnuts. He has broken them to the tandem himself. They are very spirited, almost wild, and have caused Cousin Maude many anxious moments before Cousin Jack considered them safe. He says they are good tempered, really, only young and a bit wilful. And it must seem very odd to the rear horse to find his nose so close to his team-mate's tail. The mare has been broken to the saddle, and when she has been well tested for a lady, and found to go well, I am to have her for my own mount.

    So I must put you to the trouble of sending my dark blue habit with the velvet and bead trimming. I shall not again make the mistake of requiring my second best. The one I wish to have has a little peplum, and a straw turban with a pompom. When Biddy was packing it she had a little trouble with the pompom. It may be crushed, and if it is, then will you see to the making of another. The turban is nothing without the pompom. If you will note when the first Canadian steamer is to cross, from the shipping news, it should be possible to have the box carried in her. I should then have it when the frost has gone out of the ground, and the roads about are good again. I *particularly* require to have the habit.

    A Mr. Gibbs, a friend of Cousin Jack's, in Oshawa, is giving a series of dinners, to introduce his new house to his friends. Some of these expressions of hospitality are for the benefit of his townspeople, and some, as was the dinner of last evening, to collect friends together from more distant regions. He has spared no expense, in either his house or grounds, to provide an impressive stage for entertainment.

    I hope to see Mr. Gibb's house by daylight; it presents such a romantic appearance by night. There is a very long curving drive from the road to the house. We seemed to be passing through a park, for the shadowy glimpses of trees were surely grouped by man, not nature.

There must be a stream running through the property; several tiny bridges showed brightly in the moonlight. Here and there were inexplicable mounds of darkness. Cousin Maude said she thought they might well be fountains, wrapped against the frost. She hears that there are to be deer, when summer comes, and a shelter is to be built for them.

We sat down forty-six to dinner. All the faces were strange to me, but one. Do you remember that I spoke of a Mr. Andrew who crossed with us on the *Scotia*? He was there, and we had just a moment to recall our meeting on the Atlantic, before we were led into the dining room. We sat down at about half after seven and did not rise until nearly midnight. Cousin Maude had Mr. Andrew on her right, and tried to bring him into animated conversation without much success. Our glances met once or twice, and I think he would have perhaps talked more, with me. We might have reminisced about our friends on the *Scotia*.

Lacking much of common interest with either of my neighbours, both middle-aged men with strong Methodist convictions, I concentrated on the meal and the dignity and richness of the room itself. The room was a lofty one, with a fine plaster ceiling, with most intricate pendants. Because, I suppose, the house is still so new, no decoration has yet been put upon the plastered walls, which are pure white too, and one with the pierced cornice which runs around the tops of the walls, using oak leaves and a simple rose as motif. The room is lit with clusters of brass candle sconces; there must have been four score long wax candles to light the room. Mr. Gibbs evidently feels that oil is a suitable fuel for the lamps on the street, but that candles serve better at home.

There were ten courses, in all, and one of the gentlemen assured me that much of the dinner had been brought from Webbs in Toronto, undoubtedly. Certainly much thought had gone into the choice of wines; there were most delicate small oysters, and a range of elaborate moulded jellies and flummeries, quite apart from the beef and chickens which formed the main course. Dessert came in with highly polished apples, of course, oranges, nuts, raisins, etc.

The Gibbs have a number of guests who are staying with them, from Toronto, Ancaster, and London, I believe. And there are two men from Quebec, business associates with Mr. Gibbs, who live in Montreal. But the conversation about the table was not of business, but of religion and provincial politics. Both these subjects are of the greatest importance here. And there was much speculation as to whether the bill which is to secure the union of the provinces, now being debated in England, will actually be passed. There is much difference of opinion, and very strong feeling about this matter.

You will see to the sending of the habit *at once*, won't you?

> Your affectionate sister,
> ISABELLA.

7

The Chatelaine

Word of grace to women; word that makes her the earthly providence of her family, that wins gratitude and attachment from those at home, and a good report of those that are without.

Success in housekeeping adds credit to the woman of intellect, and lustre to a woman's accomplishments. It is a knowledge which it is as discreditable for any woman to be without as for a man not to know how to make a living, or how to defend himself when attacked. He may be ever so good an artist, ever so polished a gentleman; if deficient in these points of self-preservation you set him down for a weakling, and his real weight in society goes for very little.

So, no matter how talented a woman may be, or how useful in the church or society, if she is an indifferent housekeeper it is fatal to her influence, a foil to her brilliancy and a blemish in her garments.[53]

The young woman newly married and settling into a house of her own did not lack instruction from the printed page, in these years. She and her mother might well have been smothered in it. Mrs. Beeton's monumental work on cookery and household management, newly conceived, was available to the Canadian ladies in 1860. Mrs. Beeton's unassailable edicts showered from the domestic sky like meteors. From the United States numbers of periodicals and hardbound books of domestic lore slipped easily into the hands of the Canadians. And the Canadian ladies themselves were not to be entirely outclassed by the writers of these invaluable pages.

No one, of course, thought to vie with the majesty of Mrs. Beeton. And there were great areas of Mrs. Beeton's vast essay which, although fraught with wisdom, did not easily apply to the ladies in Canada West. Taste and customs had developed differently, moulded by the necessities and climate of what the British travellers liked to call "our dependency." People in all walks of life had shown no uncertain signs of "independency."

Mrs. Beeton's rules for keeping servants in their place, infinitely useful and at the same time perfectly invisible, brought smiles to the face of a Canadian lady faced with the problem of keeping four or five girls in her house at peace with each other, and working together to the advantage of the establishment. Gentle manners were required to train a willing servant in "our dependency." But it could be done, and it was done, although there were many incidents of Sarah flouncing out of a house forever, sometimes after only one's day's work, because there were too many fires. And of Mrs. Wilson's Lucy rushing off to work in the straw hat factory, instead of acknowledging her duty to Mrs. Wilson's linen room.

There was a curious artificiality, a kind of lofty and elaborate unreality in the strictures which the *Lady's Books* brought across the American border. A lady with a large house to manage, a staff to train and keep with her, children to educate and keep healthy, well fed, and appropriately clothed could never have had the time to consider the ordinances laid down in such publications very seriously. Her considerations must deal with more permanent values than the length of the fringe on the table cover this month as compared with the accepted length (more or less beads to be employed) as advocated last month.

In the train of Mrs. Beeton and the *Godey's Lady's Book*, both given pride of place in hundreds of households, came Canadian publications dealing with domestic matters, written to suit the peculiar Canadian need. Very often these books were compilations, combining the wisdom of one writer and the experience of another. Sometimes the admonition, the advice, the little moral tale to point up some estimable principle, is signed merely "By a Lady." It was not necessarily elegant, in the sixties, for a lady to admit to having written a piece of prose. An author, and particularly a lady author was perhaps not precisely socially undesirable, but there is no doubt that there was something equivocal about the practice of the craft.

Pages such as these which follow were written by Canadian Ladies for the enlightenment and improvement and guidance of their sisters.

MANNERS FOR MEALS

For breakfast the coffee is set before the mistress, the cups and spoons ranged in their saucers in front of it, in two rows if there are many of them; the meat and plates, which should be warm, before the master; salt, butter and castor at the corner to the right of both, head and foot, if the table is a large one, when two sets of these things will be convenient. Otherwise put them in the centre with the dishes in regular order around them, and relishes at the corners. To meet this order it is a trifle to have dishes in pairs of the same size, and use them always together for different things.

Fruit, whether berries, baked apples, or pears, is served first at breakfast, then oatmeal or wheaten grits, now found on every good table in cities at least, then meats and vegetables, with toast, hot cakes, and coffee following. Hot rolls come wrapped in a napkin to keep them warm, griddle-cakes between two hot plates, and all meats covered. Baked potatoes are scrubbed with a manila brush, the ends cut off, rinsed twice, and eaten without paring, as the best flavour goes with the skin. This is the custom with the best society in this country and abroad.

Eggs are washed with a cloth in cold water before boiling, and eaten in egg cups from the shell, chipping the small end off, or broken into larger glasses, or held in the napkin and eaten from the shell with entire good form, in either method. Where individual salt-cellars are used they should be emptied after each meal, and the salt thrown away, that one person may not use it after another, and they should be very small, that there be less wasted.

Butter should be piled round a lump of ice in little pats. To be very nice, as many have learned to like it from living abroad, it should be churned daily from perfectly sweet cream, worked without being touched by the hands or with water, and without a particle of salt. Thus it has the delicate flavour of cream at its best.

Honey is especially a breakfast delicacy, and so is maple syrup, which should be served in small saucers to be eaten with hot biscuit. A basket of crisp cakes, toasted rusk and crackers, will accompany coffee . . .

For lunch the coloured table cloth may be used if ever, though their use is gradually dropped because the colours do not wash well. White cloths with striped border in colours, or fine gray or unbleached damask, with napkins to match, assist the easy half-dress style of this repast. Cups of broth and thick chocolate, with light meats, hashes, croquettes, and stews. Salad and fruit are the staple variety, and rather more attractive than the cold meat, tea, and cracker fare too often set apart for this hurried meal.

Nowhere is negligence more annoying than at luncheon, and the cloth, glasses, and arrangements should be fastidiously neat to do away with the disagreeable feeling that everybody is too busy with drudgery to look after comfort. Insist that the girl who waits on the table has her hair neat, her hands washed, and a clean apron and collar on. An unkempt servant will spoil the best dinner appetite was ever sharp-set for.

Ceremonious lunches mean an hour's visit with a meal, at which salads, shell-fish, chops, in paper frills, and broiled chicken play a part, with ices, tarts, and fancy cakes for dessert. Mixed drinks, like Regent's punch, or claret cup, with ale and beer, are more in keeping at lunch than wines. These drinks are served from the side-board the malt liquors in com-

mon goblets, the claret cup in tumblers, the punch in small cups. Beef tea is taken from cups held in small saucers, or in small Chinese Bowls, with little saucers. The absence of all ceremony with the presence of light charming detail makes the luncheon attractive.[54]

A DINNER PARTY

Written invitations are on note sheets of mill-finished paper with side fold, the fancy rough and the highly glazed papers of eccentric shapes and fold being out of use. The large envelope, nearly square, allows the sheet to be doubled once to fit. Cards have the same finish, neither dull nor highly polished. The cipher of initials entwined is preferred to the monogram, and occupies the corner of the note sheet.

Guests arrive at any time during the half hour before dinner, and after leaving wraps in the dressing room, are met by the host and hostess at the door of the drawing room. Introductions follow if the guest is a stranger. If the party is given in honour of any distinguished person, or favourite visitor, the other guests are brought up to him or her and presented.

It is an omen of success for her evening if the hostess can make conversation general before dinner. To this end, have some novelty at hand, either in the shape of a personage whom everybody wants to meet, or a new picture, a grotesque group, a rare plant in the drawing-room, the latest spice of news to tell, or a pretty girl to bring forward. Whatever the attraction, bring it on at once, to prevent that very stupid half hour.

For dinner, the family table wants to have less the air of hotel arrangements. More delicate napery and ware, whether the latter is only "seconds," or the finest eggshell china; lighter, more convenient knives and forks, and heavier teaspoons, nice thin glass for drinking, thick cut crystal for sweets, with above all things a well kept cruet stand, make the difference in favour of home taste and home comfort. Keep all cracked and nicked ware from the table. Buy nothing that cannot be replaced without regret, but let each article be the best of its material. There is choice in the quality of stone ware and blown glass as well as in the shape of each. The plainest is always most satisfactory of inexpensive things.

Small can-shaped pitchers of engraved crystal, holding about a quart, are placed with ice water between each pair of guests. The napkins are folded flat, with a thick piece of bread on each, a cruet-stand and silver salt cellar is at each corner, and a silver butter dish at each end. The small individual salt cellars and butter plates, have an air of hotel arrangements which it is desirable to avoid at home dinners, though entirely admissable and convenient at breakfast. If wax lights are used, there should be as many candles as guests, according to the old rule. These are in branches held by Sevres and Dresden figures, above the heads of the guests. Nor are wax lights by any means the extravagance they seem.

Dinner napkins are from three-quarters to seven-eighths of a yard square, and should match the cloth, for which Greek, Moresque, and Celtic filigrees and diaper patterns are preferred to large arabesques and fruit pieces. French napkins of fine fringed damask, with crimson figures of lobster and crawfish woven in the centre, are sometimes used at first and removed with the fish.

Decorations must be choice and used with discretion. Flowers should be fine but few, for cultivated senses find that their odor does not mingle pleasantly with that of food. All artificial contrivances, like epergnes and show-pieces, tin gutters lined with moss and filled with flowers for the edges of a table, or mirror plates to reflect baskets of blossoms, are banished by the latest and best taste. The finest fruit grouped in the centre of the table, set off with leaves, the garnished dishes, the lustre of glass and silver, and the colours of delicately painted china, need no improvement as a picture. A low silver basket of flowers at the sides, and a crystal bouquet holder with a delicate blossom and leaf, sparingly introduced, are all that is allowed for ornament's sake.

Large dinner services of one pattern are no longer chosen. The meats and large dishes are in silver, the sweets come in heavy English cut crystal, and each course brings with it plates of a different ware.

The old fashion of furnishing dining-rooms in dark and heavy styles is reversed. The room is light, cheerful, warm in colour, the chairs broad and substantial, the table lower than it used to be, two points which add sensibly to the comfort of those who use them. Have the chair feet shod with rubber tips which come for the purpose, or if on castors, cover the wheel with rubber so that they can move without noise. See that the room is light and especially warm, for people want comfort at meals of all times, and they feel the cold more in sitting.

THE CALLERS

In the big cities, in the small cities and in the large towns, much of the social intercourse was maintained by the paying of calls. Old ladies and young ladies, old gentlemen and young, called upon each other. Half a dozen ladies and gentlemen might be expected to call any afternoon. All of the ladies in the house must not go out at the same time, someone must remain at home, to receive the calls.

When a member of a family returned from abroad, or a new member had been added, a bride or bridegroom, a visiting friend or relative, the newcomer was welcomed by callers. The omission of such a courtesy was well marked by the head of the house, and his lady.

Friends were expected to call when there was trouble in the house – illness or other distressing circumstance. A servant might be sent to inquire, in some cases. Absence was noted. "All my friends have been kind and attentive excepting Mrs. Davis, who has neither called nor sent to ask after me."

A death in the family brought every friend to call or to leave a card. The fulfilment or neglect of such obligation was marked with appreciation or censure.

Early in the afternoon coachmen were commanded to bring the horses, and the ladies of the house, usually in pairs, or attended by a gentleman, called upon and left cards upon, appropriate people.

Much of the calling was of less significance than the duty call on the stricken, being merely the social currency of the day among friends, acquaintances, and relatives.

Ladies sat at home with their needlework, prepared to be called upon. In the garrison cities a favoured house might well receive a clutch of half a dozen officers, glorious in scarlet and gold, in an afternoon. There was circumspection required, too, in the matter of making calls. Not all, however respectable and worthy, might be received. Callers upon the lady to whom the card was offered need not necessarily be received by her. The servant might well say that Mrs. George was not at home, or it might be thought to be too near the dinner hour, and the caller would not catch a glimpse of his quarry. Apparently such a rebuff was by no means infrequent and was held to be no offense. The caller might be persistent and call again. Or he might take umbrage and call never more. But his coming would be reported and noted, and his card picked up and read and official comment given, before the day was done.

Married daughters and sons, living in the same city or town, were expected to call upon the parents' house several times a week. But the call was a formal, or at least a semi-formal event, and worthy of being noted as such in a journal. It was a "call" not just a running in but acceptable in the morning, because of the relationship. There would be an exchange of news, a reading of bits of letters received from abroad, a gossip, a congratulation, a deploring. But unless with specific invitation, there would not be a prolonging of the call to either luncheon or dinner. It was commented upon, however, in the journal which the spinster daughter of the family kept. "Eleanor called this morning with Mr. Blight (a tiresome fellow whom Eleanor had married). Eleanor and Mr. Blight were invited to dinner, but Mr. Blight would not allow Eleanor to come."

The return of a daughter of the house, now a matron, signalized the reception of many visitors. And each visit must be returned, within a very short time – certainly not as much as two weeks. If the person upon whom the call was being made was away from home, or "not at home," a different situation, but calling for the same response, cards were left. The caller inquired for the individual upon whom it was his pleasure and duty to call. The obligation was complete on the caller's side, when the card had been left and the inquiry made. It was transferred then to the object of the call. A young lady during a round of duty calls might very well report herself "disgusted and disappointed" to find the ladies at home and receiving, whom she had intended to honour in the breach. Or by the card.

> In town, leaving a card with the corner bent signifies that it was left by its owner in person, not sent by a servant. Bending the edges of a card, means that the visit was designed for the young ladies of the house, as well as the mistress of it.
>
> If there is a visitor with the family whom you wished to see, a separate card should be left for that person, naming him or her to the servant. A card should also be left for the host, if the call was designed as a family matter, but more than three are not left at one house.
>
> From three to six are proper calling hours, and a visit may be from five minutes to half an hour, never longer, unless with a very intimate friend.
>
> A gentleman leaves his umbrella in the hall, but carries hat and cane with him, keeping the former in his left hand, never venturing to lay it on table, or rack, unless invited to do so by the lady of the house. Her not doing so is a sign that it is not convenient for her to prolong his call.[56]

8

The Fashionable Years

It was an extremely well-dressed decade. Dresses, shawls, hats, and shoes were extraordinarily pretty, in the sixties. As in all fashionable periods, there were reasons behind the flowering of beautiful clothes. In the sixties there were two dramatically different influences. One was that of the dashing mustachioed Garibaldi, who with his famous "One Thousand" all blazing away in their red shirts, landed on Sicilian shores and defeated, against all odds, the Neapolitans with their many thousands. The other was the wedding of Edward, Prince of Wales, to the elegant and stately Danish Princess, Alexandra.

Garibaldi caught the imagination of the fashion designers, as he had the romantic attention of all the world. "Garibaldi shirts" in scarlet, made of fine materials, became the rage. The ladies succumbed to the lure of bright and dramatic colours (it was a vivid and somewhat swaggering age) and matched their stockings to the scarlet shirts.

The wedding of the Prince took place only three years after he had travelled through many of the towns and little cities in the British American dependencies. The girl who had danced with the Prince of Wales (there were some thought to have danced too frequently and thus drawn attention to themselves in a scarcely decorous way) read and re-read the large and lavishly illustrated book which showed the charming princess and her bridal suite in delicate watercolour reproduction.

Women in the Canadas who had been getting their Paris fashion sheets and the *Illustrated London News* for years, bent, ravished, over the pictures of their sisters across the Atlantic clothed in these brilliant colours. They noted the bright red stockings, the high silk boots made of the same rich silk as the dress, the hair piled high with jewelled combs to keep enormous chignons in place.

New colours with captivating names appeared in the *Illustrated London News*; there was a new way to make the colours, invented – who could tell how – from coal tar. The first of the new colours was called "mauve," and there were two colours named after battles recently fought, "Magenta" and "Solferino." Magenta was a rich and violent shade, a bluish kind of red, and Solferino was a very bright pink.

The ladies compared the new, violent, certainly extreme colours and the styles of the *Illustrated London News* with the delicately rich and ultra-feminine, softly-coloured costumes in Alexandra's book. Decisions were made and the dressmaker established in the sewing room, stiff brown paper patterns in her hand. The newly invented sewing-machine was introduced to the seamstress. The willow "judy" was brought out from under her sheet, and the work began.

Decision as to a costume was not to be taken lightly. The many yards of material required amounted to an investment in itself. Then there was the trimming, no inconsiderable item for a dress which used fifteen yards of silk or poplin or fine wool, without counting the collar and undersleeves, the sack, or the Irene jacket which would transform the costume from a reception dress to one in which the owner could walk outside. The ruching, fine pleating, fringing, and vandycking, the rosetting, the bias binding, and the braid, would be piled mountain-high on the sewing table before the dress was built.

Such construction would not have been possible, at home, before the marvellous invention of the sewing-machine. The "Little Wanzer," and the IXL spurred the seamstress on to miracles of construction.

And what to choose? The drama of Garibaldi or the grace of Alexandra?

There were ladies in Alexandra's party wearing the Solferino but softened with the delicate chinese silk, no doubt. "Lilac and silver brocade", "rich grey poult de soie", and the same gleaming material in "Mauve, with fine Brussell's point." And there were velvet moire "antique dresses" for inspiration and the beautiful thought of "a rich peach poult de soie, handsomely ornamented with blonde, and rich tunic of tulle, fastened with bows of rich peach glacé silk." There were crinolines caught up in a clutch of roses, lovely enough to make a girl swoon.

And Alexandra's shoulders were very bare, very bare indeed, with almost a swell of breast showing and beautiful ringlets on each shoulder. On her lovely head was perched a pillbox hat, made entirely of flowers and with a veil hanging down behind.

Young ladies in Canadian drawing-rooms left the bridal book about on the centre table and sighed a little, trying their reflections in the mirror with such a show of shoulder and such a flowery hat.

The material was good in the dresses of the times. As in the soft furnishings of the houses, so in the wardrobes of the ladies, a relish for colour, and the gleam of velvet, the sparkle of beads, the livening touch of satin bands on a wool dress, drew the eye to the wearer.

The clothes were gay in the sixties: tiny hats with long streamers, wreathed in flowers and fruit and feathers to make a flattering foil for the demure high close-buttoned necks, the tiny tailored tucks, the statuesque drape and fold of the wrap. The shoes were excessively impractical and pretty: high boots made of soft leather laced up the inside, or of the same silk as the dress, perhaps, or of grosgrain silk with facings of the dress silk, and very high heels, also covered with the silk. Demi-high boots appeared made of foulards or grosgrain brocaded with gold leaves or flowers, extremely light and pretty. A black, grosgrain silk, demi-high boot could be laced over the instep and show revers of red morocco piped with white. The heel of such a boot would be very high and covered with the silk of the shoe. An advantage of having the costumes made at home would be that the torn shoe might be mended with the scraps left from the sewing.

Alexandra's elaborate wedding gown need not have excited excessive envy in the hearts of the Canadian girls. Their own wedding dresses were beautiful enough. Valenciennes lace, crystal beads, tucks and gores, and white persane made the dresses, and they topped them up with tulle veils and wreaths of orange blossoms.

Not every girl chose to be married in white. Often the wedding dress would be an especially handsome one, made of heavy silk moiré or velvet and with much hand-work in the trimming. The purples or warm browns often chosen as colours for the splendid dress made it useful for many occasions after the wedding day.

Underwear, French corsets, chemises, and long petticoats were tucked and frilled as elaborately as the gowns. An under-bodice, worn over the corset, fitted and tucked and tightly buttoned, gave firm support for the bodice of the dress. The crinoline tied at the waistline supported the vast circumference of the skirt.

No coat could adequately cover the monumental dresses. The short, full coats called "sacks" ended at the point where the crinoline began to swell. Some dresses were made with the fitted "Irene" jacket which was an integral part of the costume itself.

There were cloaks which could contain most of the crinoline, and capes shaped to do the same service, capable of billowing out over the undulating skirt. There were fine wool shawls for winter – from Kashmir for those who could afford the best; from Scotland for those who loved the brilliance of the Paisley pattern. In summer chilly shoulders were protected by gauzy wool shawls.

The seemingly casual styles of mantle and cloak, and the rhythm of their movement, combined with the meticulous tailoring which was always employed in their construction produced costumes of great elegance and charm. And the gentlemen who attended these well-dressed ladies were equally carefully and richly dressed. The silk hat (than which there is surely no more elegant article of wear) was in common use. The gentleman with his tall hat, his almost knee-length, nipped-in, double-breasted jacket, with revers of grosgrain or velvet, presented a very *soigné* appearance indeed. In the evening his set of carbuncle buttons matched his set of studs. With broad satin ties draped around high collars, pale trousers, a nice taste in flowered waistcoats, glossy boots, a fine heavy gold watch chain looped across his middle, a Canadian gentleman in the sixties was an ornament to his times.

Children were dressed as smaller specimens of their race. The little girls wore hoops, as their mothers did. Feathers and flounces, bows and embroidered petticoats were their due also. As with the furniture provided for the children (duplicates "in small," but with the same care for material and workmanship), so with the clothing.

Little girls shared with their mothers the practical style of the "undersleeve." The elaborate silk and velvet, braided and gored and gussetted dresses, lined and boned, could not be washed. Fuller's earth, once in a long time, could be depended on to remove the grease and oily accumulation. But it was a time-consuming, messy business. The answer to freshness was the collar and the undersleeve. The sleeves of daytime dresses in the period were usually large and flaring, seldom reaching to the wrist. Undersleeves, readily tacked to the inside of the dress proper, made of fine linen or muslin and trimmed with the lace of a matching collar, made a very acceptable adjunct to the dress. The type of the set of undersleeve and collar might make the basic dress more simple or more fancy. They had the supreme advantage of fitting into almost any dress, and gifts of collars and undersleeves were happily received and valued.

Lovely accessories – parasols, fans, reticules – were much worn. One might almost believe that some small impish deity had been at work in the sixties, determined to demonstrate how charming women could be with the materials put in their hands.

The crinolines swayed; the veils blew coquettishly in the wind; the beaded and glittering reticules dangled from hands clothed in fine kid gloves, pink or purple or blue or green or cream, scented with a perfume which would last forever. And if the sun shone, since now the hats were small – mere wreaths of flowers and straw – and would not protect that cherished complexion, the gloved hand carried a parasol. It would be a "flax grey silk, trimmed with steel chains, looped by medallion heads of jet, and a black carved handle." Or it might, to suit a costume, be a violet moiré, with a rich insertion of wide cluny lace. If she chose, the lady might have a "white silk parasol, trimmed with black lace and small ornaments made with the scarlet tips of black birds' wings, and an ebony handle."

Fans were equally provocative. Lace and needlepoint and ivory, with mother of pearl sticks or jet or feather throughout, created fans for the ladies to protect themselves from the heat of the fire or the heat of the day or the heat of some young man's glance.

Was it Alexandra, or not? But, in any case, towards the end of the sixties, about 1867, the necks of the daytime dresses began to open a little. And at once, jewellery appeared to fill in the gap. There had been no lockets for thirty years, and here they were again, larger than before, with sometimes an opening at the back, a little glass box, in which to put a wisp of the hair of the beloved. Two tiny frames were exposed, when the locket was opened, to house the pictured face of mother, father, or sweetheart.

The dashing styles of the sixties, with the love of strong colours which brought the Garibaldi shirts and the bright red stockings brought brilliantly coloured jewelry too. Necklaces, brooches, and bangles were heavy and elaborate. There was a tremendous revival of antique jewelry. For a fashionable dinner a woman might wear, fashioned in gold, "a fine horse chariot, masks, acorns, or floral drops."

> *Garnets are now exceedingly fashionable. We see combs with very rich tops formed of garnets and carbuncles; ear-rings, pins, sleeve and dress buttons, studs, buckles, belt-clasps, and bracelets formed entirely of garnets.*[57]

Small precious stones set in larger ones were sought after and admired. And every lady must have in her jewel casket at least one "parure." This would be a set of jewels, all patterned in their settings after the same design — necklace, a bracelet, and ear-rings. The necklace might be a gold flexible snake chain, with a fringed pendant, a bangle, and a pair of ear-rings. Or the pendant might be a much more elaborate one with a series of medallions, graduated in size, with enamel and pearl edgings, and a mixture of precious stones. Anthony Trollope, always conscious of women's adornments, provides a heroine with

> *a short chain of Roman gold with a ruby pendant. And she had rubies under her ears, and a ruby brooch, and rubies in bracelets on her arms.*[58]

GUIDANCE FOR LADIES IN MOURNING

> *Black feathers can be worn six months after the loss of a parent, if the wearers are young children. An adult should not wear them under a year.*[59]

The Canadian *élégantes* did not depend entirely upon London and Paris for guidance in fashions. Philadelphia, much nearer home, provided the full fashion fare which their own Canadian periodicals lacked. It was possible, for instance, to send an inquiry to *Godey's* today, and in the next issue or so of *Godey's Lady's Book*, a code and creed of fashion as indisputable as the laws of the Medes and Persians came to the hands of the inquirer. From the heights of the wisdom of Philadelphia these edicts were communicated to the eager hands of the Canadians.

> *At the request of some of our patrons, a few hints on mourning will be given.*
>
> *For widows, or first mourning for anyone, we have Bombazine, which ranks first, and is always fashionable; it can be had of different textures to suit the climate. Besides this, we find Canton cloth, Tamise, Madonna cloth, Biarritz, Reps, double-width delaines, and a variety of other materials.*
>
> *Black crêpe collars are for first or very deep mourning, then white tarlatane, and lastly linen.*
>
> *Crêpe undersleeves are seldom worn, being extremely unserviceable. The dress sleeve is either tight to the wrist and worn with a black crêpe cuff, or else it is a little loose and finished with a crêpe fold or trimming.*
>
> *As a wrap, a double wool shawl, a plain cloth paletot, or a tight fitting garment like the dress may be worn.*
>
> *The bonnet is of the Ristori or Empire shape, covered with*

crêpe, and with it is worn a long double crêpe veil tied under the chin, with a ribbon through the hem. Sometimes it is fastened at the side of the bonnet by a band or knot of crêpe.

When it is desirable to lighten mourning, a single crêpe veil is substituted for the double one, afterwards it is shortened and still later veils of black net trimmed with ruches or folds may be adopted. Veils may also be very prettily decorated by running in patterns with soft silk.

A shower of beads and bugles brighten up bonnets; a white cap takes the place of the black one; and gradually flowers creep in – first white, then pearl, and lastly purple.

The dress materials we have mentioned with the exception of bombazine, may be worn for most every kind of mourning; the different grades being defined by the various trimmings; first crêpe, then bugles, then ribbon, and lastly velvet.

Alpaca, and Algerienne, a kind of poil de chèvre with a very lustrous surface, are both very good wear for half mourning. A very good walking suit for full mourning is as follows:

Firstly, very small hoops, no larger than a barrel; over these a black cloth petticoat about four inches from the ground edged with a narrow fold of crêpe plaited on one edge only. The overskirt is formed of small gores half a yard wide, and fits without any fullness over the petticoat. It is eight inches shorter than the petticoat, of the same material, and trimmed in the same manner. A tight fitting basquine like the dress, trimmed with crêpe completes the costume. The bonnet is of crêpe with long veil.

For distant relatives, suits of silk without crêpe are frequently worn but for three months.

The ornaments for mourning are jet, enamel, filigree silver. In gloves, at first we see black, then steel, and later, pearl and purple.

Mourning watch-cases of black wood, ornamented with a monogram of silver are suspended from the waist by a chatelaine of Russian leather studded with silver and caught to the belt with a silver hook.[60]

9

The Sixties and the Simple Faith

I send you by Teresa two Bibles, the one a plain, family Bible convenient for daily reading; the other a Bible with a Devotional Commentary & marginal references printed in full. I hope you will find it instructive and useful. I have not written anything in either of them. I leave that for you to do.[61]

The Bibles were sent by Egerton Ryerson to his young married daughter, evidently in the full conviction that she would have daily use for them. What she would write in them would perhaps be her own personal reaction to a comforting phrase or an admonition. She might mark the page and note on the margin the verses which she felt might have been directed especially to her. There was not even that small shade of doubt in such a reader's mind when the verse or the verses struck truth to the heart. It had indeed been sent to the reader; the hand of God had turned the page. Christian belief was very strong in the years about Confederation in the Canadas.

In the lower province there had never been lack of faith, nor was it necessary now to provide more material manifestations of it. The French province had always clung to its belief. But in the upper province, where for so many years whole communities spent many months of the year without even a visit from an ordained man of God, there had been much backsliding, much forgetting of the Word and the Law.

Prosperity brought people together again. And when there were even a few families within driving distance, the little churches were built and congregations grew. The sect to which a family came to belong often depended, in earlier days than these, on how far the church which they might expect to attend was from the farm. Horses which have worked all day for six days needed their rest on the seventh. So Mennonites became Lutherans, Methodists became Baptists, and Congregationalists were metamorphosed into Presbyterians to favour the weakness of horseflesh.

The sixties saw many tall steeples raised to the glory of the Lord. The outward manifestation of the inward faith took shape in red brick Gothic structures in the cities, the towns, and the villages of Canada

West. Church and Chapel alike found the need for a place to worship worthy of their faith. And men were found who gave the money and gave it freely, gaining much satisfaction from being able to give such rich and enduring gifts to the people of their community and to the praise and glory of their God.

The relationship of God to the Canadians in these years was a very personal one. There was an indestructible tie between Man and God, if only Man recognized it and made himself worthy. Perhaps, of the nonconformists, the Methodist spires reached highest to heaven in Canada West, although, of course, there was no competition in that regard with the great Anglican Cathedral in Toronto. But Methodism was strong and vital, and held within its ranks rich men and generous men, who with their wives were very faithful to their religion and very energetic in the furthering of it.

About the dinner tables of the Methodists and their guests there was much talk of religion. Religion shared with politics as the major interest of the day. Men and women were intensely interested in the progress of their church, and a very much stronger line was drawn then than now between one who was a "church member" and one who was not. It was not given to everyone to be acceptable. But perhaps the dinner parties with the excellent food and the delicate, well-chosen wines did their part in swelling the ranks of the church membership. And many rich men offered proof of their stewardship in the bricks and glass and mortar of a fine new church.

Seventy years later a regional historian could say, of one of these:

> The Gibbs family were prominent Methodists, and had great influence both with their money and by their personal efforts, in the building of the beautiful temple of Methodism which was for long the most dignified place of worship in the town; the steeple particularly, never fails to excite the admiration of all students of church architecture. The dedication of this building, almost coinciding with the date of Confederation, was a great event in the annals of Methodism and the history of the town.
>
> Owing largely to the generosity of the Gibbs family it was more elegantly furnished than many Canadian churches of that date. The opening sermon was preached by Morley Punshon, the most eloquent preacher that English Methodism had produced, and quite the greatest orator yet heard in Canada.[62]

In some villages the little Baptist church which had been raised in the early days of the settlement was relegated now to the service of some small struggling sect, and a fine new edifice called the Baptists to worship. And certainly there were transactions in which one man or one man and his family made themselves fully responsible for the cost.

The spacious imagination of the sixties could embrace not only a fine house, a good farm, and a stable of fast horses for the men themselves, but visualized too a country which could offer universities to its young men, could assemble great libraries, and feel a sense of profound responsibility to provide appropriate buildings for the worship of God. There were men in the sixties in both the Canadas who conceived it a duty to give bounteous aid to the young, to the sick, to the poor. There were among them men who became generous benefactors to hospitals and who endowed chairs in universities for advanced instruction in mathematics and the sciences. At least one theological college owed its being to a private benefactor, and a wealthy brewer was known to have built a private church. There was an ever-present recognition of the presence and power of God among the people. And among people both great and humble a profound faith.

The Anglicans, the Methodists, the Presbyterians, the Baptists, and the members of the many small and fervent new fundamentalist sects which grew up and flourished in these years held one common unassailable belief in the future life. Simple and sophisticated people alike have left ample proof that "he is not dead; he is gone before," was an ever-present comfort to them.

The people had need to so believe, since death was such a frequent visitor in houses great and small. Families were in almost constant expectancy of news of death of relatives, friends, or distant friends.

The birth of a child was attended with acute anxiety and the anticipation of necessary resignation to the will of God, since only by His mercy will it live. Attended by the same Providence the baby might live to become a child, but he might be claimed at two or four or six in such mysterious circumstances that there could be no explanation, but that it was the will of God. His mother, a strong and healthy woman before her confinement, could deliver her fine, strong baby easily and in three days be dead of a mysterious fever which could be neither guarded against nor cured. Husbands and mothers waited, held in a helpless suspense to see if this time the hand of God would smite or bless them.

Letters and diaries are full of references to the resignation which the writers were trying to teach themselves to feel, and to the simple remedies which they were employing to prevent grief from descending on their heads. A little laudanum for the baby or a little opium in case of contagion from cholera; raspberry vinegar for a woman thought to be dying from inflammation of the lungs and pleurisy. The doctor comes and applies his leeches, suggests a liquid diet, and then, perhaps, nothing else can be done. The fault is constitutional, and the cure is not in human hands.

But when the garnering has been done, then the faith must be called forth. And it was called forth. There is no doubt that the task was easier for the simple woman than for her more sophisticated sister, but the difference was in degree, not in kind. So that a woman who had lost her husband might still wear a shining face, secure in the knowledge that it was but a matter of time till she would join with him again under the loving eye of their Saviour, and lead an even more blessed life.

> *I never saw anyone who looked more truly happy than Mrs. Johnson did. Her whole trust is in our Saviour and her desire and prayers are that she may be found worthy to join her husband in Heaven. She feels no sorrow for his death, feeling assured that he has gone to his Saviour. I wish I could feel the humble confidence and trust which she feels, and not sorrow for those who are gone.[63]*

So did a woman of great wealth speak of a widow of a minister. And yet she herself was not lacking in faith. She walked to the cemetery to sit awhile beside the grave of her most beloved daughter, and could say in her journal, that evening, "It will not be long before I shall be with my darling Emily again." The unalterable conviction is hers that the parting is only for a little while.

Men and women liked to keep about them some physical contact with the dead. A woman would wear perhaps for years, and perhaps never surrender a mourning "brooch" or ring. Within an oval frame, outlined with jet and pearls, protected by a tiny crystal, a circle of braid of hair, perhaps a mother's or the pale downy hair of a baby who died in an instant, giving no sign. At one moment the baby was there, fat, smiling, and happy. The next, the little face was blue, and a terrible choking sound ended its earthly life. In the next life, of course, the young mother knew that she could welcome her baby again. But the grief was cruel, and many times a day she rubbed the ring softly against her cheek.

When it was impossible, through illness or the severity of the weather, many a lady read the service at home in her own room, gaining spiritual comfort from the familiar words. The gentlemen would walk to church in their furs, but all was not lost to the lady who stayed at home. She had her guide and her comforter with her. In illness and in health her God was there, ready to be called upon.

After a severe illness a lady recorded her experience in her journal.

> *During the attacks I thought I was dying and although I felt and still feel that my Saviour will receive me, yet I trembled when I thought I stood on the very threshold of eternity. I sent for the Bishop and his conversation and prayers enabled me to face death with more composure. God grant that when the time comes we may be willing and glad to go, and to say Thy will Oh God be done.[64]*

10

Canadians in Paris, 1867

It was a magnificent show, the Great Paris Universal Exhibition of 1867. It was the grandest there had ever been and the grandest there was ever to be. The powerful states of France and Prussia were already polishing up the great new guns, some of which were on view in the Exposition itself. War and turmoil and struggle for power in Europe soon wrote "finis" to such extravagant and grandiose frivolity for the French.

But now there was peace, splendour and glitter, and lights and music and all manner of richness. The world crowded the Paris streets, and citizens of the most colourful countries on earth jostled each other on the Champ-de-Mars. They had been invited to send of their best, and they had sent. Now they were come to see the novel, the precious, the splendid, the amazing new inventions and the good fruit of the earth. There were ninety-four classes open for entries. The Canadians entered exhibits in sixty-five of them. Some had only a few items, but in some there were scores.

From *Haut Canada*, from *Le Bas Canada*, from cities and villages and hamlets, from farmhouses, from ateliers, from mills and factories, boxes and bales, bundles and casks went out across the Atlantic.

Startled French organizers of the Great Fair were provided with oil and water-colour paintings from Canada which clearly showed maturity as great as many of the pictures from Europe. They were in receipt of wines from Canada, when they had thought no wine would dare to challenge their own. But here they were, *vin ordinaire, rouge et blanc*, from Cooksville; cordials and liqueurs from red, white, and black currants. *Superbe!* These from the French province, *bien sûr*.

An exhibit of interest, whose character and provenance could be easily understood, was a collection of insects. It came from a Reverend C. J. S. Bethune, of Cobourg. This place appeared to be a village in *Haut Canada* and not a city in Bavaria. A splendid vocation for a reverend gentleman, skipping about catching butterflies.

A Mr. J. T. Jones, of Bowmanville, *Haut Canada*, sent (and the astonishment was intense) a set of dentist's instruments. The Frenchman stared at this display and made inquiry. It was disturbing, to find this kind of thing from the country of the savages. But the facts revealed that these Canadians were very forward in the manufacture and the use of dental equipment. To the extent, indeed, of teaching other, older countries in their use.

Both the Canadas sent maple sugar and syrup. Refined sugar and crystallized sugar spilled out from box after box. Chicory and spices, syrup of maize, and fancy biscuits ventured across the "vexed" Atlantic to vie with the acknowledged best confections in the world. Was there no province of the civilized nations which these Canadian exporters would not seek to usurp?

Linens in variety from the villages on the St. Lawrence and shawls and flannels from the villages and towns of the western province joined with exhibits of superb blankets from both. The convent-educated seamstresses of French Canada sent lace collars, and exquisitely embroidered "cradle and baby linen." Eleven mills in *le Bas Canada* sent linen. Counterpanes embroidered with millions of all but invisible stitches on fine Canadian linen were tenderly dispatched across the Atlantic. And to the city of superlative hats, at least one show of ladies' straw hats was found worthy to go. Leather and furs, raw and dressed, were draped in opulent profusion in the Canadian exhibit.

Le Reverend Docteur Ryerson, Directeur de l'Instruction pour le Haut Canada, Toronto, sent an exhibit of school books, as did *l'Honourable P. J. O. Chauveau*, incumbent of the same lofty and responsible position dans *le Bas Canada, Montréal*.

It is pleasant to speculate on the sensations of a small, dapper, bearded Frenchman, as he opened an entry from Canada. He knows, and most of the world with him, that Canada is a country inhabited by the exotic, the beautiful, the unattainable *belle sauvage*. It is a region occupied by moccasined aborigines, armed with the tomahawk, dwelling in houses made from birch bark or the skins of animals. And now this box! "What will it contain?" The scalp, perhaps, of some ill-fated white man who crossed the path of the savage. The Frenchman's hands tremble as he seeks to unite the strong hemp knot. Perhaps it will be a primitive utensil, thumped together by rough untutored hands, and probably smelling of them.

The rope is undone, the coarse cloth folded back. There is a fine cloth within. A delicate odour comes to the sensitive nostrils of the Frenchman. His wary hands seek under the more delicate cloth below. It is soap! It is an entry of fine milled soap. It was possible, of course, the Frenchman knew, that in places other than the beautiful beloved France, people did make soap. But this soap from Canada! He looked again at the forwarding. There was no room for doubt. Even the name of the city from which it came was familiar to him – perhaps it was not a household word, but it was almost a French word, and he knew that there, far across the Atlantic, which he would never see nor anyone whom he knew would see, there was a land which Frenchmen had discovered for their king. And it had been lost again. Perhaps it was no great loss, since the gold and diamonds and great jewels which the explorers had sought were proved, after all, not to exist. But the names were still French, and this "Montreal," this strange community in the bush, peopled by aborigines and uncouth white men, this Montreal had sent to France, and not just to France, but to Paris itself, the very heart and centre of fashion, the dictator absolute of the world of perfumes, pomades, and the finest of all soap – this Montreal had dared to send soap to Paris. The little Frenchman held his head and called his assistants to pronounce him mad. How dared this Montreal to send competing soap to Paris? But they brought more and more boxes to confound him.

Photographs signed by one William Notman, he too, of this Montreal – lifelike, lively, vivid photographs. What, what was this? A painting, surely? But no, it was a photograph too, and in such rich and vibrant colour! The Frenchman rubbed his finger across the seeming canvas. But it was not canvas; the graining was perfectly canvas, to the eye, but the finger could not find the grain. It was impressive painting, upon, perhaps, a photograph. The Frenchman called his assistant. "What is it then, a painting, or a photograph?" But the assistant did not know, and they pondered there. Should it go in the Class One, "Paintings in oils," or to the Class Nine, "Photographic Proofs and Apparatus?" There were nine packages in this class from the country which the Frenchman had thought inhabited almost entirely by savages.

What else might they find or not find to stagger the preconception of the New World?

Here were maps – well, that might have been expected – maps of Upper Canada, Toronto, reports and publications of St. Anne or Ste. Anne – of no interest and of little importance. No one would care, naturally, about the Map of Upper Canada. But – look at this: "Diagram of Thermometric Observations in 1859 and 1866." What had these savages to do with "Thermometric Observation?"

Shaken, the Frenchman repaired to his two-hour luncheon, eating his thin soup with loud sups and striking his thick slices of bread petulantly into his bowl. This exposition, this *trop beau* show, was sapping to the morale. And in the afternoon it was no better.

"Paper, Stationery, Binding, Painting, and Drawing Materials." What in the *nom d'un nom* had these savages to do with the materials of the literary man, the artist?

Yet, here they were: cloth-wrapped parcels and rope-bound bales, Quebec and Quebec and Quebec and again this Montreal and Toronto and Hamilton. The little Frenchman looked again; there were dozens of them, scores of them. From Ancaster and St. Hubert and Brooklin and Streetsville and Rivière-du-Loup. At least that was a name which meant something, and one could understand the meaning of that. A Wolf River, *mais naturellement*. There would of course be rivers of wolves, in Canada.

What was within these fine great heavy boxes here from Guelph and Belleville, Hamilton and Toronto, and yet again, this Montreal? They were SEWING MACHINES! And can these savages yet sew? And make the machines with which to do the same? There was of an impertinence in it. The Frenchman had seen few in Paris itself.

They were not large sewing machines, but rather delicately constructed little affairs, mounted on iron enamelled trays, some with scalloped edges, gilded and painted with roses and shells. The Frenchman doubted that such a thing would do its work. He diffidently turned the handle with his left hand, unadvisedly leaving his right index finger under the needle shaft. A swift response from the needle brought blood. The man regarded the machine with new respect and lifted the exhibits carefully to their appointed place in the Canadian section.

Five years before the observant Mr. Russell had noted, in the 1862 London show, that

> The display of the natural and artificial products of the far-reaching lands watered by the giant St. Lawrence at the Great Exhibition of 1862 came to the eyes of most of us with a sort of shock. It was surprising indeed to behold such evidences of wealth given by a dependency which was associated in the popular mind with frost and snow, with Niagara, Labrador, and French insurrection – Moose, moccasins, and Indians. There we saw an exuberance of growth in timber and in cereals – in all kinds of agricultural produce, combined with prodigious mineral riches.[65]

In 1867 the prodigious mineral riches, the iron and copper and lead were still there in their astounding quantity and quality, gypsum and marble and unctuous talc, oil of petroleum from many towns, whetstone and plumbago. And now the manufactures from these gifts of the earth were legion. Railway wheels and models of trucks, bricks and cement, sets of bells, salamanders, refrigerators, bolts and switches and mining tools went forth to Paris. There were many models of merchant vessels, and a set of models of ships built in the dockyard of Quebec. There were telegraph apparatus and fire alarm bells, pumps and balances. A machine for taking the distasteful smell from coal oil appeared in the Canadian section.

By July 24, when the judging was not more than half finished, Canada had received three gold medals, thirteen silver, twenty-nine bronze, and forty-five honourable mentions.

●

Letter Six.

MR. CHARLES LAWSON, MILLER AND MERCHANT OF HAMILTON, CANADA WEST
VISITING THE PARIS UNIVERSAL EXHIBITION,
TO HIS WIFE AMELIA, "LAWSONHURST," HAMILTON, C.W.

· · · · ● · · · ·

Hôtel Continentale
14 April, 1867
Paris, France

My Dearest Amelia:

It is a matter of great regret to me that your indisposition and the undiagnosed one of little Charles should have prevented your coming with me this year. You would find much to interest you here, more than two years ago. There has never been anything like this show, anywhere on earth, I should think. I hope that my Aunt Truman and Elizabeth Gibson will be able to stay at Lawsonhurst until I return. I hope it may be only a matter of a few weeks.

We arrived in Liverpool after a very fast journey in the *Peruvian*, only ten days. We crossed the channel with, as usual, more pain than we experienced on the whole voyage across the Atlantic. But here we are in safety, and go each day to view the marvels of the exhibition. They say that there are seven Kings here: the King of the Belgians, the Queen of Spain, the Sultan of Turkey, the Emperor of Russia, among them, and I don't know how many princes and royal personages beside. I can't say that I have seen any of them yet, to recognize. But we met Mr. and Mrs. Robinson from Toronto before we had been inside the Canadian section for ten minutes. My father saw D'Arcy McGee looking at the China woman. There's a family of them here on show. The poor little creature looked very miserable, he said. I think Mr. McGee has something to do with the show, maybe. A party of Blackstocks and Gibbs, from Oshawa passed within a few yards of me, but the crowds were too heavy for me to go through in time to speak to them.

But I did see the little Empress, herself. She has a most tidy little palace in the Exposition grounds, and was just being bowed into it when I spotted her. She visits the Fair every day, it seems, and this fancy little palace is for her to be private in. Aunt Adams was much struck with her fit out. She'll very likely tell you what was so astonishing about it. All I could see was that she seemed to have shrunk somewhat alarmingly. This is due, Aunt says, to her not wearing a crinoline. The ladies of fashion in Paris have shed their crinolines as if they were dangerous diseases. The craze hasn't struck the ordinary people yet, and I saw in the *Paris Soir* that M. Somebody says that it is not safe for any modest woman to walk in the streets of Paris without a crinoline.

I've been looking a little into the drapery line, as you suggested, here. I am a bit tempted to lay in a little line. Your brother in Toronto seems to find it does well, but I feel my ignorance.

All the silk pieces that I see look pretty plain, to me. I hear that many of the Lyons weavers are about starving since the figured silk is all out of style. The weavers confine themselves to the one style, figured or plain. The empress is ordering special figured patterns to help them out. There's no doubt that she sets the style. Maybe we could start out with an "Empress Eugénie" line?

I've been keeping in mind too, as you asked me, something to cover the chairs and for new curtains in our bedroom. It seems that chintz is considered to be old fashioned now. The style is leaning to wool stuff, some with gold patterns in it, and heavy warm colours, reds and browns and greens, I see here. What would you prefer? I've no doubt I can find something in Mr. Woodcock's shop in London. I don't quite know my way around the Paris wholesalers.

Letter Seven.

MRS. ADAMS, WIDOW, SISTER TO THE ELDER MR. LAWSON,

TO AMELIA, WIFE OF CHARLES LAWSON.

· · · ● · · ·

Hôtel Continentale
17 April, 1867

My Dearest Amelia:

    I cannot but regret that you are not with our little family party. There are so many things which you and I could enjoy together and not consider them tiresome, as I am afraid your dear husband and my brother do. My brother John is only three years older than I, but fatigues much more quickly. And in any case is interested only in the Foreign Pavilions. It is well that he has handed the business on to your Charles. You and I, my dear, would find wandering along the streets where the newest styles are shown very pleasant, I am sure. Although the crowds are beyond imagining; one is continually jostled. But the days are so soft and pleasant, I long for a rewarding companion. Mr. Andrew joined us here, on Saturday, but he is very low in spirit. This morning he said that it is twelve months to the day since his dear Augusta died, and their baby with her. He feels the loss of his wife very deeply, and much alone, with no other children to love him, and his parents long since dead. I try to make him more cheerful, but I am an old woman, and poor company for him. He will not be entertained. He must marry again, of course. Could you not find some gentle, loving woman, among your acquaintances, who could prove a worthy successor? She need not have money, I think. Mr. Andrew is a very successful brewer, your husband tells me.

    But the fashions here! You have for many years I know had the news from your Paris fashion sheets, but the changes have been so great since I was here three years ago. You have my word for it that there are striking changes this year. Even in mourning. It is now almost fourteen months since dear Mr. Adams died, and I begin to think about shedding my bombazine. You cannot imagine the novelties being offered, in the way of caps and bonnets, mantles and new black silks. I shall bring a pattern of "gros de lustrine," a very striking new silk, and a dress length of black and white lutestring silk, for myself. This is a very rich double-sided silk. I tried to interest your husband in it, but he is not sure of his judgement, nor, I think, of mine. He must wait for you. But should I find it in a pretty blue I will bring a pattern of it. It gives the impression, almost, of being made from bands of ribbon, the join being invisible, but the selvage edge discerned. I shall have mine made to do duty for both reception and outdoor summer wear, with separate pagoda sleeves, and a pretty small cape, just to cover the bodice, and boned to fit it exactly.

    All Paris (the "chic" women) take their style from the Empress, of course. The "Empress Peplin" has taken Paris by storm. It is a belt with basque tails cut square in front and back, and very long at the sides. Women who wear the peplin cannot wear a crinoline, and it is startling to see fashionable women without them. The French pretend to like the new style. M. Paparin, one of Mr. Adam's former business acquaintances, said to me that the peplin makes an epoch in history and deserves our gratitude for with it the fall of the crinoline is assured. What irresponsible nonsense! And yet, my dear Amelia, the truth remains, that one's opinion is swayed by what one sees. However people satirize, it cannot be denied that whatever is the prevailing mode in attire, let it be ever so absurd in appearance, at first sight, it will never LOOK as ridiculous as another, or as any other which no matter how convenient, comfortable, and even becoming, is totally opposite to the style generally worn. Perhaps I can look to the moment when even I will cast off the hoops!

Pearl grey is the most fashionable colour here, trimmed often with light blue or cerise vandycking. There are some rich violet silks shown (Mr. Lawson thinks these too brilliant) and foulards in nankeen are new. The hats are extremely small, nothing more than a little patch of lace or crepe or tulle placed on the crown of the head and edged around with a frieze of pearl or amber or glass beads. The veil is usually fastened on behind, and after being tied beneath the chignon, is gathered together and fastened in front with a brooch or a flower. The chignons are ENORMOUS! It would be considered vulgar, at home, to have such a QUANTITY of false hair mounted upon one's head. Some of them are plaited and end in two long ends hanging down the back. This may be beautiful, but not in my eyes.

Walking in the Bois a day or two after we arrived we saw such an extraordinary occurrence! A lady and a gentleman were cantering past when the lady's horse shied, alarmed by the sudden flight of a bird from a tree before him. The lady jerked back, and her entire chignon flew from her head. Her escort swooped down from his saddle and snatched up the bundle. He placed it unobtrusively under the skirts of his jacket and the pair rode on, seemingly unconcerned, as if such a contretemps were by no means rare.

How strange it is, and how very often it happens, that in the midst of crowds of literally, millions of people, one so often suddenly sees acquaintances from near one's own home, and whom one very rarely sees at home. As we strolled in the gardens before the Tuileries we were much surprised to see Mr. Burnham from Ancaster. Mr. Burnham was not accompanied by Mrs. Burnham. He had as his companion a young woman of obviously foreign extraction. His attitude and manner with the young lady were such as would scarcely be tolerated in a public place at home. I judged his acquaintanceship with her to have been very brief. I did not bow.

Letter Eight.

ISABELLA MOORE TO HER SISTER

CONSTANCE IN DUBLIN.

· · · ● ◉ ● · · ·

Bradsbrook, C.W.
1 May, 1867

My Dear Constance:

    I am much offended by the tone of the letter which reached me this morning, from you, dated 12 April. You will recall that there is but a seniority of seventeen months between us, and until you have become a married woman I feel no obligation to surrender my opinion to yours. And certainly I have not "expressed myself to scandal" by riding with Captain Harrison. Captain Harrison is a gentleman, and a very brave soldier.

    It is essential that I should have my riding habit, and as soon as may be. Of course I can not go to the expense of having a new one made here, when I have an almost new and becoming one lying in its box in Fitzwilliam Square. The dark chestnut mare of the tandem team makes an admirable, spirited, and good-tempered mount for me. She is more suited to me than any I have ridden before. Cousin Maude kindly lends me her old habit, but I am a taller woman than she, and of quite a different build. I feel at a disadvantage in it.

    We go to Hamilton in June, for a visit with Cousin Maude's sister, who spent Christmas here with us, and I am most anxious to have my own habit when we are there. The Lawsons frequently open their house to officers on leave, and evidently go into society a good deal. I am going to find my wardrobe inadequate enough. Will you have Biddy carefully fold my blue taffeta in a separate box, and tie it with the riding habit box. Had you done as I asked, some months ago now, (with special reference to the pompom, you may remember), I should have had the use of the habit long since.

    Mr. Charles Lawson is in London now, and will be for some weeks yet. Please direct the parcel to him at the Westminster Hotel, and he will put it in charge of his aunt who is to leave England for Hamilton, on the first of June. Mrs. Lawson assures us that the carrying of it will be of no trouble to her aunt. It will accompany her to Lawsonhurst.

    I do not expect to leave Canada for some months yet. Madame de Tourville has asked me to visit her in Montreal, and Cousin Jack thinks I should not fail to do so, as being a pleasant way of seeing the lower province.

    You may ease your mind upon my conduct in this country. I am not conscious of "casting aside my womanly delicacy."

    Your sister,
ISABELLA.

Letter Nine.

AMELIA LAWSON TO HER HUSBAND,

IN LONDON, ENGLAND.

· · · ● · · ·

Lawsonhurst, Hamilton, C.W.
1 May, 1867

Dear Mr. Lawson:

I was happy to have your letter from Paris handed in this afternoon. You may be reassured about Charles' health. Dr. Tomlinson leeched him twice, the week after you left us, and once again last Saturday. I became anxious because he bled too much, and I could not stop it, and had to send for Dr. Tomlinson again. But the little boy seems quite well now. Dr. Tomlinson thought it was congestion. I paid him five dollars. Both children drove out to the farm with old Tom to cut some asparagus. Tom wanted to set out the melons, but I persuaded him that it is much too early.

Elizabeth Gibson is a very agreeable visitor. She had lots of calls today. Mrs. Clarke and Miss Clarke called, and Captain Phillips with Mr. Grey called upon Elizabeth. The gentlemen are to return for croquet this evening and to heavy tea. Captain Phillips has announced his engagement to a Miss Jordan of Toronto. She has only three hundred a year, and he has nothing but his pay. I am glad his attentions to Elizabeth will now be done. Such a match would be quite unsuitable, but I am afraid she thought herself to be in love with Captain Phillips. However, Captain Baring and two other officers met her at the train, and drove her here. She looked quite flushed and excited when Captain Baring handed her down from the phaeton. I wish he would propose for her. She will have nothing when her father dies. I believe that a gentleman from Barrie wishes to marry her, but he is so much older, and with six or seven children, and poor besides. She is very devoted to small children and would make him a useful wife. But he would do better to look for a woman with money. He is said to be very amiable, and in his condition it may be difficult.

Mrs. MacPherson and her daughter Mrs. Burnham called. Mrs. MacPherson is at the end of a visit which has lasted two months, and goes back to Montreal very soon. Her daughter goes with her. I think Mrs. Burnham is a pleasant pretty woman, but for a married woman she talks too much of the regiment. She knows all, all, all, about the 47th. It is rumoured that the 47th is to leave Hamilton in a months' time, for London. There is to be a great ball given by the 47th, before they leave. The streets will be dull without the redcoats. Mrs. Burnham will suffer. She was fortunate to be able to keep her mother with her while Mr. Burnham is away. His ship is expected in a fortnight, and she will meet him in Quebec. There is gossip that Mr. Burnham finds the Quebec society much more attractive than Hamilton society. If there is truth in this rumour, Mrs. Burnham may feel justified in accepting the attentions of several officers, and of Captain Fitzgerald in particular. He walked home alone with her, from the review, after the fireworks.

To touch on the subject of the pattern for the curtains and chairs. I do not believe that I should like a heavy woollen stuff for the curtains. The old carpet is red, and will still do. The heavy colours you speak of might give an appearance of heaviness which would, I think, be depressing to the spirit, especially in the spring and summer. I like a gayer aspect, in a bedroom. I should like, if possible, to furnish with something which would do for both winter and summer. There is such a dislocation when the change is made that I should vastly welcome a pattern which would be agreeable all the year round. It is absolutely necessary I agree, to have the pipes down and up, and the carpets up and down again, twice a year, and that seems enough, without altering curtains and chair covers. The girls grumble at all the work. It is harder and harder to have really willing help. And although Mrs. Mitchel in Montreal is offering $10 a month, she is unable to get a girl who will do the laundry too, even for that amount. But Hamilton is not Montreal, happily. Lucy is leaving us to work in a straw hat factory, but I have news of Mrs. Grainger's Kate, whom Mrs. Grainger does not require any more, her household having been reduced. They rarely sit down more than six to dinner. Kate will have six dollars.

And to the curtains – chintz may be considered old fashioned in some people's eyes, but not in mine. If it is not satisfactory, it must be that poor quality material has been used, and that the glaze is the kind which will not last, and the dyeing with fugitive colours. I have in mind a good firm piece, perhaps of French or English make, well designed, and with a pretty pattern which will not tire our eyes. Not a cheap Indian print.

Will you not look in the London shops, since by now you will have left the Paris ones behind, and see if there cannot be found a good piece?

Sarah will have her birthday before you can return – hard to think it is seven years. You will not forget to bring her some trinket, will you? A locket, perhaps?

I am sure that Mr. Merrill in Montreal will have some excellent chintzes, and if time does not allow you to search, I could, while Elizabeth Gibson is here and with the children, go to Montreal to see what I can find. Having lost the opportunity of the holiday in Europe, a trip to Montreal would be quite agreeable. Your Aunt Truman is willing to accompany me. It must be only a very short holiday since, as you will recall, we are to have the Bradys and Miss Moore at Lawsonhurst in June.

I have had this letter by me, hoping that I might send it by hand, and now Mrs. Clarke, who goes by the Damascus on Friday, will take it from me this evening. And I have not told you my ideas for the drapery line, to which I have given much thought. I shall try to write them out in an orderly fashion, and send them by my next.

Mrs. Burnham will not go to Quebec to meet her husband. Only

Mrs. MacPherson's maid will go with her, to Montreal. The explanation of this sudden change in plan is that there is doubt whether Mr. Burnham will stop in Quebec after all, and that she might miss him there. Telegraphs are not reliable. Captain Fitzgerald does not go with the 47th to London. He has leave and has taken rooms at the Mansion Hotel for a fortnight. Aunt Truman thinks Mrs. Burnham will soon be looked upon as a light character, and that if Captain Fitzgerald is to blame, Mr. Burnham will have no other recourse but to horsewhip him. Mrs. MacPherson and her daughter had a great spat, about the change in plan.

●

Letter Ten.

AMELIA LAWSON TO HER HUSBAND,

IN LONDON, ENGLAND.

• • • ● ● • • •

> St. Lawrence Hall,
> Montreal, C.E.
> 24 May, 1867

My Dear Mr. Lawson:

You will see that I have taken your acquiescence for granted and that I am now in Montreal. Your Aunt Truman and I arrived here early yesterday morning, and have already met a number of friends and looked in several shops for chintz. I confess myself much flattered that you will come to no final decision about the drapery business until we can discuss it together.

We took tea with Mrs. MacPherson, last evening. There was a large number of callers come to meet a Mr. Borrett, a young gentleman who is a fellow of Cambridge, I believe, now travelling in North America in the interests of broadening his knowledge. Each night he writes an account of his day's discoveries and impressions, with the object of sharing them with his father on his return to England. Mr. Borrett is a much-travelled gentleman, very well read, too, and I confessed to a curiosity to learn what opinions such an observant visitor might form, at first glance. Mr. Borrett has promised to have his clerk make a fair copy of some of them, to give to me, which I think very civil of him. I shall wait for them, to include in this letter.

A Miss Porter, whose acquaintance Aunt Truman and I made in our journey by the *Spartan*, speaks very highly of the *Grecian* as being superior in every way to the *Spartan*, although I believe that the *Spartan* is a stronger ship, and a champion at running the rapids. But the *Grecian* presents a very gay appearance. Her wheels are set higher than the deck, and there is a very handsome circular stand, with a decorated canopy for the band. Miss Porter says that in the evening there was always music, from a very nice toned piano to amuse the passengers. On this occasion a lady sang "The Brook" and "Robin Red

Breast." They are, Miss Porter said, "very appropriate airs to beguile our ears while our eyes feasted on the enchanted seas." I should, I think, enjoy something a little more sprightly. Miss P. seems a far from frivolous young lady, over serious. She has written down in great detail an account of her trip, with her mother, of six weeks duration in the west, going as far by steamer as Hamilton, and then on to London by train. She means to publish this work, and with the proceeds build a music college. I cannot but think she is over optimistic.

The *Grecian* has gone to Quebec, and on her next trip but one, we plan to go home in her. The fare from Montreal to Quebec is $3, and with more leisure I should like to go by the river to Quebec, and perhaps the Saguenay, too. But the object of this excursion is chintz, and we bend our energies towards chintz, and then home, since I am not yet quite content about Charles.

Mr. Merrill agrees with me that there is beautiful and lasting chintz to be had, and that ladies of individual taste will not be done out of it. He had a number of bolts, any one of which would have been pretty enough. But we have fixed on one, hoping to gain your approval with both the idea of chintz and this pattern. Mr. Merrill has put the bolt away.

It is a glazed woodblock print, French, and I thought it exceedingly handsome. The design is of garden flowers, drawn perfectly, from nature. There are tulips, both open and closed, cabbage roses with their leaves prominently displayed in the rhythm of the design, paeonies, small cluster roses in buff, with large single roses in pink. The tulips are striped, either yellow and red, or purple and pink; the paeonies are dull red and buff, with red centres. All colours are soft, rather than brilliant. The design and colouring (the background is soft grey green) bear every mark of a truly French elegance.

We go home on Thursday, in the *Grecian*. Elizabeth is to go to the 47th Ball, and I am to chaperone her there. I hope she may enjoy herself, but she is quiet and does not draw attention to herself. In spite of the total unsuitability of a match between herself and Captain Phillips, I think there is no doubt but that she was in love with him, and his engagement to Miss Jordan has come as a shock.

Elizabeth shall wear my white worked muslin to the ball – the one with the seven flounces and the very wide crinoline. We have taken out the undersleeves and the collar, and tried it upon her with my green and white enamel parure with the amethysts. She is a little too tall for perfect grace, but the ruffles on the sleeves coming down her arms almost to meet the bracelets diminished the effect of height. Carrie dressed her hair most cleverly, placing three ringlets on each shoulder, and a bunch of fresh violets at her breast. Captain Baring's eyes will brighten when he sees her so, I believe. I feel quite sure he is in love with her. I should be very glad, shouldn't you, if it should end in marriage?

When may we hope to hear that you have finished in England, and are on your way to Lawsonhurst? The Bradys and Miss Moore are to be here about the 17th of June and will stay perhaps a fortnight. Miss

Moore is as you know, a lively young woman, and very amiable. I anticipate a very pleasant visit, and hope very much indeed that you will be with us. The 63rd are expected to be here by the first of July, and perhaps we may expect a ball or two.

MR. BORRETT'S FAIR COPY

Montreal, by Steamer from Quebec . . .

This was my first introduction to the river steamer of the New World, and truly they are an institution to which nothing that we have can for a moment be compared for comfort and speed combined. The American river-boats, of which the Canadian is a copy, is nothing more nor less than an immense floating hotel – a mixture of every kind of life – fast life, slow life, busy life and lazy life, all under one roof.

The saloon is a fine handsome room of great length and good height, fitted up with exaggerated decorations, extravagant, and is I think, tasteless.

All along either side are the state cabins, each and all a good bedroom in itself, comfortably arranged and extremely well ventilated; and around them, on the outside runs a sort of open deck or platform, where the passengers sit and promenade at their ease. At 6 P.M. was served in the saloon at the lower end, which is set apart as a dining room a handsome "high tea"; and after tea there was music, cards, chess, and so, till late in the evening, when after a final moonlight walk outside, the passengers turned in. I found my bed very comfortable, so did my companion, in so much so that we both had great difficulty in rousing ourselves on reaching Montreal, where we arrived in the morning at 7:30.

We have taken a walk round Montreal, and are greatly astonished with what we have seen. To people arriving with the idea of finding the inhabitants dwelling in log shanties and brushwood huts it must be a surprising sight to come upon a fine handsome city, with splendid buildings and noble churches, and all the indications of affluence which are characteristic of a wealthy commercial city. I certainly never expected to find that Canada had its Paris – the buildings of Montreal surpass those of many a fine city on this (or the other) side of the Atlantic. . . . The French Cathedral, the Palais de Justice, and the Post Office are all perfect in their way.

The Montmorenci Falls are far finer than anything of the kind I have seen in Europe.[66]

II

Concerning the Duty of Women

> *It is as easy to marry*
> *a rich woman as a poor woman.*[67]

Since to live, money was necessary, and to live with the comfort and elegance appropriate to gentle living, a great deal of money was necessary, prudent young men and women in the sixties looked well to such security before entering into an engagement to marry. It would have been considered rash not to consider the material advantages of a union.

Young people naturally intended, in time, to be able to maintain the kind of home from which they came, but an establishment of some size and dignity was expected to be provided for a newly married pair. It was not unusual, however, in either Canada West or Canada East for the first year or two after marriage to be spent in the family home of the bridegroom. Such an arrangement was apparently not resented, and the bride made her new social contacts from her husband's home.

Talk of financial settlements before marriage caused no embarrassment; firm legal commitments, expected and agreed to by both parties were made before the wedding could be arranged. And very often the agreement was by no means easily reached. A father who was marrying his daughter into a very wealthy family, and who himself was not overly prosperous, might balk at handing over too great a percentage of his goods to his prospective son-in-law. The young man about to enter into marriage with such a young woman, however much he loved her, might feel that he was offering enough in himself and his prospects, without also settling upon her the annual income which her father seemed to feel was absolutely necessary for her happiness. So there would be lawyers and wrangling, often enough, before the conclusion of the affair. But there would be little use in wrangling and lawyers once the marriage was consummated.

Two essential characteristics for marriage, to the prudent, were money and amiability. A young lady, perhaps a very young lady, left without the protection of her father who would have given more thought to his daughter's happiness than the guardian left to look after her, might be persuaded to marry someone to whom she was not much attracted, on the somewhat dubious grounds that "He has Money, and is, I daresay, amiable."

Amiable or temperamentally thoroughly disagreeable, the young lady upon her marriage surrendered herself, her whole future, to a large extent her property, and, at least, her earthly prospects of happiness to her husband. If he truly cherished her, she might have her opinion asked for and respected. But she would acknowledge him to be her master in his house and in his marriage. The word "obey" was pregnant with meaning in the Canadian marriage relationship of the sixties. There was little thought that Mrs. Atkinson's view would prevail over Mr. Atkinson's opinion, should they unfortunately differ. Not even the most spoiled of wives would expect such a conclusion. There may be tears and bitter ones, but they are shed in private, and there is no thought of disobedience. What Mr. Atkinson says is law.

If Mr. Atkinson is cruel, and cold, unreasonable and extravagant and seems to prefer the society of other women to that of his wife, Mrs. Atkinson must bear with it. If Mr. Atkinson is kind, and affectionate, careful of his money (and hers), and lives peacefully in the company of his wife, then Mrs. Atkinson is blessed and may bask in her luck. But her duty to her husband is an absolute duty. Next to God, she must revere and obey. And she must guard her reputation sedulously, as a married woman.

Marriage settlements were as varied as the personalities, financial standing, and circumstances of the people concerned might be. A handsome residence with linen and plate might go with a bride. On the other hand the gift of a pair of ponies, with harness, cutter, and trap, and perhaps the young lady's piano and sitting-room furniture could be considered a handsome enough dower by a father. The father of the groom to be would very possibly not agree and protest that there must be investments to accompany the gifts of "kind." The bride's father, on his part might feel that the hundred pounds annual settlement proposed for his magnificent daughter would not go far towards clothing her as she ought to be clothed. Perhaps a diamond parure would go some distance towards making the offer acceptable.

And undoubtedly there would be the consideration of what might be expected to come to her after the death of her father. It was not only in the novels of Trollope and Jane Austen that it was known to a nicety that "Mrs. Prime had her two hundred a year," or that "it is hard for a gentleman to live on seventy pounds a year."

Similar calculations were anxiously made in the offices and drawing-rooms in the Canadas, and similar conclusions reached.

Old women and old men, and young ones too, when taking their pens in hand to retail news of the marriage market, never failed to comment on the material prospects of the match.

"I hear that the Honourable George Atkinson is to be married to a very young lady (seventeen), who has thirty thousand pounds. Mr. Atkinson is not very young, not very rich, and is a widower with five or six children." From a distance of a hundred years one can only hope that Mr. Atkinson was amiable, and invested his wife's money to advantage.

If by the merest of chances, Mrs. Atkinson, in the absence of her husband from the fireworks, should be seen walking from the parade ground to her home with Colonel James, Mrs. Atkinson has laid herself open to suspicion. Should Colonel James find occasion to speak a few private words with Mrs. Atkinson after the reading from Shakespeare in the drawing-room of a friend's house, and then, Mr. Atkinson still being absent, if Colonel James should once again walk with her, to protect her, perhaps, from footpads in the streets, then Mrs. Atkinson must begin to take care of her good name. For Mrs. Atkinson's good name is the unequivocal possession of Mr. Atkinson, and any man who asperses it may expect to find Mr. Atkinson's hand on a horsewhip.

> *It is true that people will make ill-natured remarks without grounds, but when a married woman knows that she is a subject of such remarks, and that they annoy her husband, it appears to me that the remedy is simple and easy. She should avoid the gentleman who caused such remarks, and if necessary cut him. What can all the men in the world be to a right minded married woman in comparison to her husband, and even if should that husband be a brute her duty remains the same. She has in the sight of God promised to love honour and obey and cleave unto him until death. The lot of some women is very hard but there is another and better world where those who do right receive their reward.*[68]

AND BY HER HE HAD NINE SONS AND FOUR DAUGHTERS

In spite of the very great danger and likelihood of mortality that attended the birth of children in the sixties, a young lady marrying then might expect to produce a large number of babies. Big families were welcomed and not only in the French province. Six or seven children made up a very usual family, and there are many records of a woman having given birth to a dozen or more living children. There are many more records of a man being father to more than a dozen, but investigation shows that in most cases of fourteen or sixteen children in a family the first wife has had no more than eight or ten to call her own. It must have been a woman of great courage and belief in her own capacity who would take on seven or more children born to some other woman, and know that she would probably have as many herself.

The Canadian mother of many had much more responsibility in the training of her family than the English mother in similar circumstances assumed. The tradition of the ever-powerful English Nanny was never successfully transplanted across the Atlantic. Nurses there were, of course, but there is little evidence that the relationship of the mother to the child was quite as remote as it commonly seems to have been in England. The training, early teaching, and the "bringing up" of the family was very largely the mother's responsibility. It is natural to suppose that in the family of "nine sons and four daughters," the father would take an active interest in the developing capabilities and manifestation of growing intelligence in the sons once they were out of petticoats. Perhaps very early he might choose George or Malcolm or William or Maurice as his likely successor, and begin to test and prepare him for his destiny. Two or more sons might be expected to inherit the family concern, and there would be places for the others in the expanding Canadian economy. A cousin or friend in Montreal, having only daughters, would take in a likely boy. The members of the business aristocracy were known to each other. Perhaps the eldest, who, disappointingly seemed to have no head for business, but was interested only in animals and trees, could be given charge of the river farm with prospects of another farm or two, if he should make a good thing of it. There was the law, always a good profession, and one which could lead to a brilliant career in politics. Fathers looked over the range of towheads and black for one which would have the height of head above the ears, and the length behind it to indicate brain power. A gentle, bookish boy may perhaps take to the church. But for good to come of that there must be a vocation. Ah well! They would declare themselves, and their mother would keep them in health, and she herself would see to the training of the girls.

It was likely that the daughters would marry, and very likely that they would marry into established, prosperous families. But they might not. There was much marrying of Canadian girls to British officers. Perhaps such marriages did not always result in what Frances Monck warned her maid Conway against: "I told Conway what a terrible life was a soldier's." But there was always doubt about the financial prospects of girls who married into the army, no matter how enchanting the officer in the scarlet coat. She would be whisked away from her home and her country almost inevitably, and must be prepared to hold herself as a gentlewoman should, wherever she might go. The household arts must be taught to all young women. It was the duty and satisfaction of the mother in the house. A clever and conscientious lady saw to it that her daughers were well versed in the principles of household management and the preservation of food, meat, fruit, and vegetables. She might ensure that a girl should learn to cook, both simple and elaborate foods, to bake bread, to store a quantity of jelly and jams of her own make. Perhaps, when she married and had an establishment of her own, such occupations would be quite unnecessary. But she should have the knowledge of how to make a spotted dog pudding, and be prepared to go down into the kitchen and show the new cook how to do it.

There would never be the despair and confusion in a Canadian kitchen that reigned in a comparable kitchen in England when the cook walked out forever, with the policeman.

Mothers in the sixties arranged to have their daughters taught to play the piano or the violin, or trained to sing acceptably for company.

Girls also must be taught to do decorative needlework; a sitting-room in which ladies waited for their callers was furnished with embroidery frames, upon which skilled fingers created flower pictures and landscapes built upon old designs and their own original ones;

needlepoint and Berlin Work and crewel for fire screens, and table covers, and bits of tapestry worth framing for their own intrinsic beauty.

Young women were encouraged to sketch with charcoal and pencil. A girl showing a special gift must be given drawing lessons and learn to manage water-colour and perhaps oils, for the essential cultivation of her talent and for the decoration of her home. A black velvet panel bearing a profusion of lilies, iris, roses, and violets painted in oils might be made to bloom in the drawing-room. Virginia creeper glowed crimson on the bell pull. Small family portraits in pencil or ink from the fingers of a daughter became treasures in the house, when the children had grown up and gone and perhaps the subject himself was dead.

And prominent among her accomplishments, a lady must have an ability to give pleasure to her guests, to entertain graciously, to put her guests at ease and be at ease herself, with a thorough knowledge of the complex and inexorable social code of her day.

The lady who had a mere four daughters had all this training to establish satisfactorily, and beyond this there was more. She must see that the spiritual life was fostered and fed. The governess, the school, the reading aloud while the girls worked at their frames, the new periodicals and the new books served for the intellectual nourishment. But to the mother whose life was lit by the light of the promise of the life beyond this was not enough. It was her duty to guide her family towards the hope of life eternal, to persuade them towards the un-utterable joys of the spirit.

AND THE GREATEST OF THESE IS CHARITY

In the sixties in Canada the gentlemen built the churches, endowed the universities, and provided the libraries, but the small personal charities were left in the hands of the ladies. It was they who found the money and gave assistance to the poor and the unfortunate. Clergymen in pecuniary distress were apt to call upon a lady for help. It was nearly always forthcoming, and certainly it was very often greatly needed.

A popular custom employed for the relief of private distress, usually in the case of a lady who for some reason had fallen on her luck and to whom the misery was not an accustomed one, was the raffle. A lady in the interests of such a person, would go about the town, calling on her friends to say that Mrs. Parkins wished to raffle a few pieces of silver, being in need of ready money. Tickets for such a raffle might cost as much as two dollars, and found ready sale among the generous. Gentlemen properly might be expected to pay more for their raffle tickets, and find themselves after a three dollar gamble, in the possession of a gun or even a horse.

Sometimes the need for ready money, in case of a lady, was the result of curious circumstance. Mr. Peterson, the father of six young children, left his wife and family to seek new fields and richer returns for his talents in California. News of Mr. Peterson was slow in coming, and then there was no more news of Mr. Peterson. But Mrs. Peterson was not without enterprise. A raffle of Mrs. Peterson's goods was arranged by a lady, and the money resulting sent the six young children and their mother in search of the wandering father and husband.

There was the ever present duty to the poor. The poor were the responsibility of the ladies in the big houses. They were to be called upon, given encouragement, advice, perhaps a piece of fine scarlet doctor flannel to relieve the soreness of congestion in the chest, or of a face ache. It was the part of a lady to lend an ear to the call of distress. Jellies and cordials and strengthening soups went out to the houses of the unfortunate from the houses on the hill. All illness was a mystery then, even more than it is now. It was attributable to the cold or the damp or the falling of the leaves when summer was gone. There was power, some believed, in the waxing of the moon, and if it came in time, there would be healing. Mysterious illnesses might be discovered to be no recognizable disease, but the result of a fragile constitution.

A visiting lady could bring comfort to a house where the mysterious ailment was affecting an old man or a child. Old men particularly feared the waning of the year, lest with it they might wane too and go on into extinction. A visit from a lady, especially if she brought a clergyman with her, comforted the old man and taught him to know that his fate was not in the falling leaf, but in his Saviour who held his life in His loving hand.

An afternoon a week was reserved, often, for regular visiting of poor and ill. Sometimes a visitor could tell by the overly-bright eyes and flaming cheeks of a child that it would scarcely benefit from calomel or rhubarb. She would stop her horse by the doctor's house, and bid him to call on the child at her expense.

Some ladies found, with experience and study and joy in the work that they themselves could heal specific ailments, and grew herbs with medicinal qualities and prescribed them. A lady kept her little store by her and gave to those who asked. The soft fluffy grey leaves of "lambs' ears" were good for cuts and ulcers. There was coltsfoot tea for coughs, a bunch of dried lemon verbena to make a refreshing tea, the root of valerian to quell hysteria.

Salves and ointments from treasured secret recipes were concocted from beeswax, and mystery – the soft kind to draw out the poison, the hard to heal. Little round wooden boxes of such as these went out in the reticule, on the day for visiting the sick, in case there should be need.

The mysteries of healing were not all to be found in the steeping of herbs, or the making of poultices. There were a few visiting ladies in those years whose own spiritual vigour was so great that they could, while praying with the sick, lay their hands on a fevered head, and feel strength flow from strong to weak. In the morning, the fever would have gone, and health restored.

12

Literary Life

> *I have put up two or three French Books for you to read — I send two numbers of* Revue des Deux Mondes. *— I wish you would write out a translation of the admirable Article on the Future Modern Societies. It is the best view of the Relations of Protestantism & Romanism to Modern Civilizations & their probable destinies that I have ever read. I will revise the Translation and have it published in some form, or parts of it, as "Translated by a Lady."*[69]

There had been story tellers before the sixties in the Canadas, of course. They were both native and immigrant, and for the most part had told stern tales of great hardship and the fearful battle between man and the untamed forest, the cold, the hunger, the intractable land, and the intractable people. By the sixties some of the hardness and violence had disappeared from the literature emanating from the Canadas. Stories, poetry, essays, and reporting on the wonders of nature had taken preference over pioneer tales of wolves, sudden death, starvation, and the ever-present menace of forest and snow.

The famous Canadian writers of the late nineteenth century had not yet appeared. But not all young women were content to sit in rich drawing-rooms working heavy wool into thin fabrics, making heavy glowing pictures out of thread and silk. Nor were those who passed their educated fingers over paper and canvas, clasping brush and pencil in their hands entirely content. For some there had to be words to tell of what they saw and felt and knew of the sudden beauty of the sunset or the night or the flowers, without being taught.

And young men lifted their eyes from the carving of wood or the keeping of ledgers, and were moved to write poetry. They wrote sonnets and sagas and dramas in verse. Some of them published volumes of lyrical verse, and now, perhaps for the first time, it was truly Canadian poetry. The rivers and the hills and the songs the poets sang of them were of Canadian rivers, of mornings and evenings where the canoe slips along between banks of Canadian colours, where the shapes of the hills are Canadian shapes. And the men of our own times who know of the quality of true poetry, can find it in the verses of the poets of the sixties. The names of Sangster and Heavysege are the names of the best of these poets.

Between the early pioneer tales and the sophistication of the latter years of the century not a great deal of memorable fiction came out of Canada West. But Canada East had one great story teller in Mrs. Leprophon. She wrote of the life in the high society of Montreal and of the complexities of life in Quebec when British rule was new; in all she produced nine novels. She drew a pattern for Canadian historical novels and built her own on an elegant structure. Her *Antoinette de Mirecourt*, with another one or two of the novels went into very popular translations. The writers who followed her and published their historical romances owed much to Mrs. Leprophon.

One might be brought to believe that there was a magnetism at work during the 1860's, which drew men of outstanding talent, in some cases a talent amounting to genius, to the writing of books. Rich literary fare from the United Kingdom and Europe was served forth to the Canadians in the sixties. It was varied, imaginative, immensely instructive, critical, and abundant. The writers whose books, and whose serials of books, appeared on the counters of the Canada West Mechanics' Institutes, the private libraries, and the shelves of the booksellers were among the greatest names in English language writing of all time. Their books are on our shelves today, honoured and read.

Many of the greatest – including Dickens and Thackeray and Trollope, to name but three – were writing their best then, and the magazines which carried their serials were immediately available to Canadians. Dickens, already, of course, famous and much read in North America, produced *Great Expectations* and *Our Mutual Friend* in the sixties. Trollope published *Framley Parsonage*, *The Small House at Allingham*, and *Phineas Phin*, in these years. The polished witty prose of Thackeray crossed the Atlantic – sometimes in as many as twenty-four monthly parts – in the *Cornhill Magazine*, of which he was the first editor. Messrs. Rollo and Adam of Toronto hastened to inform the readers of their *British American Magazine*, that it was only a matter of letting them know, and the *Cornhill* with the stories by the famous Mr. Thackeray could be in their hands. *Lovell the Widower*, *The Adventures of Philip*, and the charming *Roundabout Papers* appeared in monthly instalments, in the *Cornhill*.

Browning, Carlyle, Gaskell, Kingsley, Le Fanu, Hawthorne, Ruskin, Swinburne, Collins: these were the writers who were putting forth their best in the sixties. This was the bountiful fare provided for the reader. Among the women writing, and writing with extravagant output, perhaps Mrs. Gaskell was the most prolific. She turned out books and stories almost every year. *Cranford* came out in the fifties, but the sixties found Mrs. Gaskell, pen in hand, furiously covering her paper with words for which there were thousands of readers waiting. *Sylvia's Lovers* and *Mr. Harrison's Confessions* came out in the sixties. And there was mourning among the readers of the *Cornhill Magazine*, when an abrupt unsatisfactory end was reached, and *Wives and Daughters*, appearing in that magazine, was announced to have no possible proper conclusion. Mrs. Gaskell had died.

George Eliot made literary history in the sixties. Thackeray as editor of the *Cornhill Magazine* offered her £10,000 – an incredible sum, for a projected novel. In the end (the way of authors) the novel brought her £700. This was *Romola*, whose fame has faded in the hundred years. But her masterpiece, *The Mill on the Floss*, was an offering of the sixties, and *Silas Marner*, *Felix Holt*, and the poem "The Spanish Gypsy" followed in the same decade.

Le Fanu with *Uncle Silas* and Wilkie Collins with his *Woman in White* and *The Moonstone* brought to the shelves of the reading Canadians the fearful forerunners of the heart-stopping, breathtaking, hair-raising, horror-type tales.

Poetry flourished in the sixties, some truly great poetry among the mass of published verse. From England came Elizabeth Barrett Browning's *Poems before Congress* early in the decade. Her husband published his *Dramatis Personae* and the world-famous *Ring and the Book*; within this period Tennyson published *The Holy Grail*, the *New Arthurian Poems*, and *The Passing of Arthur*. Rossetti, Swinburne, and Macaulay swelled the poetry sections of the libraries. Emerson and Longfellow sent their poetry north from the United States.

Lorna Doone dates from the sixties; Hawthorne was writing then; Mark Twain had become a household name, and his *Innocents Abroad* appeared at the end of the decade. Ruskin, Carlyle, Blackmore, Meredith, Ouida, Parkman, names which all men know now, were new and valued at that time.

With all this richness from which to choose, it is not remarkable that the Mechanics' Institutes and the private libraries vied with each other to place the latest book of these writers on their shelves.

There was a hot debate in the sixties, and a certain amount of bad blood between the town of Oshawa and the town of Hamilton in Canada West, on the question of which could show the best collection of literature. Hamilton taunted Oshawa with having less-educated people than were in Hamilton. This judgement was made on the grounds that the Hamilton Library had many more books than the Oshawa Mechanics' Institute could boast. Oshawa retorted, and with spirit, that there were many more periodicals and better ones, on the shelves of the Oshawa institution "to afford a pleasing recreation to cultivated minds, and to promote literary tastes."

A superb selection of excellent magazines was available. It was a wonderful time for the periodical. English periodicals flourished and made their way to Canada. American periodicals flourished and made their way to Canada; by the middle of the nineteenth century, Canadian periodicals flourished too, and, oddly as it seems by present-day practice, they advertised and analysed the imports very generously.

The *British American Magazine*, published in Toronto by Rollo and Adams in 1863, offered in its pages extensive quotes from contemporary British quarterlies: *The Edinburgh Review, North British Review, London Quarterly, Blackwood's Magazine*. It advertised the monthlies too.

The British Monthlies including Blackwood *(American re-*

print), Cornhill, Temple Bar, The St. James Magazine, Good Words, London Society, The Churchman *magazine*, The Exchange, *etc, etc, can be procured each month at Messrs. Rollo and Adams, Toronto.*

In addition to the notices of the British magazines, the publishers of the *British American Magazine* included analyses of the offerings of American publications, every month. "*North American Review, American Journal of Science, Atlantic Monthly, Harpers, etc, etc.*" The Canadian offerings were not forgotten either, and Messrs. Rollo and Adams were prepared to give information in their magazine as to the contents of them, and also provide the magazines themselves. On the counters of Rollo and Adams were to be found: "*The Canadian Journal, The Canadian Naturalist, Proceedings of the Botanical Society of Kingston, Transactions of the Literary and Historical Society of Quebec, Canadian Parliamentary Documents.*"

And although Canada West was evidently not to be supplied with *Le Foyer Canadien*, or *Les Soirées Canadiennes*, by the publishers of the *British American Magazine*, these two periodicals flourished exceedingly in Canada East in the sixties. *Le Foyer Canadien* regarded itself as a *Recueil Littéraire et Historique* offering its readers a collection of literary and historical articles. *Les Soirées Canadiennes* described a rather smaller circle, but with a high aim. It was a Recueil de Littérature Nationale "*consacré à soustraire nos belles legendes Canadiennes à un oubli dont elles sont plus que jamais menacées.*"

Les Soirées approached its aim with vigour and conviction. Every issue was headed by a poem of impressive length and, usually, great moral significance. Flowers, virtue, children, are frequently the subjects of the smaller, lyrical poems. Sometimes, although the tone impresses the twentieth-century reader as cloyingly sentimental, the verses are neat and occasionally beautiful. A strikingly lovely maiden sent mad by the death of her lover who was drowned on the way to the wedding, wandering in a lifetime of bewilderment is the type of much of the poetry. Her name is probably Madelon, and she is pictured as spending much of her days picking flowers.

>   *pour orner une bière
>   ou, dans le froid sepulcre,
>   entraina sa raison.*

Les Soirées printed long, long, long stories written by men who went to California; awarded many many pages to a description of Italy or an immense poetic eulogy on the wonders of French-Canadian voyageurs and forestiers; with a long article on the Micmac Indians, to give full measure. Full measure was what the readers of the French magazines liked, and there was no stinting, no skimming just the cream off the top. If the subject should be shipwreck, and it often was, the reader was spared no distress for the drowning. A man who was to be executed for good and sufficient reason, made an excellent subject for a French pen. The man's state of mind before he committed his crime, while he was in hiding, when he was captured, his possible remorse or lack of it, the condition of his family, with particular attention to the grief of his very ancient father, the tears of his children, the consumptive hopelessness of his wife – all these were given full attention. And the moral was drawn with a black pencil.

Le Foyer revived old French songs and poetry, guided its readers to the love of virtue for its own sake, and when one of its Presidents died, it gave seventy-two pages to his eulogy, and published his *généalogie* back to 1685.

> *This is a sceptical age – in mundane things as in heavenly nothing is taken for granted, or received without inquiry. Like the old pagan Coifi, who in the time of the Saxon Redwall, rode full tilt against the false gods of his fathers, and hurled a sacrilegious lance within the holy precincts of the fane, do we assail with bold defiant brow, the unquestioning faith of our ancestors; and with profane hands raze to the ground the goodly edifice of ancient credulity. There is no superstition so sanctified by antiquity; no prejudice so hallowed by the time honoured adherence; no custom so venerable by long observance; whose just claims to respect, the analytical, curious, doubting mind of the nineteenth Century does not test and examine. There is no subject too sacred for argument, no being too exalted for criticism; meekness and reverence are old fashioned qualities, thrust aside to make way for more exalted virtues [!]*
>
> *We are taught to believe in nothing but what we can understand; pursue only the practical; cultivate only the useful. True superstition and prejudice have received their death blow; but devotion and humility have suffered in the conflict, as also that sweet handmaiden of rare souls, Poetry. Where is the beautiful fairy lore and simple faith of the past in elves and brownies? Where the wild songs of Sagas and Skalds? Where the romance of Tournament and Galant Prince, of persecuted beauty, and faithless knight?*[70]

There is a strange dichotomy, in these early Canadian magazines, especially in the English-language ones. There are book reviews of enormous length, dealing with most learned subjects in a most learned way. On the next page the reader finds an equally long article on the moral influence of flowers. This is written by a botanist with much knowledge, much experience in the identification of plants. And she will preface her learned piece with some statement as

> *The love of flowers is the first dawning of that high inward life that is the gift of God to Man.*[71]

The *British American Magazine* took its responsibilities to its readers seriously, and believed that they were capable of reading and appreciating the best that could be published, and that at great length. The stories are very long; the poems are lengthy; there are no illustrations, and when it comes to paging for book reviews, there can have been no limit set.

To begin a review (which was to run for a full eight pages) of a two-volume work, on *Researches into the Origin of Civilization in the Old and New Worlds*, by Daniel Wilson, LLD, professor of History and English Literature in University College, Toronto, the reviewer says:

> *These delightful volumes, fair in outward adornment and beautiful in the spirit which pervades them and the language in which the spirit finds expression, will be welcomed and read with peculiar interest by Canadians and Americans.*[72]

"Britanno-Roman Inscriptions, with Critical Notes" (London: Longmans & Co. 1867), by the Rev. John McCaul, LLD, President of University College, Toronto, was reviewed with enthusiasm and for eight tightly packed pages.

> *As a specimen of Canadian Literature, this is certainly a very remarkable volume. It is one which wherever produced, would do credit to the learning, ingenuity, and good taste of the author, and could hardly fail to obtain the high approbation of those who can appreciate such pursuits; but it could scarcely have been expected in the old world, that in the remote capital of Western Canada a scholar would devote his time to correcting by accurate knowledge and acute reasoning the errors of those who would seem to have much better means of examining the particulars requiring to be known, than himself.*[73]

The *British American* advised its readers to take note, in the *Westminster Review*, of a new book, called *Les Misérables*. It was written by a man called Hugo, and the *Westminster Review* said that it had a priest in it and named its other characters. The *Edinburgh Review* mentioned *Les Misérables* in the same month, and said it was full of screaming discords, unbelievable black on white. Readers of the *London Quarterly* could find an elaborate and learned disquisition on the original New Testament. The Miscroscope and its Revelations were to be discussed, and *Blackwoods*, the eldest of the periodicals and "always attractive and sterling," offered an account of a month's visit to the Confederate Headquarters (the twelfth of a series on Life, Literature, and Manners), an account of progress in China, and a full criticism and appraisal of Thomas Trollope's Italian novels. There was no need for a man to be ignorant. The periodicals were there.

The *British American* itself set out to provide useful information for its readers. It began, sensibly, by an extensive statistical article on British North America: eleven pages, for a start, on Physical Features, Geographical Features, agricultural capabilities, mineral resources — coal, iron, salt, building materials.

Mrs. Moodie contributed a story, Dr. Scadding produced twenty-one pages on "Early Notices of Toronto." There was some poetry, inclining to death, the grave, and the hope of meeting beyond it.

For I know each passing minute
Brings me nearer life's last shore,
And nearer that cloudless kingdom
Where we both shall meet once more.[74]

Once beyond that, there are twenty pages of analyses of the Post Office and Railway Systems in Canada and the United States, and a charming and most knowledgeable (and very long) piece on "Insect Life in Canada." Topped off with a few sketches of "Indian Life," and a bit of "Correspondence," and there was your magazine with something for everybody.

The Periodical Publishers must have been kindly people, to judge from the "Correspondence." It runs something like this.

> *D.N., Kingston. "Margaret" will appear next issue. G.T., Montreal. Not suitable. A Lady, Toronto. "Marian and Mary," and "The Spinster," respectfully declined. The publishers would like to see some prose from the same writer. H.M., London. Sentiments good, but would appear better in an essay. L.M., Barrie. "Smiley" will appear in January. Mrs. G. Perhaps a friend would bring the parcel with the manuscript to the publishers.*[75]

The literary gifts to children in the sixties were the most enchanting books ever written in the English language for the young. Edward Lear, Lewis Carroll, Charles Kingsley, Wordsworth, C. M. Yonge, W. H. G. Kingston, R. M. Ballantyne, and Maria Edgeworth were among the great names providing books for children, during these most fecund years.

Perhaps there are some people who still read, and with delight, *Guide to the Mathematical Student: Elementary Treatise of Determinants*, but there is no doubt that there are scores of thousands of people who do read with delight of Alice's Adventures Underground, which came from the pen of the same author at just about the same time. Little inimitable Alice, with her long flowing hair, accompanied by her strange acquaintances had newly found her place on the nursery book shelves in Canada West by the Confederation year.

The people who wrote for children in the sixties were almost invariably professional writers, men and women who wrote excellently for adults too. Frequently they were erudite clergymen who had been turned into professors of mathematics or history. One was thought worthy to be a chaplain to the Queen, a Tutor to a prince. The great poets wrote for children.

Some of the little brightly illustrated books were mawkish and overly given to the pathetic. These, naturally, were not from the hands of the best writers. But children died in early youth or were orphaned by disaster of water or fire and dispatched to the care of cruel, unfeeling, distant relatives. There was little disposition to shelter these lambs from the north wind of rough reality.

Virtuous behaviour was rewarded; there was punishment for calculated naughtiness. On the whole, the characters were inclined to be either very fortunate or very ill used, either very white or very black, and many words were spilled in an effort to keep the black from besmirching the white.

And there was no pulling of semantic punches. The whole richness of the English vocabulary was hurled at the reading child. Kingsley in the *Water Babies*, an erudite and abstruse work, combining quantities of scientific information with a swift-paced story of adventure and the supernatural that almost all reading children loved and love, went impishly out of his learned way to include lists of verbs and adverbs well calculated to puzzle any reader, great or small. He lists them in almost alphabetical order; a child making his way through them, dictionary in hand, would have given himself a generous helping of instant education.

Words like "contumelious" or "phantasmagoria" were dropped into the children's minds like lumps of enriching fruit. Children in the eighteen-sixties were fed words large enough to frighten a modern child, trained in two-syllable words, out of its tidy little mind.

There were funny books *Rummical Rhymes*, books of adventure, books about Natural History, and many books about midshipmen, and the life of boys at sea.

Adventures of Dick Onslow among the Red Skins which W. H. G. Kingston wrote, charmed as the many writers were with the savage magic of imagined life in North America, must have puzzled many youthful brows in Canada.

Early in the sixties Edward Lear published his *First Book of Nonsense*. Kingsley's *Water Babies* came out in 1863. In that year Wordsworth's *Poems for the Very Young* was read in nurseries. A *Picture Magazine* for children was available by 1864. A volume of *Arabian Nights* suitably edited for children and *The surprising, unheard-of and never-to-be-surpassed adventures of young Munchausen* appeared at the same time, in the middle of the decade. In 1866 came Alice herself, *Underground*, at first, then translated to *Wonderland*, with *Swiss Family Robinson* as companion.

Magazines for boys, magazines for girls, and magazines for children appeared on the shelves of the libraries in the houses on the hill. Christmas annuals put months of ecstatic reading into the hands of boys and girls, and were treasured and read by succeeding generations. They were storehouses of delight for children.

Even today, in Canada, hands searching in attics for remembrances of the past, may find in an old trunk, a pile of

BOYS' OWN MAGAZINE
1867
100 Handsome Pages
Tinted Paper, Plates, Correspondence, Essays
Competitions & Awards

*

Such a searcher should look well in the dusty corner under the gable window. He may well find a broken backed copy of *Beeton's Annual* or *Everyboys' Annual*, put there for the last time by some enchanted child a hundred years ago.

Letter Eleven.

MR. LAWSON IN LONDON,

TO HIS WIFE IN HAMILTON, C.W.

> Westminster Palace Hotel,
> London.
> 1 June, 1867

My Dearest Amelia:

I was somewhat surprised to learn from your letter of 14 May that you had gone to Montreal without specifically gaining my permission. I begin to think your Aunt Truman has not a good influence on you. It is devoutly to be hoped that the bolt Mr. Merrill has put away for you will be acceptable. Mr. Woodcock, whose warehouse I have been investigating is a very large and well stocked one. If I do decide to extend my merchandising to include a line of soft furnishings I shall certainly import from Mr. Woodcock. And he assures me that there is very little to be had in chintz worthy of our taste, no matter what we choose to pay for it. I hope you have not been too precipitate. If such an occasion should arise again, I should be obliged if you would not be in such haste to make such an important choice without consulting my taste. But since the matter seems to be concluded without the least reference to me, we shall consider the matter to be a fait accompli, and I have directed Mr. Merrill to have the bolt sent to Lawsonhurst. You will see to the making up immediately. Although I suppose no matter how swiftly the work goes now the room cannot be newly furnished before the Bradsbrook contingent comes.

There are a number of Canadians at the Westminster. Mr. John A. Macdonald and his wife have been here, but we missed them by a few days. D'Arcy McGee must be still in Paris, I think, but we see familiar faces almost every day hereabouts. Lord Monck was here for the Queen's birthday on the 24th. My father longs to go back to Canada. He and old Mr. Warren from Uxbridge walk in St. James's Park every day and grumble about the exorbitant cost of the Paris sojourn, "Tilled up pretty fast for me," my father mutters, every day or so. Perhaps I should be content to let him make the journey alone, but I fear for him. He seems frail. I shall be very glad indeed to go home myself. I find the poverty in England so depressing. But since Mr. Proctor, whom I particularly wish to see is not yet come from

New York, I think I must contain my impatience. I don't want to cross my path with his on the Atlantic.

Aunt Adams has gone to Brighton to spend a fortnight with her daughter Susannah and Mr. Reid. The Reids would much like to have her stay longer, but she is determined to be in Canada for the first of July, and is drawing the time pretty close as it is. She is much concerned about the doleful state of young Andrew. I have asked him to come to us at Lawsonhurst, probably to coincide with the time of the Brady visit. I think Aunt Adams has a scheme for interesting him in Elizabeth Gibson. But I don't like the thought of providing husbands for impecunious young ladies. I'm afraid I can't give any opinion about the possibility or the desirability of Elizabeth Gibson pleasing Captain Baring to the point of his making an offer. The poor girl has nothing, and will have nothing. She is probably an estimable young woman and seems agreeable. I realize fully that you would not have left our children in her care unless she was both. But I beg you not to be hasty in putting ideas into Elizabeth Gibson's head.

I hope very much to be at Lawsonhurst for the first of July, to join with the town in the celebration. This will be a day which both Sarah and little Charles should remember all their lives. The *Great Eastern* is due out of Southampton on the fourteenth, I believe, and I shall hope to be aboard her.

Doubtless you will have the plans for the day well in hand, however, whether I am there or not. You seem to be showing what I can only call undue enterprise.

Kiss the children for me. I shall bring the locket and a trinket made of aluminium, for Charles. This is a very marvellous new material, very strong and light and silvery in appearance. The Emperor has ordered a dinner set of it, but I think I should put it in the kitchen if I consulted my own opinion. Tastes differ. Thousands of people at the Exhibition stared at an ordinary rocking chair, such as we have at least a dozen of, in our house, as if it were the most extraordinary invention. And thought nothing, apparently, of a thousand electric lights strung among the trees in the Tuileries when the Empress had her great ball. I don't know quite what I think about this electric light invention. It is said that it will quite throw gas and oil out of any competition. But I shall have to wait and be convinced. It seems to me an invention for simple, foolish, tricks and not for a permanent use. The ladies at the ball, some of them, had electric frogs and rabbits and skull-and-cross-bones poised in their headdresses, winking and grinning and performing such kinds of foolishness. I assure you we shall wait before we tear out our beautiful sconces at Lawsonhurst, and put in these glaring lights. Perhaps, though, it may be a coming thing. In any case, we now have seen it in France, and if there should be any enduring worth in it, we shall have it too.

Aunt Adams has packed a great quantity of sheet music, some of which I think is for you. She is greatly moved by the new waltzes which we heard in Paris and which have not taken long to reach the London bands. The new one by *Strauss* which is called "The Beautiful

Blue Danube" was played, under the composer's own direction, at the great party in the Tuileries. It is a very pretty melody, and I feel sure a sheet of it will be in your music parcel.

●

Letter Twelve.

MRS. THOMAS TRUMAN TO HER LIFELONG FRIEND
MRS. ALBERT ADAMS, AUNT TO MR. LAWSON
OF LAWSONHURST, HAMILTON, C.W.

· · · · ● ● · · ·

Lawsonhurst,
2 June, 1867

Dear Rachel:

    I thought you would have been back in Canada long since. You must be finding plenty of entertainment there, first Paris and then now London. Well, you are fortunate in having the means. Had Thomas lived to make the fortune which he was well equipped to make, I should have been as well able to please myself as you do. But I do not complain, and Amelia Lawson is as kind to me as ever a daughter could have been. I have rented my little house in London for another year, so must make plans for when I go from here. Amelia suggests that I stay at Lawsonhurst for a few weeks after Mr. Lawson returns, which date seems to be uncertain.

You have not said that you were able to buy me the little clock in Paris which I wanted, so that I may have some gift to leave this hospitable house when I do go. If you could not find one at the price which I suggested, perhaps you will have picked up some other handsome curio. I should like it to have come from France, rather than England. Perhaps a little ebony box, nicely carved, or a fan handsome enough to lie on the drawing room table. It must, alas, be not too costly.

Amelia I think is sadly disappointed that she could not go abroad this year. I wonder a little how Mr. Lawson will feel about her rushing me off to Montreal, with her. She insisted that we go, and it was a very great pleasure to me, Amelia making all the expenses. But Mr. Lawson, in spite of the great kindness of his disposition, is, I imagine, rather a strict disciplinarian.

But the children of course were well cared for. Elizabeth Gibson is a most trustworthy person, and she is even more dependent upon the hospitality of others than I am. It is a common misfortune which tends to bring us together. Certainly if one has no means of one's own the essential thing is to cultivate an amiable disposition. Some people do not have the faculty, such as poor Mrs. Metcalfe. It is certainly well that she is independent, because people cannot like her, and I do not know who would have her. Even her sister Mrs. Burnham, 'tis said, does not invite her except for dinner, and that very infrequently. When Mr. Burnham went abroad (some months ago now), it was felt that the appropriate thing would have been for Mrs. Burnham to have joined her sister in Mrs. Metcalfe's big house. But it seems that there is very little visiting between the sisters, and that Mrs. Burnham has not been in Mrs. Metcalfe's house for a twelvemonth. I believe that Mr. Metcalfe would have welcomed the society of Mrs. Burnham, but as it was Mrs. MacPherson was forced to come from Montreal to stay with Mrs. Burnham in her small rented house, so that there should not be gossip.

Apparently there is gossip, in any case. You will know that Mrs. Burnham refused to go with her mother to Montreal, when circumstances forced Mrs. MacPherson to return. And evidently there was, according to your letter to Amelia, some attraction rather than pure business which kept Mr. Burnham abroad. But I dislike all kinds of such rumours, above all things.

There is no doubt that Eliza Davidson did have a child. But my belief is that it was born before she was married and not immediately afterwards, as Mrs. Metcalfe told me. They said that old Davidson went roaring into the brewery and took Jim Holliday out by the collar, and shouted so that all could not help hearing, that Holliday should and must marry Eliza. What a sad thing for poor Mrs. Davidson. But you will remember that she was a Coates, and all the Coates girls were very pretty and sought after and weak. Mrs. Davidson has not far to look for precedent.

You have not said when you come again to Hamilton, but surely for the first of July? Amelia talks of great celebrations about that date. Captain Baring who is now calling upon us almost every afternoon or evening, when his duties permit, is also much involved for plans for a ball, or a great picnic, or something or other, all of which seems destined to end in a firework display which will amaze the heavens themselves. And all this, mind you, without any word from Mr. Lawson. Elizabeth Gibson is invited to remain, as a matter of course. Captain Baring and Elizabeth and another officer, sometimes one, sometimes another, drive out very often, on the pretext, or so it seems to me, of finding just the most perfect situation for the picnic, if picnic it is to be. Amelia has set her heart on Elizabeth Gibson and Captain Baring making a match. Perhaps he is in love with her, I cannot say. I think Amelia should discover whether Captain Baring has money or not, before she presses this scheme beyond helping. His father is said to have an estate in Devonshire, but estates in Devonshire have been discovered, more than once, to be very small holdings, and I believe too that Captain Baring is a younger son. Amelia will not listen to me, however, and is convinced that Captain Baring is or will be, a person of property, and that her friend Elizabeth must have him.

I daresay the poor girl would be happy enough if he should propose for her. A gentleman in Toronto is said to be anxious for her, but he is poor and with very little of the gentleman in his appearance, I hear. She must settle herself before her father dies, or there is no prospect for her but to be a governess. She is out now with the curate, visiting the poor.

It was kind in you to ask for a suggestion for a gift for myself. There is nothing that I stand in need of. Amelia will have a sempstress here, and has offered to let me have a few days of her labour, although I do not know what kind of work she can do for me. There is a new hand sewing machine, a Wanzer, in the upstairs room which Amelia has cleared out for her, but Mrs. Briskett is not pleased with the machine. There is another kind now, it seems, which is noiseless, and which hems, fells, tucks, quilts, binds, and braids. If at all possible, Mrs. Briskett wishes to employ one which will embroider too. Amelia warmed up pretty fast on hearing these demands from Mrs. Briskett. She told her that the Wanzer, manufactured right here in Hamilton had won the prize at the great Exhibition in Paris, even over the Singer, and that unless she could use the machine which is at present in the sewing room, there would be no need for her services. Mrs. Briskett will come here Monday week.

I saw Mrs. William Alderhouse in the town this morning. She was driving quite unattended and with feathers in her hat. Mr. Alderhouse has been dead, I am sure, only eleven months this day fortnight. Everyone knows that Mrs. Alderhouse was a skilful driver, before her marriage, but she will certainly lay herself open to criticism by behaving this way, while still in deep mourning. Her driver was a jet black pacer, and she seemed to be having a hard time to keep the animal pulled in to its gait. I am almost certain that she was laughing.

Mrs. Metcalfe called this morning for money for the curate. Mr. Donaldson, is going to have to leave after the New Year. There will be no money then, it seems, to pay him. The Bishop says that the vestry will not increase the pew rents, and that is the reason. Mrs. Metcalfe says the money she is collecting is for a gold-handled umbrella. Mr. Donaldson already has a serviceable black-handled umbrella, and Amelia said she did not think Mr. Lawson would feel obliged to subscribe, and she could not in his absence. It occurs to me, and Amelia agrees, that a curate with only a hundred a year could do quite well with his old umbrella, and be given the money.

If you persist in your idea of a present for me, perhaps a nice silk petticoat quilted with down, which Mrs. Briskett could alter to fit me, or a pretty pattern for a dressing gown, or some such small article. Have you seen one of these new Paisley shawls? My old Kashmir is quite serviceable, of course, but when has but one shawl one tends to tire of the colour. But I should not care for a printed shawl, should you? It must be woven, or nothing. Mrs. Metcalfe has such a handsome red Paisley. I daresay they are quite common in London.

Will you go directly to your house in Ottawa, on your return, or do you come here? Perhaps one of your daughters longs to have you. What a fortunate person you are.

Yours affectionately,
JANE TRUMAN.

13

The Sound of Music

The 17th band had played in the Governor's Garden in the afternoon, and there was a very large dinner party at Spencer Wood, later.

After dinner the 25th string-band played outside the verandah. It was all like a scene in a play – the moon made a silver path on the river, a ship standing out so clearly on the water that the rigging could be seen quite plain, and the "Band discoursing sweet music" the while. The KOB's play so exquisitely. The redcoats of the officers formed a very good foreground to the picture. The servants had dancing at one end of the verandah.[76]

It was all very pleasant and comfortable and gay. And yet the Honourable Frances was not quite happy. She found, when she went to the band concerts, even if the exquisite playing of the KOB's or some other regimental band was to be heard, that her musical taste was to some degree offended. She found herself disappointed that they played only "popular" music. What was she listening to? She was listening to Offenbach, and Strauss, and perhaps to one of Beethoven's Waltzes from *Gertrude's Dream*. In spite of her disapproval of the choice, her silken slippered feet might find themselves tapping to the "Rataplan March" from *La Fille du Regiment* or the "Spanish Retreat."

Dance bands today and regimental bands and what few are left of small-town bands still play the lovely dance music of the 1860's.

"The Offenbach Quadrille," an arrangement by Charles Valentine could be purchased as sheet music for as little as four shillings. "These quadrilles on Offenbach's favourite airs are exceedingly pretty, and capital to dance to."

Crinolines swayed to the divine rhythm of Mozart's Favourite Waltz. In *The Bohemian Girl* Offenbach provided both waltzes and polkas, and Strauss tossed off hundreds of waltzes besides the 1867 "Blue Danube," for the delectation of the dancers of the sixties. Sheet music piled up fast on the pianos, and there was always someone in the house who could play. Magazines frequently carried words and music of the new songs to the pianos of the young ladies. There was often an evening of singing, when neighbouring young men and women joined together and made music of their own. A new song from a popular composer was a valued acquisition.

The same dichotomy of dissimilar characteristics being received and enjoyed at the same time as that of the literary offerings of the day existed to some extent in the popular songs. Soulful contraltos sang, wistfully, "Where I fain would be," or "The Ivy Leaf," or perhaps "Robin Red Breast," titles almost unequivocally guaranteed to produce the most dreary response. "Little Bird So Sweetly Singing," advertised as a thoroughly bird-like song, originally written for Mlle Liebhart, "My Pretty Jane," and "Madeline," are characteristic productions. "She Wore a Wreath of Roses," in modern times so parodied that one can be astounded at the original, is spirited enough, and "Bonnie Dundee" was the choice of many singers bearing towards the hearty.

"Claribel" composed a song which was intended to be an answer to "Come back to Erin," and was advertised as being in all respects equal to that classic. It was called "Kathleen's Answer" and published in a magazine which provided a gold mine of musical wealth to its subscribers.

A musical periodical could publish, on one page, a sentimental ditty written for a sentimental tenor voice, "Thro the green, green fields, My Love," and on the opposite page, complete with a red, white, and blue illustration of The Drum Major himself, his rollicking song.

> *Marching thro' the Park*
> *Marching thro' the Park*
> *You hear a drum*
> *Go Rum Tum Tum*
> *As we march through the Park.*

Bosley and Company, already publishing all varieties of songs, added descriptive notes to their advertisement, so that the lady or gentleman ordering by mail might be sure of what kind of thing he was buying.

"Only a Lock of Hair" was described as a song of "plaintive simplicity." "The Wrecked Hope," "full of melody and feeling – an excellent song for the drawing room" offered stout competition for the "Lock."

Music, once published, seems to have come at once into public domain. Sonatas for the Piano-Forte or the Harpsichord were openly advertised as being freely revised or rearranged from the Adagios or Last Movements of some celebrated composer's work. A "Sonata in which is Introduced in a varied Stile Handel's Favourite Voluntary." The young ladies with the nimble fingers for the Piano-Forte were well served.

And on the other hand, a great deal of serious and beautiful music was available to the Canadians. As early as 1864 *The Barber of Seville* was presented in Quebec. For some years to come, although there was sporadic attempt at opera production in the large cities, the major share of opera fare was provided by travelling companies from outside Canada.

Canadians flocked to concerts, in the sixties. When Jenny Lind came to Toronto in 1851 to sing in the St. Lawrence Hall, then newly completed, she had a sell-out house. Tickets cost four and five dollars, and all were bought. The orchestras playing in these years had their favourites among the composers. A typical programme would include overtures or symphonic movements from *The Marriage of Figaro* or *The Magic Flute* or *William Tell*. Hamilton rejoiced in the warmth and vivacity of Haydn's music. When the coming of a concert in which his *Surprise Symphony* was to be the major work, the music hall was full. Mozart's *Symphony in G Minor* could fill a concert room in Quebec. Almost every programme in Canada in the sixties contained a fair representation of music by Handel, Mozart, and Haydn. Excerpts from Beethoven's *First*, *Second*, and *Fifth Symphonies* were often heard. The operatic favourites were Bellini, Rossini, and Donizetti.

Piano factories flourished in many towns, large and small, in the sixties. Toronto, Montreal, Saint John, New Brunswick, Kingston, St. Thérèse, Bowmanville, Halifax, Quebec, and London had their factories. Many other communities sent out pianos. Heintzman in Toronto was building more than sixty pianos a year in the late sixties. Fox in Kingston turned out "about five hundred pianos per annum."

Organs had been made in both the Canadas for many years, and during the sixties the names of Canadian organ makers became famous at home and far beyond the boundaries of British North America. In the cities and in the villages, when a new organ had been bought, perhaps with money from one man or woman or the concerted effort of a whole congregation, no finer instrument could have provided than one which may have been made right in the home town. There were two organ factories in Toronto and two in Hamilton early in the fifties.

All types of pipe organs were built, from the little ones for chapels to the great ones destined for cathedrals. Good organ builders came from smaller places too. The name of Casavant from Ste. Hyacinthe, Quebec, is known throughout the musical world. The Casavants were building their organs in the sixties.

A PORTRAIT IS TAKEN

Toronto was the meeting place and dwelling place of many of the painters who by the sixties were producing an abundance of pictures. In 1867 the Society of Canadian Artists was formed. The society did not live long, but the start was made. The Toronto painters rubbed shoulders in downtown Toronto. A year or two before Confederation Henry Perré had his studio at 101 Adelaide Street West, Paul Kane was working at 20 Toronto Street, and the wealthy and famous were able to find Berthon at 39 King Street West.

There was an extraordinary rich and varied output of painting in these days. Men trained in Europe, under such distinguished painters as David (as in the case of Berthon), men nourished in the glow and precision of the Dutch painters, and native Canadian painters with little or no formal education, but possessed of the gift, were covering vast areas of canvas or sheets of paper, and painting delicately upon ivory in all regions of British North America, by Confederation.

> *this portrait was taken in 1845, by Mr. Berthon of Toronto, by desire of the gentleman of the law.*[77]

By the sixties gentlemen of the law, of the church, and most especially of the government were desiring their portraits to be taken. And the gifted and superbly trained Mr. Berthon stood ready with brush and easel at their hand. The gentleman of the law who sat for his portrait in 1845 was Sir John Beverley Robinson, Bart., Chief Justice of Canada from 1829 to 1862. He must have been well pleased with the picture, for he caused his three daughters, Emily, Louisa, and Augusta to sit for their portraits, too. The naming of three streets in Toronto had already secured promise of immortality to the girls, and the Berthon picture could do nothing but add to their fame. The artist posed them together, all smooth, bare, plump, white shoulders and ringlets and ribbons and lace. "The Three Graces" was an admirable acquisition to a famous father's house.

One after the other Berthon painted the great men of Canada West, and when the province became Ontario, the Lieutenant-Governors in succession sat to him. His famous portraits include "a stately and impressive picture of the Honourable and Right Reverend John Strachan, D.D., Lord Bishop of Toronto." Mr. Berthon's first Chief Justice looks down with dignity from the wall of the great library in Osgoode Hall. Of another Chief Justice's portrait ...

> *Fully arranged in judicial robes, with black knee breaches and silk stockings, the figure is posed conventionally beside a chair, with book in hand, with glistening white hair and luxuriant Victorian side whiskers, the presentment of the Chief Justice is the embodiment of judicial wisdom and old-world courtliness. Indeed virtually all of Berthon's portraits of men seem to breath the atmosphere of gracious dignity, stately ease, and comfortable assurance.*[78]

The romance of the Indian way of life, which had for so long inspired the imagination of the Europeans who had never seen them and who never would, caught the Canadians now. Canadians began to see that there was landscape in Canada too: stupendous mountains and magnificent rivers and tremendous sunsets and waterfalls not to be equalled in the old lands from which the types and criteria for pictures had come.

The painters set forth to spy out their own land, forgetting, if they could, the conventions of the old. Lucius O'Brien journeyed through the wildernesses of the West to paint the Rockies and Selkirks. His motive was to make an exact copy of the wonders of nature. He painted in water-colour and also produced vast oil paintings in which he strove to portray with truth and beauty a sunrise on a river, the mist in the mountains, the wonders of a waterfall.

Paul Kane, travelling with the Hudson's Bay Company men and canoes produced, in a very arduous three years of travelling, masses of Indian documentary pictures. Krieghoff, that spirited and uninhibited painter, was turning out his gay and brilliant pieces with immense abandon in the years before Confederation. Officers bought them for a few pounds and sent them to England, where people could not believe that any sunset could be like that.

For the man who wanted his portrait painted or required a picture of his wife or daughter, there was only the question of choosing an artist. There were many painters capable of satisfying his needs.

M. Plamondon in Lorette could paint a gentlemanly portrait, delicately designed and exquisitely finished, should the lower province be a convenient place for the sitting. And M. Plamondon could paint a golden bowl of fruit and leaves which would be above all things beautiful and appropriate for a dining-room. If something after a Reynolds should be the thing required, then M. Hamel in Quebec would be the man to choose. For portraits in watercolour, Mr. Hoppner Meyer might be consulted. And although perhaps not thoroughly respectable, and thought sometimes to be given to drink, nevertheless he turned off very pretty miniatures in ivory. They would be just the thing for a remembrance of the little one, before she put off her baby ways.

Canadian painters were picking up prizes in Paris, in Montreal, in Chicago. Daniel Fowler was competing with much more famous painters and doing well. Perhaps Mr. Fowler would paint a picture for the dining-room.

> *Fowler's best papers are marked by a brilliance of colour and boldness of brushwork uncommon among Victorian watercolourists.*[79]

Grave consideration must be given before a choice was made:

> *A man that can paint like that should wear a gold hat.*[80]

John Arthur Fraser, the man who was forced into such a statement as he stood before one of his own works could perhaps be justified in so saying. He did glorious paintings of mountains and sunsets and spectacular subjects. But his fame rests on a technique which he perfected of transforming photographs into paintings. Working as head re-touch man with the great photographer Notman, Fraser achieved a tremendous success. With his dexterity in handling water-colours he painted over light prints on drawing paper succeeding so well that it was difficult for even artists to detect the photographs. And in the case of his miniatures, they resembled in every way the real thing done on ivory, with rich backgrounds, broad draperies, and clear flesh colours. They were a pleasure to behold, and ultimately became one of the principal features of Notman's business.

Perhaps a photograph by Mr. Notman retouched into a painting by Mr. Fraser might be the answer to the problem.

*University College,
Toronto, circa 1871*

Ontario Archives

1.

2.

1. A Methodist Mansion
   Thos. Bouckley Collection

2. Sir John's "Tea-Caddy Castle," Kingston

3. A House in the Italianate style from the Rear, Woodstock, Ontario

4. Classical proportion in Toronto
   Toronto Public Libraries

3.

Whitby Court House, 1853   Thos. Bouckley Collection

Place D'Armes, Montreal, watercolour by Kreighoff, 1878   Toronto Public Libraries

Government House, Halifax, Nova Scotia   Public Archives of Canada

Spencer Wood, watercolour   Toronto Public Libraries

King Street Golden Lion
Toronto Public Libraries

At the Sign of
the Golden Griffin, 1873
Toronto Public Libraries

Toronto's Eighth Post Office under Construction
Toronto Public Libraries

Mount Uniacke, West Front Bedroom as in 1875   Nova Scotia Archives

Confederation Chamber, Charlottetown, P.E.I.   National Film Board of Canada

14

The Glamour of the Garrison

Conway has been invited to the grand ball next Monday, given by the 25th sergeants to the 17th sergeants. I am letting her go with Sergeant Lambkin (orderly), and his wife. Mrs. Lambkin is to wear a black silk, with low body and short sleeves, and is taking dancing lessons. Happily Conway won't wear a low dress.[81]

There were soldiers everywhere, in the heavily garrisoned towns in British North America. The British soldier, smart as paint, brought a sword-swinging fascination to the social picture, a swagger which the native militia, no matter how valiant and worthy, could never display. Fresh from his triumphs on the other side of the world, marked with the sun of India, blood-streaked from the horrors of the Crimea, knowledgeable about the exotic civilization of the Chinese, he offered inexhaustible glamour to the young girls in the garrisoned towns.

Fresh influxes of these glorious creatures were continually landing at Quebec in the middle sixties. The Civil War in the United States seemed to go on and on, and what might not happen if the North should win? There was little credence given to this opinion, but if it did, might it not then very well, swollen with the pride of victory, turn to its neighbour expecting easy conquest there? And what then? For the defences of the Canadas were pitifully inadequate. Mr. Russell, of the *Times* of London, found the fortifications defending Toronto so weak that any reasonably well-equipped battleship could flatten them in half an hour. Oh yes! There was need of a garrison!

Regiment after regiment they came, and they lit up the landscape with scarlet and green and bearskin hats. The young ladies in Montreal and Toronto, Niagara and London, twittered discreetly, adjusted their crinolines, and laid plans for conquest. They were one with the young ladies of Jane Austen's creation who "drooped apace," when the regiment was about to leave Meryton, and could not have understood Miss Bennett's relief at their going.

Perhaps Quebec most of all gained the greatest entertainment from the presence of the garrisons. The physical situation of the city lent itself admirably to the recreation of the visiting warriors. The great river itself, the magnificent citadel, the aura of valiant deeds which lingered about Quebec, and the added ingredient, that of being at once in a foreign country and at home, heightened the responses of the strangers.

An acid minded English lady visitor, lorgnette in hand, found much to deplore, in the soldier-dazzled society of Quebec.

> *the society is very much French, elegant, hospitable and frivolous, while the tone of morals is vitiated by the large number of military – they (the young ladies) have no accomplishments except the ability to play modern dance music. Their time is all spent in an endless bustle and round of amusement. There are balls nearly every night kept up to a late hour, 4 or 5 and the young ladies run about to each other's houses to discuss their conquests of the preceding evening, after they have arisen at eleven o'clock. If they are in the house they are sitting in their drawing rooms elegantly dressed while officers and other gentlemen lounge in after breakfast and remain for hours generally in the afternoon escorting the young ladies to the public promenades, or to the drives in the neighbourhood in their tandems.*[82]

It was discouraging to find that the garrison glamour extended right through all the strata of society. Lady visitors from abroad, all confirmed journal keepers, tended to level their lorgnettes at all who came within their range, and there was much wounding and slaughter. Commenting freely on the manners and customs one found in "our dependency," she noted that:

> *It might be expected that the Bishop's family would move in a different class of society, but no. Miss Mountain is a muffin and received officers the whole morning while pretending to be crocheting and in winter drives a tandem sleigh to Montmorenci Falls. Any young lady who is not a "muffin" in the winter is totally despised.*[83]

The garrisons defended our boundaries, fought sham battles on the heights of Quebec, winter and summer, and in the summer afternoons played cricket where Wolfe and Montcalm had fought. The Quebec garrison eleven journeyed to Montreal to play the Montreal garrison, avenging a defeat on the Spencer Wood grounds on two hot August days.

There were reviews on the Plains of Abraham; sparkling columns of superbly trained soldiers, attended with bands who played exquisitely, arrayed there for the Governor General to review and for the people of the city to admire. Hearts were lifted with the stirring marches, the perfect discipline of the drill, the flags, the click of rifles, the clip of heels. The scarlet of the Guards, the green of the Rifles, flashed with scarlet and white, the glitter of brass, and the dignity of the tall bearskins wove an inimitable tapestry on the plains. Dust swirled about the feet of the marchers, above the glossy knees of the horses, about the spurs and the swords of the mounted men. And all was glory, radiance, and pride.

And then there came the evening, and all was not yet done. There was a ball, and all attended who were lucky. Sometimes the viceregal party brought its special allure to the ball, and Frances Monck recorded her pleasure on many pages of her journal.

> When we with difficulty got up the very great Citadel Hill, we found everything very nicely done, the soldiers had decorated the stairs and anteroom like a miniature Guards' ball with two tall soldiers and two pipers on the landing and flags and designs done with bayonets and stars, and theatre scenes painted by Col. Fane. The string band was of course, exquisite. There were many pretty faces at the ball – and again – after dinner, we went to the militia ball. The music hall was beautifully decorated with artificial flowers and fir branches; the refreshments were served on the stage, with a scene at the back. There was a very good supper, and I was so hungry. Col. Sewell gave me pretty little flags for a cake – I have French, English, Southern and Yankee flags. There were two bands, the R.A., and the 25th, in the gallery.[84]

The officers and men of the garrisons added colour, if not grace, to the skating scene. They spent their money on horses, brilliant harness, low-slung sleighs, elegant high-wheeled phaetons for summer, and rich fur robes for their sleighs. To own and drive a tandem was the height of an officer's desire, and many of them attained it. And in their glorious equipages they drove their enchanted muffins through snowy lane and leafy track.

In winter they slid through deep tunnels of snow, ice flying up from the horses' hooves like miniature storms, the snow like starch beneath the runners; and always the wild sweet music of the bells accompanied them. In summer they clattered at breakneck speed down the rough, narrow streets of the city and on out to see the marvellous Chaudière or Montmorenci with the water freed from its ice, the Cone gone. And some of them found, as did more than one British visitor, that Montmorenci gave more to the heart than did the great Niagara. The soldiers and their muffins were stilled there, moved by the wonders of the canvas which nature had painted for them. But joy was their search, and they did not stay long in the eerie cavern. Back to Quebec, and the band concert in the gardens or the preparation for the play. Perhaps, though, it might be the last day for the regiment in Quebec. With the coming of the first ship a cruel ordinance had decreed that the 17th, with its glorious officers, must leave. The muffin hearts were sore to think of such injustice. Misery, arrant misery, when the 17th had gone. But yet, when the 17th goes, will there not be another regiment arriving? And who could tell what magnificent officers and men there might be among them? And there were invites out, already, for a Sergeants Ball! The hearts of the muffins healed a little.

Perhaps there would be clever and amusing actors, in the 25th.

The 17th had put on such hilarious comedies, the muffins had all but died laughing.

The garrison players merited Viceregal patronage. Mrs. Monck went off to the Music Hall, one winter's night, in a hooded sleigh, with the Governor General himself.

> *The play was* Macbeth Travestie. *The prologue was very well spoken by Col. Robertson, and the acting of the first piece was capital.*
>
> *Capt. E. was very good, and looked so hideous in a yellow coat covered with red hearts. Mr. Stoney made a most lovely woman. Every one was in uniform, and the room looked gay.*
>
> *In one scene they all had a ballet in night-gowns. The band was lovely. In the witch scene, where they made apparitions, was Mr. Collis, in a nightgown, followed by his enormous Maltese dog, also in a night dress and night cap; it ran in on its hind legs. Such a sight I never saw; the house almost came down with applause. Lady Macbeth, in a pink sunbonnet and watering pot, was delicious.*[85]

The 25th came, was welcomed, fêted, entered to a certain degree at least, into "muffinage," and on a soft day at the end of April, when there should be beginnings, instead of endings, the 25th itself was slated to go. But there was one last evening of garrison theatre, before they must tear themselves away. Mrs. Monck came down from Spencer Wood to see the last play:

> *The first play,* Aladdin, or the Wonderful Scamp, *was very well done; but the second one,* Little Toddlekins, *I liked much the best. The puns in the first were almost too marvellous to understand.*
>
> *The man who acted "Barney Babbicome" in the second play once forgot his part, and, pretending to talk to Amanthis, said, "Speak Louder", meaning the prompter. They all acted beautifully. The women were done by a drummer and Mr. Stoney (25th). The band was so beautiful, and they sang part of the "Farewell Valse," the men with broad grins on their faces.*[86]

15

Summer Time

> *The Montreal Fox Hounds, a subscription pack, which would do credit to any Leicester field – are ably managed and hunted as long as the season permits. They seldom or never fail to "find," and, meeting always within easy distance of the city, they afford a healthy means of exercise to the lover of the chase.*
> *Since the garrison has been here of late years, the races and steeple chases have become quite an institution – cricket and baseball afford plenty of amusement to the less ardent admirer of sports....*[87]

The short sudden Canadian summer brought the people out of their hot winter houses as by a magic. Where there had been cold winds and icy roads and snow piled second-storey high, there was now the long bright day, the fresh green of grass and trees, and the sparkle of the running water. The people came out to play.

Railways, steamers, stage coaches, hotels, summer resorts courted their attention, promising excursion and pleasure. What had been seen in the winter and marvelled at, must be seen in the summer, to compare. If Montmorenci stunned the senses of the traveller and sport lover in the winter, her falling waters were a thousand times more effective, capable of drawing out poetic rapture and spiritual exaltation in a most extravagant measure.

> *... having descended a stairway from the bank to a platform projecting to the very edge of the precipice, I then beheld with enraptured amazement, the beauty and sublimity of the cataract – the rolling and tumbling of the water over an almost perpendicular ledge of solid rock, to the depth of 280 feet, and then hiding itself in the misty folds of its fallen dignity. From below the Falls, a magnificent view of them is also obtained; and when the tide is out, it is easy to creep along by the base of the mountain crags, until one feels himself enveloped in the ethereal spray, and beholds, as it were, the overshadowings of the Almighty. Magnificent prospect! How beautiful and trans-*

> *porting to the reflective soul, and how refreshing to the feelings that are jarred and wounded by the jostling world. The spirit bathes in the fountain of delight, and feels a longing to be at liberty to revel amid the sparkling effervescence of the pellucid element.*
>
> *The mystery of their beauty and enchantment is neither embodied in the thunder of troubled waters, nor in the grandeur of imposing magnitude; but is beautifully revealed through the emblem of purity and simplicity. So sweet – so lovely they appear, that the fancy is impressed with the solitude of a lovely virgin bathing in the crystal fountain of innocence, and gently gathering up around her the white mantle of modesty.*[88]

A summer day's excursion could make use of a variety of transport – the "cars," the steamers, the stages. All were prepared to play their separate and cooperative parts to provide entertainment and transportation. The livery stable could provide horseflesh to take the traveller to whichever of these public transport systems he required first. The hotels of the time advertised the services of "attentive ostlers," and were prepared to provide "good stabling." "Fine Livery Stable Attached," "A good Livery in Connection," assured the patron that he could have a horse.

The coming of the railways and the spreading of the nets of steel over the provinces lessened the work of the stagecoach, but by no means relieved the stage entirely.

In the year of Confederation there was a stage from Beaverton to Orillia (where one could get a boat for Muskoka) twice a week. During the winter a stage ran daily from Orillia to Barrie. One could go all the way from Toronto to Durham, a distance of one hundred and forty miles, for four dollars "through ticket." A forty-cent fare took a traveller from Claremont to Stouffville, and for the curious amount of thirty seven and a half cents he might go from Oshawa to Raglan.

> *Passengers from Orillia to Muskoka Lake, with its beautiful and romantic Falls, will take the steamer Fairy, which runs daily during the summer, touching at the Indian village of Rama, McPherson's landing, and terminating at the Severn, from which place stages are taken to Muskoka Bay, where connection is made with the* Wenonah, *for the Lake and Falls.*[89]

Native Canadian and traveller alike found interest and refreshment in these excursions – whether it was an extensive trip from Hamilton to the Saguenay and up that river, or just a day around a northern lake. Mr. Day was impressed with the convenience of the combined railway and steamboat excursion and wrote a detailed description of how it could be done.

> *The extent of the Northern Railroad, as the line is now termed, is 94 miles; fifty one miles of which runs through the county of Simcoe, close by the Lake. It enters Simcoe at Bradford, forty-*

three miles from Toronto and passes along the eastern side of West Gwillimbury, near to the mouth of the Holland River; A branch runs down to Cook's Bay on Lake Simcoe, about one and a half miles to where the new town of Bell Ewart is springing up. At this point the "cars" meet the steamboat, which makes the circuit of the Lake, and returns to meet the "cars" in the evening.[90]

There was a freshness of newly-cut pine, about some of the little towns which the "cars" and the steamboat now put in the way of the traveller. The pale, painted buildings seemed to cling to the waterfront, the hills and the pines dark behind them. For them the highway was still the water.

There could be found substantial, dignified dwellings in some of the villages: a palladian type or two, perhaps, with the two-storey pillars and a simple pediment straight from the Parthenon. Square-faced, three-storey hotels with double verandahs swung about their white walls faced the river or the lake. And all about the settlement the air was fresh with the scent of pine.

Little paddle-wheelers (and some big ones too) crossed and re-crossed the lakes, seeking business and pleasure. A load of freshly-picked strawberries to be picked up here, to be sent to the markets in the city, or livestock, meat, grain, or flour to go farther (perhaps to the American port across the water), varied the voyage of the steamer. The "cars" ran close to the water's edge, as if to share intimately the triumph of transportation – up to the lake from the city in the cars, a gay and refreshing day on the water, then the steamer back to the shore, and the cars again.

English visitors great and small enjoyed the oddity of lake excursions in the Canadian provinces. Frances Monck prepared well for her party.

We are going to a lake to-day, a great excursion, and I dread the heat so. I have on a blue calico dress, and am covered with leaves down my back and inside my bonnet.[91]

The ordeal was less than she expected, evidently, and she could comment happily the next day,

We went on our expedition yesterday to Lake Beauport. We set off at twelve, and were not back till nearly seven. Most of the party went in covered waggons, but I went in an open one with Col. Gordon. I found my leaves keep out the heat uncommonly well. I also had a dust coloured cloak and umbrella. Most of the gentlemen wore straw hats, and Mr. Godley had a green veil, and Col. G. a blue one. They looked so odd.

The working men here all wear red shirts which look pretty.

We sat under the trees near the lake till lunch was ready. We then ate an enormous lunch in a small room at the inn; nearly every-one had three helps of meat.[92]

In the next month she went on an even stranger excursion. The

Governor General and his Lady, whom Frances irreverently referred to as "her Ex" took her with them to Newport, on the Fourth of July. And once again the steamer, the coach, and the "cars" served.

> ... off to Newport in the steamer at 7:30. The 4th of July is a great day in Yankeeland, and Newport is a Yankee town. They received the G.G. very well at Newport. Several quaint old men were presented to him and her Ex., on board the steamer. A large coach and six white steeds met us, followed by another large coach and four brown steeds – the town was gay with flags in honour of the day – Sergeant Lambkin was on the box of the yellow coach, and his red uniform looked very gay....[93]

Mrs. Monck took the train back to Montreal. She was fond of trains, and more than once compared the comfort of the Canadian trains to the disadvantage of the English ones, particularly in the quality of the meals which could be obtained, "Instead of those horrid sandwiches," which were served at railway stations at home. She was much taken with the car which had carried the Prince.

> *We had the Prince of Wales's car, and you never saw such luxury and comfort in a railway carriage – a large sitting room, two bedrooms, and a smoking room. The servants had a car to themselves. We had lamps, armchairs and sofas. Dick had ordered wines, sandwiches and cakes so we had food enough, and were all very pleasant.*[94]

Mr. Day with his newly-made friends made a most pleasant journey when he had the luck to have

> a special saloon carriage that had only just been built for the Viceregal service, at our disposal, thereby rendering the trip extremely agreeable. The interior of the carriage presented a unique display of elaborate ornamentation, and was furnished with elegant mirrors, a rich carpet, spring sofa and easy chairs, covered with green silk velvet. Attached to the saloon carriage was another of similar dimensions, laid out in dressing rooms, replete with every requisite for toilet purposes.[95]

Summer time was for picnics. Almost any excuse was enough to send the people rushing from their houses, basket in hand. A defeated candidate made excellent reason for his supporters to have a grand picnic in his honour.

> Between 800 and 1,000 people were present, and a band, and a deputation of twelve gentlemen were sent to excort him from a neighbouring house to where the festival was held. He passed through an arch of evergreens which had been created for the occasions. Sheep were roasted whole. Mr. B. was forced to bring home a large handsome cake with flags in his honour.[96]

Children celebrated their birthdays with tremendous family picnics. As the fashion of the mid century was for enormous families, ten children being not unusual, a family gathering could turn out to be a multitudinous occasion. Girls in the families of wealthy miller, brewer, sugar-making, and judicial groups tended to marry within the group. So there were dozens of cousins, double cousins, brothers- and sisters-in-law; there could be scores of relatives to invite to the picnic.

To the people who lived in the great houses high on the river banks, the Humber or the Don or the Grand was more road than the track through the woods which surrounded the house.

On the birthday the servant had a cart filled with pork pies, sandwiches, cakes, and meringues. There was the fruit of the season, and raspberry or ginger cordial to accompany it. The man wheeled the cart down to the river bank and stowed the comestibles away in a rowboat. Two menservants sprang into the boat and rowed it away.

The birthday girl with her sisters and brothers and any cousins who might be staying in the house, came down after them, sunshade in hand. Her aunt from England, a little annoyed but intrigued, nevertheless, with these goings on, clambered into one boat with as many people as it would hold, and the rest into another or into two more. The laden boats followed the provision boats down the river, perhaps to its mouth.

Fresh winds whipped the aunt's false ringlets back from her cheeks; her hoops stood up from the uncompromising gunwales, until her wrathy face was hidden from sight. The birthday girl perhaps twelve today, and her brothers, were the victims of uncontrollable laughter. The boat shifted alarmingly when the aunt from England rose to her feet, to attempt an adjustment of her hoops. The boys rocked the boat, perhaps unintentionally, and the aunt from England, glaring, sat down again with amazing abruptness.

Rivers, lakes, falls all called in the summertime for people to come to picnic beside them. From the viceregal set to the corporal's, ladies and gentlemen, officers and muffins took their food and drink and made a party of eating outdoors.

The never ending beauty and variety of the summer landscape called Frances Monck to fishing picnics.

> We steamed on to the mouth of the Marguerite River (out of the Saguenay), in the night, and found ourselves anchored in the most lovely bay on the morning of Monday, all surrounded with rocky and wooded hills and sands. The gentlemen were off before seven – the noise they all made was dreadful; they rowed to the shore and had breakfast there, and a fire; and after breakfast we all rowed to shore, and found they were catching such quantities of fish. The servants came on shore and laid an enormous fire, and arranged lunch on some planks near the bank on the shore; and we had a grand lunch of trout, just killed, and wild raspberries and blueberries, so good. Felix fried the trout in a pan over the fire; they smelt very good. We sat on logs and had our plates on our laps . . . [the gentlemen caught 162 trout].[97]

Mr. Day was taken fishing, from Montreal.

> amongst the few private clubs in Montreal, is one called "The
> Prince of Wales Fishing Club". It has been established for some
> years, and is so extremely exclusive as to be limited to eight
> members.[98]

It was a supreme compliment to be invited to join an expedition with the Prince of Wales' Club, and Mr. Day was very sensible of the honour. An early morning start was to be made.

> ... proceeded to the president' residence, where, besides having
> a substantial breakfast, we fortified ourselves internally with a
> spirituous concoction known in Scotland as Athol-brose – the
> most insidious and yet delicious compound I have ever tasted
> before or since.
>
> After breakfast we proceeded in a carriage to the wharf,
> taking with us a ponderous hamper well stocked with viands of
> various descriptions, and sundry bottles of wine and brandy –
> In a short time we pulled off from the shore, and were moving
> up the St. Lawrence at a brisk rate, the boat's flag, ornamented
> with the Prince of Wales' plume, gaily streaming in the wind.
> Upon arriving as far as St. Nicholas Island, we disembarked.
> Over a square of rock a snow white cloth was laid, upon which
> was spread a repast that would have stimulated the stomach of
> the most dyspeptic.[99]

He does not make very much mention of fish.

Summer resorts on the St. Lawrence, at Niagara, on Lake Ontario, vied for summer visitors. Cacouna had its enthusiasts.

> The situation of Rivière du Loup is more romantic but Cacouna
> has the advantage of purer and stronger water. Both command
> an extensive prospect of the St. Lawrence which is, here, up-
> wards of 20 mi. wide, studded with Islands and bound on the
> opposite shore by lofty and rugged mountains. And the so-
> journeyer is enlivened by numerous large vessels constantly
> navigating the broad expanse.[100]

Rivière du Loup called its faithful summer after summer. People picked up their sponges and India rubber baths and gathered with their friends at their favourite Niagara hotel year after year, for the inspiration of the Falls and the music and games provided for their entertainment. Clifton Springs was a favourite spa, whose waters were thought to be good for headaches and the improvement of circulation. Here and there on the broad verandahs overlooking some piece of lovely water, acquaintances were renewed and friendships made.

In the parks of the summertime bands played, and men in white trousers played endless games of cricket, city against city, regiment against regiment.

And everywhere there were the horses – to ride, to drive, to carry bus loads of merry-makers to picnics, routs, drums, drawing-rooms. There were driving clubs in the cities. Young men and women who belonged to the driving clubs arranged for entertainment at some recommended inn, perhaps ten miles from home. Then, driving in a kind of convoy of tandems they set out for the rendezvous, by sleigh in winter, by elegant high wheels in summer. There would be a supper laid out at the inn and then a little dancing, and home by the light of the full moon whose imminence had suggested the date for the gathering.

Men proud of their horses and their equipages paraded them on Saturday afternoon in Montreal, and many people found it enough entertainment in a week to go to the centre of the city and watch the fashionables drive by.

And on the Plains of Abraham, where once Wolfe and Montcalm fought to the death for possession of the beloved country, the fastest of the hot bloods raced.

●

Letter Thirteen.

ISABELLA MOORE TO

HER SISTER CONSTANCE, IN DUBLIN

· · · ◦ ● ● · ·

Lawsonhurst, Hamilton, C.W.
20 June, 1867

My Dear Constance:

    Since it pleases you to refuse to send my riding habit I cannot but feel a certain satisfaction in advising you that I no longer am in need of it. Indeed, should you feel any regret in not obliging me, you need feel it no longer. Amelia Lawson (Mrs. Lawson now insists that I call her Amelia, and indeed she gives me a sister's kindness) has had her almost new riding habit remade for me. There is a seamstress resident in the house, ready to make up a bolt of chintz for furnishing the Lawson's great bedroom, should Mr. Lawson approve, when he returns. She is occupied with remaking Amelia's habit for me. It is black with royal blue facings, and I may assure you that I do not mourn the navy blue at home. Amelia finds the royal blue to become me. She wishes to give me the habit, since she has become, she says, a little heavier with each child, and now that she is to have another, convinces me that she will never wear it again. It is well that I have full use of a riding dress, since I have had need of it almost everyday since we came to Lawsonhurst.

I shall tell you of Lawsonhurst, and the company we have here. Mr. Lawson is not yet returned from London, but is hoped for soon. Mrs. Truman, Amelia's aunt is with us, and a Miss Elizabeth Gibson, a serious quiet, well-educated person, perhaps three and twenty, a friend of Amelia, and most beloved of her children. Cousin Jack, Cousin Maude, and the children, of course, are here, and with myself make up the party within the house, not counting the servants, who are three, beside the cook.

Miss Elizabeth Gibson is thought to be in love with Captain Baring, one of the several officers of the 33rd who make up our little riding parties. He is perhaps the most distinguished in appearance. Amelia hopes that he will propose for her. So far he has not and yesterday did not leave my side in our ride. But we all enjoyed ourselves immensely; we took all the fences, and avoided all the roads. Elizabeth Gibson does not ride, nor does Amelia at this time. The gentlemen of the party were all officers, and we were joined by a Mrs. Burnham whose husband is abroad. Captain Fitzgerald is said to be too closely attached to Mrs. Burnham. They kept their mounts together, yesterday.

The chestnut mare Portia from Bradsbrook is my mount, and an admirable one she is. Captain Baring rides Traveller (named after General Lee's famous horse I believe; though this information will be of little interest to you, since you seem interested in nothing that I tell you, but to accuse me of impropriety). In any case, Captain Baring's horse is a tall dappled grey, as Lee's horse is. I think there cannot be a fence which Traveller could not take. It occurs to me that you might be less unhappy and perhaps less censorious if you could interest yourself in some subjects outside the range of Fitzwilliam Square and Mr. McEvoy's peat bogs in Antrim. All whom I have met are deeply distressed that the South lost the American war, and feel sympathy almost amounting to love for General Lee. Portia and Traveller went admirably together, yesterday.

Your last letter but one, in which you accuse me of having forgotten myself and my upbringing because I am enjoying the freedom and the openness of the social life here, and almost commanding me to come home, suggests in the crossing that you are considering marrying Mr. McEvoy. Before you take such a step, which can only be disastrous, do consider and take advice. Mr. McEvoy must be full twenty years your senior, and I wonder if he could be called a gentleman.

Uncle Jack who now considers himself to be my natural guardian is so kind and so approachable, that I think you might do not better than consult him, before you reach an unalterable decision, with Mr. McEvoy.

But I scarcely expect you to take an interest in my opinion. As for me, I am glad to have such a friend in him. I expect to return to Fitzwilliam Square sometime in midsummer, if some friend of Cousin Jack's or of the Lawsons is to go then. There seems little doubt that some lady will be going and may be glad of a companion. Cousin Maude presses me to stay longer, but however kind the Bradys are, I can have no permanent place in Canada, and I must not impose too long on my friends, I am to go to Montreal within a week, for perhaps a fortnight with Madame de Trouville, and after that I shall make my plan to return.

Now to Lawsonhurst. It is a large estate to be centrally located in a city – a house with perhaps twenty rooms, set in a park which Amelia says is only nine acres. It is so skilfully planted that I should have thought it must be more. It is close to the centre of Hamilton, and with a fine view of the "Mountain." The mountain is not more than a fine hill, but the Lawsons have a kind of chalet there, to which they repair when it is very hot, in the summer. They also have a number of farms on a river, not too far away, I think, and the "Lawson Mills" are on the same river, the mill wheels run by the same swift stream, I believe. The house is pure white and made of "frame," as it is called here. We should, I think, at home, call it a "wooden house." But such a phrase suggests poverty, and lack of means to run to brick or stone. There is no lack of such means here; although there is no ostentation, either, no suggestion of any article bought because it might show the owner rich. A wide verandah goes across the front and one side. The lawns surrounding the house are almost as smooth and velvety as those of some English country house. And there are set up two croquet grounds; one finds the mallets and balls in the summerhouse.

Croquet parties are very fashionable here, and very pleasant too; such a sense of exhilaration in being out in the air, which is, so far, almost always sunny and fresh. Early in the afternoon the players meet on the lawns. Everyone plays – Mrs. Truman, Amelia's aunt, who is with her until Mr. Lawson comes home, Cousin Maude, Cousin Jack, Amelia herself, of course, and sometimes as many as a dozen guests, with usually half of those officers. Sometimes partners are chosen, and play together, sometimes single players compete. Captain Baring and I played together yesterday, with quite amazing success. Elizabeth Gibson had a Mr. Donaldson, I believe his name was, a curate, to play with her. Amelia did not seem as happy with the afternoon as I have seen her be.

We played on and on, until nearly seven o'clock. Elizabeth Gibson was quite exhausted by that hour, and Amelia unusually tired and quiet. We had a "heavy tea," as it is called here, then, and afterwards several other officers came in. We sang part songs in drawing room, when the light failed, and there were plenty of dancers for an eight handed reel. We ended the evening with "Sir Roger," just as if we had been at a proper ball, and then "The Queen," the officers joining in most lustily. Captain Baring has a most pleasant tenor voice.

Amelia says that when Mr. Lawson come to Lawsonhurst we shall have a proper ball with a Quadrille band. And in the meantime there are three more parties to look forward to. Ladies and gentlemen and usually officers to call upon me every afternoon. I shall never be able to return their calls, since I am to be here only until the 27th, and the days are so full of such pleasurable activity. I do not know that I can be here for the ball, since it is not sure yet when Mr. Lawson returns. He is hopeful of being here for the July first celebration, and there is talk of having the ball before that. I am not quite sure that Mr. Lawson would be happy to have a ball in his house before he is there to direct it.

Perhaps I did not explain to you that I am engaged to go to Montreal, to be there on the first of July. Madame de Trouville, whom you may perhaps remember having been with us in the *Scotia* has invited me to visit her before I go back to Dublin, and has fixed the date for my arrival as the thirtieth of June. This engagement is of long standing now, and cannot be broken, although when I see how very comfortable and amusing it is in Hamilton, I must confess I am loathe to go. Elizabeth Gibson will certainly stay for the ball. It would be a disappointment for me, should I not stay too. Mrs. Ormiston is still in Canada West, and is to come, with her husband, now here (St. Thomas, that is, but people here think of people twenty miles away as neighbours) and I should like to extend my acquaintance with her.

It is extraordinary that there is such a broad acquaintance among the people whom I have met, here. Amelia and Mrs. Ormiston went to the same Young Ladies' Academy. Madame de Trouville's husband was associated with Mr. Albert Adams, whose widow is an aunt of Mr. Lawson's. I believe it is through this association, as well as the acquaintanceship on board ship that I am invited. Cousin Jack advises me to go. It will be an opportunity to see the lower province under most excellent auspices, he says. I am to travel by boat, lake steamer. They are said to be very pleasant and gay. But I feel that I shall be leaving gaiety here.

To-morrow there is to be a driving picnic, got up by the ladies of the Military and the ladies of the city. We shall drive, it seems, fifteen miles, perhaps, into the country, and find a pleasant secluded place with perhaps a sunny slope and a stream, and there have our lunch. I quite look forward to it.

I have not been able to send this letter, so go on to tell you that Mr. Andrew, whom we met on the *Scotia*, has come to Lawsonhurst on the invitation of Mr. Lawson. It is very agreeable to have Mr. Andrew with us. He is less sad, I think, than when I saw him in March, and we have had the opportunity of talking together more than once. He no longer wears the crêpe band about his arm. Mr. Andrew has business interests in Montreal and is well acquainted with Madame de Trouville. He assures me that I will be very well pleased with Madame de Trouville's house and entertainment. This may well be so, but the company here is so pleasant that I am loathe to leave. Mr. Andrew is an accomplished horseman, and we look to another famous ride tomorrow morning. Elizabeth Gibson finds Mr. Andrew a very sympathetic companion; perhaps more so even than Captain Baring. But she does not ride. Both she and Amelia seem to have recovered their spirits somewhat since Mr. Andrew has joined the household. I shall certainly find it hard to go to Montreal. The ball is to be put on for sure, for the 26th, Mr. Andrew who has seen Mr. Lawson very recently in London is quite convinced that Mr. Lawson will be here on that date, and Amelia determined that I must have a ball, before I leave Lawsonhurst.

The verandah is being decorated already, with scores of yards of coarse white muslin in swags, which Amelia says will keep the mosquitoes out, as well as hold bunches of flowers, one to each post. The gardens are glorious with pæonies now, and dozens of them are being sacrificed to the ball. There is to be a Quadrille band, and Amelia says we shall dance all night, probably; they usually do, until it is broad daylight. We shall dance on the verandah and in the drawingroom, which is being cleared of furniture. We hope for an evening like this one, with moonlight and stars. Between dances, Amelia says, people wander through the gardens, which will be most pleasant with an entertaining companion. The programme is over twenty dances, and we shall dance them all. Amelia will not dance. I look forward to it eagerly, I confess. And in the morning I go by the *Corinthian* to Montreal. I should have preferred a day or two longer here. Cousin Jack goes with me to Madame de Trouville, which is more than kind. He and Mr. Andrew seem to have much to say to each other, and walk about talking quietly and nodding their heads, as though in full agreement. Mr. Andrew walks in the garden with Elizabeth Gibson. They seem to talk very pleasantly and more intelligently than I could ever do about the plants.

Mrs. Briskett, the seamstress, is engaged now in making a dress for me. It is to be a travelling dress, and will be excellent for the steamer, when I once more set out across the Atlantic. It is to have a petticoat of very fine scarlet cashmere trimmed with rows of black velvet and large jet beads. The dress is of soft grey poplin bound with velvet. The skirt is to be looped up in the back à la laveuse. Amelia says I must look for a hat of grey felt trimmed with scarlet velvet, and a long veil of grey crêpe, to wear with it. There is no hope of Mrs. Briskett finishing with it while I am here, and in any case it would be too warm to wear. Cousin Maude will have her come to Bradsbrook, she says, when she has done with the Lawson curtains, and finish it with some other work there. I am to look for a black velvet sack to complete the costume when I am in Montreal.

16

Mr. Lawson Comes Home

Mr. Lawson's telegraph arrived on the 25th. Mr. Lawson himself arrived on the very day of the ball.

He flung the reins to Old Tom and leapt from the carriage. His eyes brightened with the sight of his own home, and he thought he had seen nothing so satisfying to the eye since he had left it. There was a shrill whinny from the pony shed and Diamond thrust his shaggy head out to greet the carriage horses.

The hot sunny air was heavy with the fragrance of the last of the lilacs and the first of the black locust. The rose hedge, he could see, bloomed with hundreds of little crinkled blossoms and the lilacs were beginning to come. A blur of wine and rose and white beyond the verandah must be the peonies blooming. He had the absurd feeling, but only for a moment, that they were intending to welcome him home. Then Amelia was there and the children, and he did not even see that the little white turk's cap lilies were nodding their heads by hundreds, deep in the wild garden which bounded the house.

He gazed at his wife, taking in the dressing of her hair, the smudge on her fine linen undersleeve, and the pallor of her face, the thickening about the waist, which she would never conceal with a tightly pulled lace. He kissed her and determined that this was the last party which they would have in this house until the child was born. The children ran to him and were kissed and promised presents bye and bye.

He looked again at Amelia – was she not too pale? What if this time when the child was born, she might die? Often, with the third child, for reasons that no one knew, while the child might live, the mother would not survive. But surely it could not be with him? From the upper window in the sewing room he could see the shining spire of the Anglican church. It was his money, the Lawson money which had built that spire. Not that he looked for reward, of course, but he had done what he thought was right to do and lived the good life. And Amelia – she was impulsive, too impulsive, and there was that smudge on her undersleeve, and her wisp of hair falling free of the net. But she too, even more than he, was a faithful church goer. And when because a child was ill or she herself not well enough to go to church, he knew that she set apart the hour and read the service in her own room. There was belief and reverence and worship in his house. Surely here disaster would not strike? He straightened his shoulders and shifted the burden of his imaginings from his mind. It must be that he was fatigued, not quite himself after the long separation and the journeyings. But he was pleased, on the whole, with the business which he had done. Pleased, too, that his father had seemed content to go with his old friend Mr. Warren to Bath for a fortnight, and would come home with Aunt Adams. All had been well arranged and all provided for.

But he was not entirely pleased that the ball should have been set for the twenty-sixth, and not for the first of July, which day was to be made memorable, in the minds of his children.

"There will be a great deal for the children to do to amuse themselves on the First. And to remember too," Amelia said. "And if Miss Moore is to go back to Dublin after her visit to Montreal, this will be perhaps the only opportunity that we can have to introduce her to all our friends in Hamilton. She is curious to attend a summer ball in Canada."

"I have seen little of her," Mr. Lawson said, "but she seems very lively and I see that you and she have become great friends. What about your plans for sacrificing poor Captain Baring to Elizabeth Gibson?"

"Alas! Since Miss Moore has come Captain Baring has no glance to spare for Elizabeth. All his attentions are directed to Miss Moore."

"Aunt Adams has her schemes, as doubtless I may have told you, of interesting Mr. Andrew in Elizabeth Gibson. She thinks her quiet and reserve would be just the thing for him. Women are the very devil for matchmaking. I don't know that I would have even thought of you, Amelia, if old Mrs. Metcalfe hadn't put the idea into my head."

"Do you regret the suggestion, sir?"

"You know that I have never regretted it, but sometimes I believe there may be great mischief done."

"It is certainly true that Mr. Andrew and Elizabeth do speak often and together. Aunt Truman has noticed it. It would be a very great thing for Elizabeth if Mr. Andrew should propose for her. Much more to her advantage than to accept Captain Baring, perhaps."

"For such a quiet young lady she has a good many changes of heart, it seems to me. When I went abroad she was madly in love with Phillips, then it was Baring, and now you tell me, since Baring has turned his eye towards Miss Moore, it is Mr. Andrew. Well, I must go to the stables. I haven't yet seen the horses but Dolly and Jack. Your decorations are very pretty. Do you mean to dance on the verandah?"

"I shall not dance at all. There will be music heard both on the verandah and in the dining room. Let me go with you, to the stables."

Amelia took her husband's arm and chattered to him as they walked.

"Do you know, Miss Christie and Miss Eleanor Christie have come back from Paris. They have been away almost a year now, and were much of the time at school. Aunt Truman met them at Mrs. Metcalfe's when she went with Isabella to return her call. Aunt Truman says that Paris has not improved them in manners or dress. They find it now, they told her, quite a desperate trial to speak anything but French and were very silly and affected. They would never, they said, wear crinolines again and looked most immodest. They are quite the laughing stock in Hamilton. Mrs. Metcalfe told Aunt Truman that Mr. Christie must have laid out more than a thousand dollars for each of them, for all this schooling and junketting about. She says the kind of French they speak is not like you and your sisters speak."

"No doubt it is not. But you remember that our Father spent his early life in Montreal, and learned French very thoroughly. He was very careful that we should learn it too. We might still be there, had there not been a prejudice against the English in the French province. I find it useful, very useful, since so much of our business is still carried on in Montreal, although the mills are in Canada West. We must see that Charles and Sarah have some time, too, in France, when they are older. They can manage very well here for some years yet, but I should like to send Charles abroad, perhaps to England."

"I know that many people among our friends would agree with such a scheme. But I do not."

"You do not!" Mr. Lawson looked with amazement at his wife. There was such strength and firmness in her voice.

"No, indeed I do not. William Sylvester has been sent away from Harrow. He has been there, as you know, only two years, and his health is quite ruined."

"His health ruined?"

"Aunt Truman says he has become a confirmed drunkard. At sixteen."

"Your Aunt Truman, I hope, does not repeat such rumours without very good authority."

"Sometimes I think she does relish gossip, since her days are empty and her future uncertain. But she met with Mr. Sylvester and his sister at church, on Sunday. It was they who told her. They are quite broken hearted. The only boy in a family of nine."

"I can scarcely believe it. What a disaster!"

"Mrs. Sylvester is in England now. She went at once, when the telegraph informing her came. She has established her son in a friend's house and went herself to Harrow, to inquire by what means her son had been so corrupted. They say his state is so bad that he may never regain his former strength. She might have spared herself the trouble. William's school master informed her that any gentleman should be able to hold his liquor by the time he was fourteen."

"It is an incredible, a fearful story. Surely the boy will become well again, once he is at home. Who will there be to inherit the business, if he does not? I am most heartily sorry for his father. Most heartily. And very glad to be at home myself, again."

"And I am so glad that you are come, and in time for the Ball. I am going to cut some Harison's yellow to make a wreath for Isabella to wear tonight. Elizabeth Gibson will have pink buds."

17

Old Grey City

> *Protocol is just as important here as it ever was at Versailles in the days of Louis XIV. Democratic society is just as jealous of its privileges as feudal society was. A member of parliament's wife, who is incorrectly seated at table, can give a scowl as black as any duchess who is received in audience by the king and finds no stool placed ready to support her backside.*[101]

Quebec was happy in the possession of the most fashionable establishment in the provinces. The Viceregal residence set the tone for entertainment, winter and summer. Within the beautiful walls of "Spencer Wood" there were many parties, summer and winter, music and dancing and dinners. Balls and drums and drawing-rooms brought the ladies in their lace flounces, their swaying crinolines, their frighteningly top-heavy head dresses to Spencer Wood. Officers in brilliant dress uniforms escorted them there. Lacking officers, members of parliament, judges, famous educators, dressed in their best, offered an arm to the ladies.

> *I dined at the Gov't House last night 24 gentlemen sat down to dinner. I sat second to the right of the Governor General. Afterwards Lady Monck had a "Home." The party was very large and brilliant. Lady Monck made herself very agreeable. She played on the piano and afterwards on the harp, accompanied on the piano by one of her daughters. I believe there was some dancing in the course of the evening; but I left about half past ten, and the party broke up at a quarter before twelve; it is said Lady Monck makes herself more agreeable than heretofore. The Governor General is very popular in his manners, and is very popular with all parties personally.*[102]

The young ladies in and near Quebec especially enjoyed the unique titillation of Spencer Wood's hospitality. The "Drawing-Room" in the Governor General's mansion was the most elegant social occasion to which a young lady might be bid. It was well for a bride that her invitation to a Drawing-Room should come before the other invitations which would be showered upon her. For Quebec took its brides seriously and offered them many special little attentions, and required of them much in the way of politeness, graciousness of bearing, and the acceptance of social usage. An invitation to Spencer Wood was her accolade, an indication that the stranger could be accepted into the exclusive Quebec society. For more than any other city in British North America, Quebec treasured its traditional society and had kept it to an astonishing degree intact. An entrance into the enchanted circle would be made only by one or two very selective approaches. The easiest way in was by blood relationship. If there were an undisputed connection, of even the most tenuous, such as the sharing of a great-grandfather with, say, a minister of the Crown, the door would be flung open, and the cousin and his bride, be she English or French, welcomed in.

Perhaps the newcomer may never have been seen before by his Quebec relatives. But if he should be revealed as needing a job, there could surely be found an opening for him. It could be certainly assumed that a man whose great-grandfather was the same as that of the French-Canadian minister who held the giving of jobs in his power, would be capable of distinguishing himself in any position to which the minister should appoint him. The enchanted circle opened and closed.

If the husband of the bride was already an accepted member of Quebec society, and if he were of some importance in the government or the judiciary or the army, she might expect to be invited frequently to the great house, during the course of her life. But the first time she came, she entered as a *bride*, a creature upon whom special attention was showered. She must suffer the appraising glance of the other guests and meet with their approval, or her subsequent social acceptance might well be curtailed. Unless, of course, there was a connection by blood.

A bride at her first "Drawing-Room" after her marriage could scarcely be overlooked, since tradition demanded that she appear in her full bridal costume, "with all the accessories."

As frequently happened, when Mlle. Duchesnay married M. Juchereau, one sunny day in the summer of the year 1866, she found herself resident with her husband's family in a fine summer house, a few miles from Quebec. The town house was being maintained too, with a skeleton staff, in case there was need for the family to go into Quebec, to consult a doctor or for some essential shopping, or to meet a ship whose progress up the St. Lawrence livened the summer scene.

The plan might be that a year or so was to be spent in the Juchereau house, while the young man decided upon his future. Would he build upon one of the farms, or would they find that a fine old house in the city would be their choice? There was no hurry in any case. Perhaps to see first if a city or a country life would best suit Lucie.

And Lucie was a very busy young lady that first year. Nearly all the people whom she bowed to at the Drawing-Room, had sent wedding presents. Each donor had to be called upon, every afternoon found her driving out to pay her calls, sometimes two or three a day, until the obligation was done.

Sometimes, Lucie, only eighteen herself, and her young sisters-in-law, parasols in hand, walked to the city, taking an hour and a half in the doing of it and finding great pleasure in the exercise and the opportunity for cheerful gossip with no elders to reprimand.

"Mlle. Sevigny is to marry Captain Jameson. She called with him yesterday, chez les Morins, and he is very handsome. She is calling upon all her friends, to introduce him. There is to be a ball, with they say, more than two hundred people, given for Mlle. Sevigny. M. Sevigny is to build a great banquet room, for the party. He has already started it. But the invitations cannot yet be delivered. What shall you wear, Lucie?"

Small as the Quebec society was, it seems possible to have had parties for which three hundred cards could be sent out. People with large grounds depended on the summer season to entertain. Travellers about Quebec were able to enjoy, even in the winter, "about five miles (drive) in the country – a most beautiful ride, and on either side residences of rich merchants and gentlemen, with ornamental grounds planted with rare trees."

The ornamental grounds in the summer were splendid places to give large parties.

> Mrs. — had sent me a card for her party. We did not go until 9/2 and were too early to be fashionable. The trees in the drive through the part were all hung with coloured lamps and all the lawn – thrown open for the reception of the guests. There were about two hundred and fifty people present, including a large number of both houses of Parliament.[103]

There was no resisting any opportunity of dancing. Picnics were sometimes required to provide facilities for dancing too.

> played "Aunt Sally" till all the pipes were broken! Then dancing was to begin on a board under the trees, with the band near and then went away. It was almost pleasanter sitting and talking than dancing, as the ladies' dresses flew about so.[104]

Winter evenings in the snow-and-ice-bound city were given over to games and to music, when there was no ball to engage the young ladies and the middle-aged ladies, since dancing and balls were not to be considered as the province of the young alone. Visitors, both ladies and gentlemen occupied themselves in providing entertainment for themselves and their hosts.

One of the young ladies in the house would almost undoubtedly be accomplished on the harp, and the piano could be played by another, and perhaps there would be a cornet and a violin. So when the game of casino was done or the whist finished, and the gentlemen had retired for a short while to the smoking-room, there would be music.

Sometimes charades would provide an hour or two of fun and laughter.

"We had five instruments," a young lady could enter into her diary with satisfaction at an evening well spent.

Over native and visitor alike, Quebec cast a spell of a kind which no other city in the British possessions, or indeed in the North American cities which were no longer British could conjure up. The magnificent gifts of nature and the imagination of man together produced a unique result, summer or winter. Whether in the gardens of Spencer Wood "overhanging the St. Lawrence," listening to the band and in full sight of the river and the blue Laurentians, or dazzled by the ice and snow of the winter, Quebec offered its own peculiar treasure to all with eyes to see.

The grandeur of the Canadian scene never failed to rouse tremendous enthusiasm in the breasts of the travelling note takers. Sensitive to nature, they were sensitive too to the practical, and sometimes combined the two in a startling fashion. Quebec, the city and the country about was the most stimulating, in the sixties. Once such traveller stood by a saw mill, on the St. Lawrence, and viewed the "Paper Mills Falls" with a lifting of his heart.

> *A poetic observer standing on the margin of the river near the Falls might easily transmute the Grecian imagery chanted by the Roman into actual scene before him; and can almost fancy without any peculiar and visionary flights of the imagination that he beholds around him the principal and most solitary dell of the ancient immortalized Tempe.*
>
> *"Est nemus Haemoniae praerupta undique claudit*
> *Silva; vacant Tempe" etc.*
>
> *The railway tubular bridge, about a mile above the falls, is a very fine one, and worth an inspection.*[105]

●

Letter Fourteen.

ISABELLA MOORE TO HER SISTER CONSTANCE, IN DUBLIN.

· · · ● ○ · · ·

Montreal,
30 June, 1867

My Dear Constance:

You will perhaps have been surprised not to hear before this from me. But your letter containing your decision to marry Mr. McEvoy has just come to my hand, and I hasten to wish you joy. It is possible that you may be already married, since your letter went first to Bradsbrook, then to Hamilton, and was brought here only today. I am somewhat surprised that you did not think to telegraph such a piece of news by the new Atlantic cable. I should have had it then in a few hours.

I had intended, in this letter to speak to you about my situation here, and the great kindness which Madame de Trouville shows me.

She is a descendant of someone whom all speak of as the "Marquis," and I am ashamed to ask what Marquis, since it is assumed that all know. She is obviously very wealthy, and it is said that during the winter she gives banquets to large numbers of guests which are so magnificent that four or five hours may be consumed in the serving of them. But in the summertime, although the house seems always full of visitors both English and French, there is no note of such formality.

Madame, in spite of her great bulk, is an enthusiastic horsewoman, a driver, I mean, since it would take a mighty hunter to carry her with ease, but she drives a most splendid tandem, and took me out the very afternoon of our arrival, to show me Montreal.

This lively city is the largest, I think, of the British cities in North America, having something over a hundred thousand inhabitants. Madame says that I must certainly see Quebec, before I leave for Ireland, but assures me that for fashion and excitement and the "*nouveau*," there is nothing in Quebec to compete with Montreal.

She is much more conversational in her own house, than she seemed to be in the *Scotia*. Her rooms are large, and filled with furniture, with great soft sofas and chairs upholstered in bright coloured silks. Everywhere there are evidences of extensive foreign travel – pictures and small treasures in ivory and brass and silver which can only have been carefully selected by the traveller herself, and brought home. She has two drawing rooms, both so filled with tables and overstuffed hassocks and glass ornaments and plant stands that I think she can never have a ball here. Where would the objects find a place to be hidden? Madame walks about through all this maze of inanimate objects rather as a sure footed elephant draped in silk might make his way through the undergrowth of a forest, breaking nothing, but always seeming about to trample on some valuable growth!

Montreal is preparing for to-morrow, which is the great day on which the Dominion of Canada will declare itself a confederation. There will be all sorts of military manoeuvres, and sports and picnics, and cricket matches, to celebrate. Montreal means to end the day with a magnificent fireworks display. Madame thinks we shall not have to leave her house to see it; there are a dozen rocking chairs on the long verandah which stretches from one side of the house to the other; the verandah will be our "box."

The devices which we are to see in fireworks are the emblems of the three provinces which are now to be joined to make one country, the pine is to represent New Brunswick, the mayflower Nova Scotia, and for Canada there is to be a beaver. All the cities are to celebrate so, and in Hamilton, where the Lawsons will be watching, there are to be four great bonfires set ablaze on the mountain when the fireworks are fading.

I had thought to be very sad, as I told you, to be in Montreal and not at Lawsonhurst, for the First. But I feel no regret now. Did I feel that you would receive my news with interest and sympathy, I could with pleasure tell you at length of the dissipation of my disappointment at leaving the known gaiety of Hamilton for the unknown pleasures of Montreal – SUCH a ball, we had, my dear Constance! But I doubt your interest, and will spare your eyes, from detail which may interest me very deeply, but with your own present concerns will in all probability not have great interest for you.

At the ball I made the discovery which had, apparently long been known to Cousin Jack, that Mr. Andrew had been much attracted to me from our very first meeting, on board our ship. Thinking that Cousin Jack was legally my guardian, not just my guardian through kindness and affection, he had asked his permission before proposing to me.

We are to be married in early September, in Bradsbrook. Mr. Andrew suggests that we go to Ireland on the first stage of our wedding travels. He can then, he says, look to any business arrangements which may be necessary, if the old house in Fitzwilliam Square is to be sold.

My new grey dress with the scarlet petticoat and the grey hat and veil (which I can certainly find in Montreal) will serve admirably for an ocean voyage, at that time of year. I think I shall buy a black velvet burnoose, instead of a sack.

    Your most loving sister,
    ISABELLA.

18

On the First of July, 1867

The days of isolation and dwarf-hood are past; henceforth we are a united people, and the greatness of each goes to swell the greatness of the whole. [106]

All her (Great Britain's) glory, her greatness and her power belong to us now and by doing in the future as she has done in the past, we may add to that bright inheritence (sic) some good qualities and fair virtues of our own. [107]

The Day broke fair across all Canada.

On the first of July Lord Monck heard the reading of his new commission, and took his solemn oath, his hand on the Bible.

On the first of July John A. Macdonald entered the East Block of the Parliament buildings a plain man and came out a Knight Commander of the Bath.

On the first of July the little steamer *Queen Victoria* resting in the waters of the Ottawa river might well have been content. For she had been part of it from the beginning. She had carried the men with the plan down to the Maritimes, and had brought the Maritimers back. And now it was she who had transported Lord Monck, the Governor General of the Dominion of Canada to Ottawa, to set the seal upon it all.

The Day had come, the deed was done. The city dailies sang their exultant songs.

Sensing the greatness of the day, and the importance of recording anything which pertained to it, the little twice weeklies in Canada West made detailed mention of the weather. "Confederation Weather!" they exultantly exlaimed. Some boxed in the weather report,

> *The Temperature.*
> *July 1st. Monday.*
> *Taken at noon in the shade at Atkinson's Drug Store. King Street, Oshawa. 78 degrees. Fine.*[108]

The scores of little weekly newspapers printed in the small towns sang of the brilliance of the day, the performance of the Volunteers, the great happiness which must come now to all Canada.

There were those who wept, fearful of their lost identity, and some newspapers in the Maritimes edged their sheets with black on this day. But those who sang and hoped were many more than those who mourned, when the plan was completed, and the dream made real.

The *Vindicator*, Oshawa's newspaper, provides a specimen of the recording of the day's activities in the small towns, as the editor saw it. By Wednesday, the 3rd, the paper could be had by all, from the office of the printer.

> CONFEDERATION DAY IN OSHAWA.
> *The first morning of the New Dominion was ushered in in Oshawa with the ringing of bells and the firing of cannon, including a salute from the guns of the juvenile battery.*[109]

Oshawa graciously gave way to Whitby for the full and military celebration of the Day. In the afternoon of the First, Oshawa was a "deserted village." The people of Oshawa harnessed their horses and jumped into their buggies and waggons to join with their neighbours five miles away. The stagecoachmen threw the harness onto their horses and made two or three trips to Whitby with full loads of passengers. Then they stayed themselves to miss nothing of the festivity.

A strong military flavour in the celebration was evident throughout both cities and towns. Toronto planned a "grand review" for the Spadina Avenue grounds.

> *The volunteers muster at their headquarters at nine, and are expected to be on the ground in time to receive the General, punctually at 10:30. The 13th Hussars, 17th infantry, two batteries of regular and one of volunteer artillery, Queen's Own, 10th Royals and Grand Trunk Volunteer battalions, and Captain McLean's Fort artillery company, will take part in the review. Line will be formed prior to the arrival of General Stisted, and immediately on his entry on the field, a feu de joie will be fired by the infantry, and a royal salute by the artillery.*[110]

The cities may have boasted of their regulars, their Queen's Own, their Hussars, their men of military magnificence of all kinds. But the volunteers who came to Whitby for their review on the first day of the Dominion were those same glorious volunteers who two years before had swarmed down to Toronto from the north, with full intent to take on the full military strength of the United States, if need be, should the war which seemed imminent break out.

Their aim was peaceful now, and their welcome tumultuous. "Companies from Whitby, Oshawa, Greenwood, Columbus and Brooklin" marched on Whitby, this first of July.

> *Major Button's troop of cavalry was present, with fine horses, and soldierly bearing. After the reading of the proclamation*

> by the Mayor, the troops fired a feu de joie. They were put through several movements and evolutions of a field day. The officers and men deserve great credit. The horses of Major Button's cavalry faced the fire from the squares remarkably well, some of them rushing so closely upon the bayonets as to receive severe thrusts. . . .
>
> Dinner as well as lunch was furnished to the Volunteers by the Corporation of Whitby, in the Hall of the Mechanics Institute.
>
> About 7000 persons were present on the field (to witness) the games on the agricultural grounds, and the fireworks at night. Music throughout the day was furnished by the "Battalion Band."[111]

It was a pattern of celebration which was followed across the rejoicing country. In Toronto a great ox was roasted whole. He was such an immense beast that the roasting of him took all day, and it was evening before his meat could be distributed to the poor. Glorious illuminations played about the façade of the Post Office and the Gas House. The streets leading to Queen's Park were lit with coloured lanterns, luring all to the Band Concert (the 17th and 13th Hussars). And when it was done, there would be dancing in the Park.

On the First of July there was glorious summer weather all across the new Dominion of Canada. The tall blue Canadian sky was spindrifted by tiny clouds, as if by new-born lambs in flight. The lakes and rivers shone gun-metal blue under the sun, and flotillas of sailboats and canoes and rowboats were abundantly scattered on the surface of the water. Everywhere there was something joyous to do.

The "Confederation Weather," hot, but not too hot, and continuing fine all day, brought the people streaming out from almost every house. Those who did not wish to travel far joined their friends and families in a picnic in a nearby sugar-bush or went by water to some favourite spot to laze away the day.

The school children in Bradsbrook gathered in the park across from the toll gate, and ran races and drilled determinedly with miniature Union Jacks in their hands. Jack Brady joined them there with his wife and their children. He brought a tin trunk full of fireworks and put it under the bandstand, until it should be dark enough. In the late afternoon the trestles under the maples at the far end of the playing field were spread with white cloths. The mothers built mounds of sandwiches and fried cakes and gingerbread snaps, and set out tall pitchers of raspberry cordial and lemonade.

The great bonfires bloomed on the mountain in Hamilton, and the Lawson children danced around a bonfire of their own making, stopping every few minutes to set another rocket high into the darkening air. Blue and green and red the balls danced against the sky.

The people who sat on the dozen rocking chairs on Madame de Trouville's verandah were granted a clear and uninterrupted view of the spectacle above Montreal. The glorious vast green pine grew into the air, and faded. The Canadian beaver spread his huge and fiery bulk into the sky, the Mayflower sprang up and blossomed and died in a fountain of fire. But Isabella Moore and Mr. Andrew, sitting there in the intermittent darkness, saw nothing of the Pine, or the Beaver, or the flowering of the May. When the fountaining light shattered the darkness they saw only the other's face, and in the fire shine they could almost believe in the miracle which was theirs.

A lady who was a hundred years old a few years ago remembers this: there was the dark, and then there was the light of a candle. She was in her bed at the top of the long, long stairs. Then there was the voice of her father carrying her down the long stairs. They went through the hall, and then down the other stairs that curved round on both sides. Then there was the opening of the great door, and the rush of cool fresh air, and the deep darkness.

There were the voices of people about her, men's voices and women's talking together in the darkness, and walking together across the long garden, and down to the shore of the lake. There was the voice of her mother, and her older sister and other strange voices. Perhaps they were the voices of the people who had come to dinner, the old lady thought.

"Oh! Look!" said a voice, and it seemed to the child who was a very old lady now that the sky was suddenly full of shooting stars. And there were fountains of stars, coloured red and green and blue, spraying bright balls of colour into the air. There were some which tipped their colours into the air to mirror them in the water, and some were far away, both to the right and to the left. And there were sharp loud noises, sudden, shocking, reverberating. It seemed to the child that the air was full of the echoing noises.

"This is the First of July, in the year eighteen hundred and sixty-seven," she remembered her father's voice saying. "Always remember this day, and this night," her father said. "You are a very lucky little girl, to be a child in Canada, today."[112]

This is what the old lady remembered.

Notes

Among the many keen observers of Canadian life in the 1860's, three in particular stand out: William Howard Russell, Frances Monck, and Samuel Phillips Day.

William Howard Russell of *The Times* of London was the first and perhaps the greatest of war correspondents. His letters to *The Times* from the Crimea in 1854 and 1855 are credited with rousing the British people to the shortcomings of the War Office and thus contributing to the fall of the Aberdeen government. Russell was in India during the Mutiny and in the early years of the American Civil War he travelled in what S. P. Day calls "the late United States." He reported to his paper on the Civil War and then came to the British possessions and commented on the Canadians, their unreadiness for war, their social customs, and the state of their development. He produced a three-volume work on the state of North America of which the third volume deals with things Canadian. It is from this book, *Canada; its defences, conditions, and resources, being the third and concluding volume of "My Diary North and South,"* London, 1865, that all Mr. Russell's quotations are taken.

Frances Monck was the sister-in-law of Governor General, Lord Monck. She and her husband, Colonel Richard Monck, spent the best part of a year during 1864 and 1865 with Lord Monck and "Her Ex" in the beautiful viceregal residence "Spencer Wood," a few miles from Quebec. She recorded her experiences and impressions in a book which was first privately published and then reached the reading public in 1891. All the quotations in this book attributed to Mrs. Monck are from this second edition of *My Canadian Leaves, an account of a visit to Canada in 1864-1865*, London, 1891.

Samuel Phillips Day was a correspondent for the London *Herald* in 1863-64 and for the *Morning Post* in 1865. He travelled joyfully through both the Canadas in 1862 and sent back reams of astonishingly well-observed comment on Canadian life, scientific achievement, social development, and economic prospects. He sailed and drove and rode the trains. And he thoroughly enjoyed his investigations. "Social life in Canada is of a superior order and infinitely superior to that existing in the late United States," he found in 1862. He must have been a most engaging companion, being given to tramping the country roads, singing as he went, stopping to filch a few apples from an orchard, and inspiring his friends to lyrical and amusing poetry about travelling with Samuel Phillips Day.

All the quotations from Mr. Day in this book are from his two volume *English America: or Pictures of Canadian Places and People*, London: 1864.

1. Donald Creighton, *The Road to Confederation*, Toronto: Macmillan, 1964.
2. *Ibid.*
3. *Charlottetown Islander*, September 9, 1864.
4. J. M. S. Careless, "George Brown and the Mother of Confederation," *Canadian Historical Association Report*, 1960.
5. P. B. Waite, "Edward Whelan Reports from the Quebec Conference, *Canadian Historical Review*, vol. 42.

6. *Ibid.*
7. *Diary of Mercy Ann Coles.* Mercy Ann was the young daughter of George Coles, a former premier of Prince Edward Island, who at the time of the Charlottetown Conference was the leader of the Liberal Opposition.
8. Harvey (ed.), *Whelan's Union of British Provinces*, Charlottetown, 1865.
9. *Ibid.*
10. *Diary of Mercy Ann Coles.*
11. Donald G. Creighton, *op. cit.*
12. *Diary of Mercy Ann Coles.*
13. *Ibid.*
14. *Ibid.*
15. W. H. Russell, *Canada; its defences, conditions, and resources, being the third and concluding volume of "My Diary North and South,"* London, 1865.
16. *Ibid.*
17. Frances Monck, *My Canadian Leaves, An Account of a visit to Canada in 1864-1865*, London, 1891.
18. Charles Horton Rhys, *A Theatrical Trip for a Wager! Through Canada and the United States*, London, 1861, published for the author by Charles Dudley.
19. *Ibid.*
20. *Ibid.*
21. Mr. Russell.
22. *Diary of Mercy Ann Coles.*
23. Anne Wilkinson, *Lions in the Way*, Toronto: Macmillan, 1956.
24. Anthony Trollope, *North America*, New York, 1862.
25. Sir George Bell, *Rough Notes by an old Soldier*, London, 1867. This was later arranged and edited by his kinsman Brian Stuart as *Soldier's Glory*, London: George Bell & Son, Ltd., 1956.
26. *Ibid.*
27. Mr. Russell.
28. S. P. Day, *English America: or pictures of Canadian places and people* (London, 1864), 2 vols.
29. Mr. Day.
30. *Ibid.*
31. *Ibid.*
32. *Canadian Handbook and Tourists Guide*, Montreal, 1867.
33. Anon. in *British American Magazine*, 1865.
34. Mr. Russell.
35. Mrs. Monck.
36. Mr. Russell.
37. *Ibid.*
38. *Ibid.*
39. *Ibid.*
40. Mrs. Monck.
41. *Ibid.*
42. *Ibid.*
43. *Ibid.*
44. Mr. Russell.
45. *Ibid.*
46. *Ibid.*
47. Mrs. Monck.
48. *Ibid.*
49. *Ibid.*
49A. Lord Frederic Hamilton, *The Days Before Yesterday*, London: Hodder & Stoughton, 1920.
50. Mr. Day.
51. *Ibid.* Mr. Reynolds, the Sheriff of Whitby, had had this vast house built for himself. He found it a little too expensive to maintain, and it early became the home of the Ontario Ladies College. "Trafalgar Castle" houses the young ladies still.

52. Private family papers.
53. *Home Cook Book*: compiled by the ladies of Toronto and chief Cities and Towns in Canada, Rose-Belford Publishing Company. The *Home Cook Book* went into an almost incredible number of editions – some of them, surely, very small, since the edition of 1877 from which this quotation is taken (as well as a long quotation to come) is described as the fiftieth edition.
54. *Ibid.*
55. *Ibid.*
56. *Ibid.*
57. *Illustrated London News*, January-June, 1867.
58. Anthony Trollope, *Phineas Phinn*, London, 1869.
59. *Godey's Ladies' Book*, January, 1867.
60. *Ibid.*
61. Egerton Ryerson, *My Dearest Sophie*, Toronto, 1955.
62. D. S. Hoig, *Reminiscences and Recollections*, Oshawa, 1933.
63. Diary of Amelia Harris (unpublished).
64. *Ibid.*
65. Mr. Russell.
66. George Tuthill Borrett, *Letters from Canada and the United States*, printed for private circulation, London, 1865.
67. W. M. Thackeray, *Pendennis*.
68. Diary of Amelia Harris.
69. Egerton Ryerson, *op. cit.*
70. Mrs. Holiwell, *British American Magazine Devoted to Literature, Science and Art*, Vol. I, 1863.
71. Catharine Parr Traill, in *British American Magazine*.
72. Anon. *British American Magazine*.
73. *Ibid.*
74. *Ibid.*
75. *Ibid.*
76. Mrs. Monck.
77. William Colgate, "A Canadian Painter of Eminent Victorians," *Ontario Historical Society Papers and Records*, Vol. XXXIV, Toronto, 1942.
78. *Ibid.*
79. Duval, *Canadian Watercolour Painting*, Toronto, 1954.
80. Quoted in William Colgate, *Canadian Art*, Toronto, Ryerson Press, 1943.
81. Mrs. Monck.
82. Isabella Bird, manuscript journal.
83. *Ibid.*
84. Mrs. Monck.
85. *Ibid.*
86. *Ibid.*
87. *Canadian Handbook and Tourists Guide*, Montreal, 1867.
88. Willis Russell, *Quebec as it Was*. Mr. Russell, the proprietor of the famous Russell House in Quebec, wrote this little book which went into a number of editions. This quotation comes from the 1867 reprinting edited by Charles Rogers.
89. *Simcoe Gazeteer*, 1866-67.
90. Mr. Day.
91. Mrs. Monck.
92. *Ibid.*
93. *Ibid.*
94. *Ibid.*
95. Mr. Day.
96. Diary of Amelia Harris.
97. Mrs. Monck.
98. Mr. Day.
99. *Ibid.*
100. Mr. Russell.

101. Robert de Roquebrune, *A Testament of My Childhood*, Toronto, University of Toronto Press, 1964.
102. Egerton Ryerson, *op. cit.*
103. Isabella Bird, manuscript journal.
104. Mrs. Monck.
105. Willis Russell, *op. cit.*
106. *British Colonist*, Halifax, July 2, 1867.
107. *Daily Telegraph*, Toronto, July 2, 1867.
108. *Oshawa Vindicator*, July 1, 1867.
109. *Ibid* July 3, 1867.
110. *The Globe*, Toronto, Monday July 1, 1867.
111. *Oshawa Vindicator*, July 3, 1867.
112. Among the members of a family which has played a prominent part in the life of Canada, this little girl was subsequently known as "Cousin Marion."